Phyle Based Semasiological Infoduct Distribuenda

AF720504

Alba Y.

Phyle Based Semasiological Infoduct Distribuenda

First Edition September 2025

Written by Alba Y.

TABLE OF CONTENTS

CHAPTER 1

INTRODUCTION

1.1 GENERAL

World Wide Web (WWW) is three decades old now and has freed up the process of information exchange among the people of the world. A huge amount of information can be created, accessed, or shared and can potentially be used by people to start their ventures. WWW has contributed to various aspects of our life that it seems difficult to imagine one's day without it. Although, there has been drastic improvement in accessing the digitally stored information but the underlying information can only be processed by the machines and presented to the user to understand it. The content written in natural language over the web can only understand by human beings, and thus impose a challenge on the human capacity to process such vast information. The transition from the "machine-readable" to "machine-understandable" is the vision of the semantic web [1]. This would mark the beginning of a new era comprised of the Internet of Things, intelligent agents, blockchain, etc. This would surely be the beginning of a new era, in which there would be intelligent personal agents, and the concepts of bitcoin, blockchain, that will revolutionize the web.

1.2 EVOLUTION OF WEB

The evolution of the web can be reflected in the growth of connected information and connected people. The connected network and WWW had created vast learning and business opportunities for people around the world. On March 12, 1989, Tim Berners-Lee proposed sharing the information with multiple computers, and its first implementation represented "Web 1.0", known as "read-only web" [2]. In this phase, only the organizations created the information and present it over the web for the users to only access them and read them. There was very limited interaction from the user end.

The web communities started working to make websites interesting and easier for the general users to use and contribute to information creation. The year 2004, mark the new wave with the rise of social collaboration through blogs, discussion forums, and social networks, and that era was called "Web 2.0". In this era, the users are not just be the consumer of the information but also the producer of the information and also known as the "Social Web". The big player which largely took over the Web 2.0 is Amazon, Facebook, Google, Twitter, Wikipedia, etc. They had created platforms for the thousands of users to contribute in creating interesting information which is not possible for any single organization to create on their own. This has revolutionized the way people use the web. And now, with the adaptation of machine-understandable language and realizing the potential of semantics, we are heading towards the "Semantic Web" [2].

The authors in [3] have described about major web evolution in terms of the connection between the information and connection between the people as shown in Fig. 1.1. It describes the technical advancement of how well the information could be linked with each other and this increases the social richness among the connected people. The graph shows the transition from the era of PC's to the internet era and slowly and gradually moving towards the four versions of web evolution.

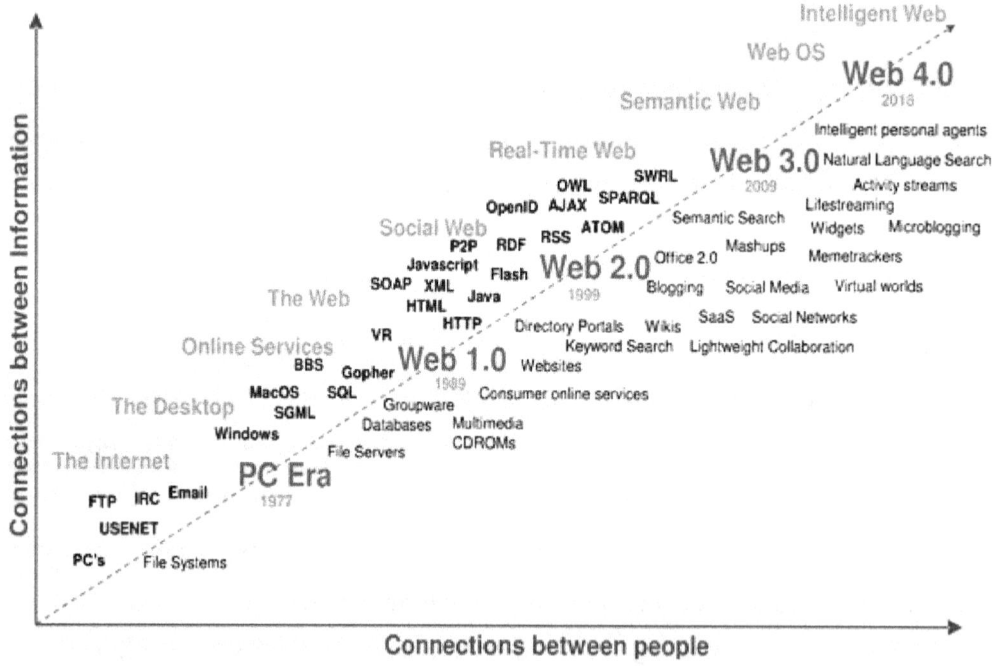

Figure 1.1: Major Waves of Web Evolution

1.3 LIMITATION OF SOCIAL WEB

Social Web provides various online tools and platforms over which users can share their thoughts, suggestions, perspective, and experiences. The end-user is not just using the services of the application but also can take initiative to get involved as a participant.

CHAPTER 2

STATE-OF-THE-ART TECHNOLOGIES IN SOCIAL AND SEMANTIC WEB

2.1 INTRODUCTION

The era of the Social Web has been growing tremendously over the web. Users are getting allured towards new paradigms tools and services of the Social Web. The amount of information available on the Social Web is produced by sharing of beliefs, reviews, and knowledge by various online communities. Interoperability and portability of social data are some of the major bottlenecks of social network applications like Facebook, Twitter, Flicker, and many more. Combining Social and Semantic Web is a very challenging task. Various studies have been conducted in describing the structure of information and maintaining relationships among the plethora of web documents. Most of the social networking sites provide limited means for users to publish and access social data rather than integration of social data [9]. The era of social websites has gained tremendous height during the last 6-7 years. These have become the medium of marketing and promotions in innovative ways [10].

As the number of social websites increases, the need to achieve portability of social data also increases. It has led to the idea of aggregating social data with the help of semantic web technologies. On the other side, Semantic web consists of various ontologies to deal with social datasets available on different sites to allow interoperability through machines rather than XML based approaches [11]. It also examines how semantic web technologies can be used in achieving interoperability among Social Web applications. Various research work related to the study of extracting ontologies from collaborative tagged systems and the development of ontology as a unified model for social network had been presented [12] [13]. Various services such as searching, recommendation, trend analysis could be provided through combining Social and Semantic Web in single entity.

Researchers in [14] briefly described privacy issues in the context of Semantic Web and Social Web in their article titled *Social Semantic Web* and presented various suggestions for reducing the gap between Social Web and Semantic Web. The article also includes a survey of semantic web applications like *semantic wiki* which is used to annotate unstructured data.

2.2 OVERVIEW OF SOCIAL WEB

Social Web is a collection of social data published and shared by millions of users which are being spread over various publishing media, networking media, discussion media, and sharing media as shown in Fig. 2.1. The term Social Web was given by Howard Rheingold [15]. The use of the latest Information and Communication Technologies (ICT) has changed the Social Web by introducing various second-generation web applications like Wikipedia, blogs, social networking sites (Facebook, Twitter), content sharing sites, and community sites.

These applications allow users to create their accounts and maintains user profiles based on different preferences. Similarly, community-driven websites such as *Quora, Digest, Academia* connect a group of people to share their common interests and respond to queries via comments or live chat assistance. Content sharing sites enable users to post their informative content on Social Web. The content may be images text, videos, etc. It has enhanced knowledge sharing through Social Web.

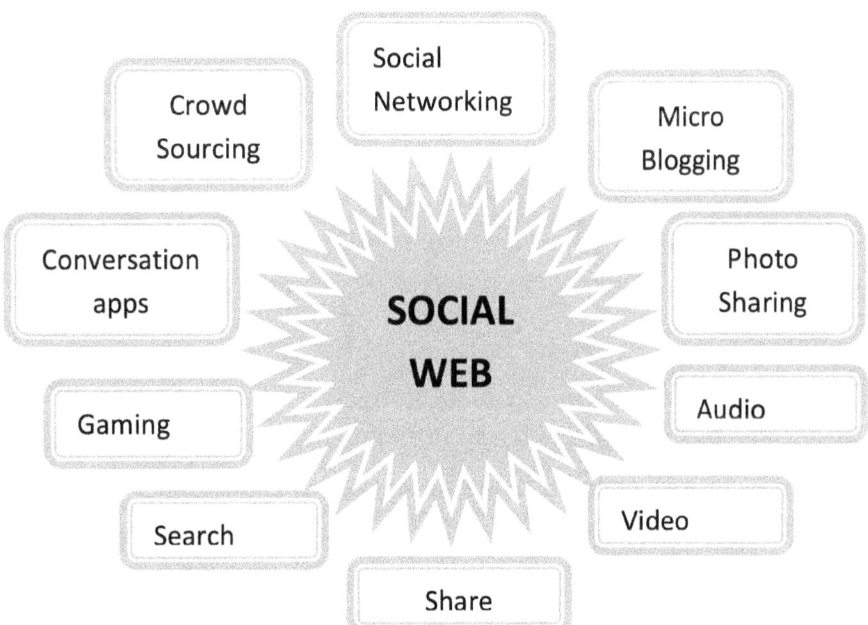

Figure 2.1: Overview of Social Web

2.2.1 Issues in Social Web

Some of the most common issues in the Social Web are addressed below:

- *Lack of efficient Indexing:* Indexing means the generation of metadata. Folksonomy or collaborative tagging is the main source of the metadata creation on the Social Web. But due to social web ambiguities and inconsistency, proper indexing could not be achieved. With the use of the semantic web, it is possible to convert folksonomy to ontologies and generate metadata in Resource Description Framework (RDF) having triples- *subject, property*, and *object* as shown in Fig. 2.2. In this example, 'Usha' is a subject, 'birthPlace' is a property and 'Faridabad' is an object.

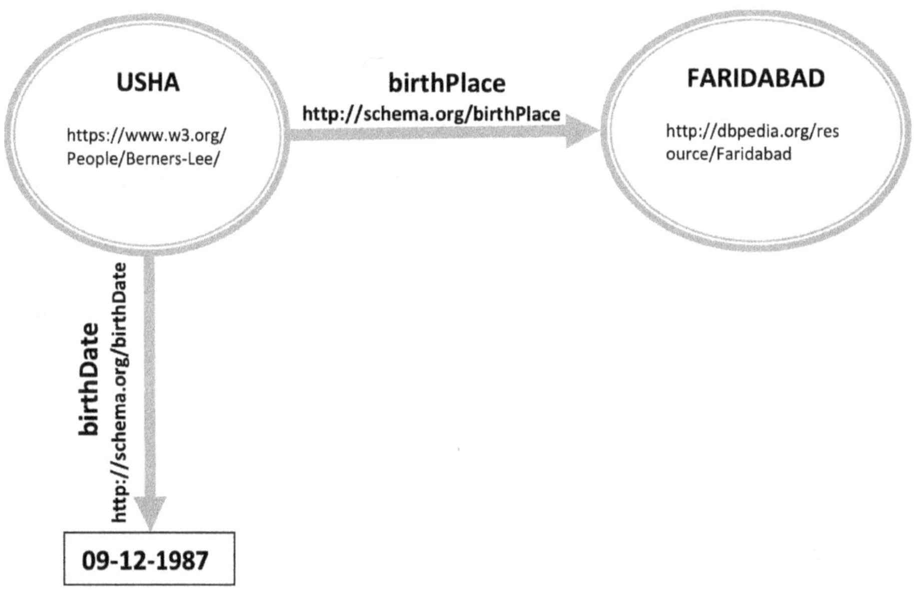

Figure 2.2: Sample RDF Model

- *Difficulty in extending and reusing data due to lack of standards*: Social networks focuses on publishing contents of the website like text, songs, images without having standardized underlying architecture. It has led to portability issues and a lack of knowledge representation. To overcome this challenge, the standard must be defined for content generation and its storage. This can be achieved using semantic based applications and browsers which allow users to publish content in RDF format, which eventually leads to integration of social websites with multiple data sources.

- *Fake Identity Management*: - Users make use of different names, aliases and nicknames to create their profiles in different groups. Each group has its terms and conditions that ensure user's privacy and does not allow other people to access some of the personal information. Therefore, it is difficult to differentiate between fake and genuine users.

The next section describes the Semantic Web technologies and how Semantic Web can be used in achieving interoperability among Social Web applications

2.3. SEMANTIC WEB TECHNOLOGIES

The idea of the Semantic Web as envisioned in [4] focuses on making data machine-understandable as much as it is friendly to humans. The Semantic Web technologies have been represented in a stack often called the "Semantic Web cake" or "Semantic Web stack" as shown in Fig. 2.3. The stack shows the layers of technologies required to realize the full Semantic Web vision. The bottom layers of the stack have been fully realized. The Ontology vocabulary layer has been partly realized and is actively being developed. The upper layers are still not quite mature in the web applications, although these have been deployed within local or enterprise levels projects. However, the Semantic Web stack is itself evolving frequently along with new technologies, research, and practical challenges identified.

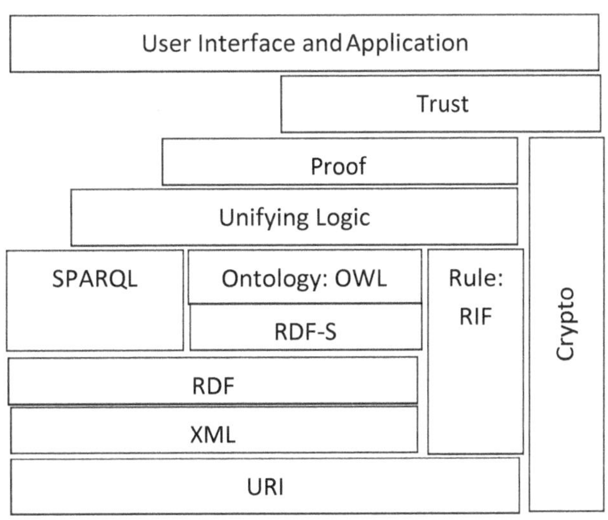

Figure 2.3: Semantic Web Stack

2.4. ACHIEVING INTEROPERABILITY IN SOCIAL WEB

Ontologies define the structure and decide on the standards to represent any domain, it can greatly contribute in achieving interoperability. Although there are large numbers of ontology created for different domain, but they have not been adopted by many businesses. The Semantic web has also standardized some ontologies to maintain interoperability and portability across various social applications. The most famous ontologies/vocabularies include FOAF (Friend of a Friend), SIOC (Semantically Interlinked Online Communities). A brief description of these ontologies is discussed in the following subsections.

2.4.1 Friend of a Friend (FOAF)

FOAF [16] is a simple RDF ontology that helps in identifying "who is who" and links them with other persons by using XML/RDF format. It includes mainly three components- ontological definition, ontological properties, and empirical properties. One of the most common classes in FOAF ontology is *foaf: person.* It holds various properties like *foaf: name, foaf: email, foaf: gender, foaf: knows*, and many more. Fig. 2.4 shows the sample *foaf: person* class of FOAF ontology.

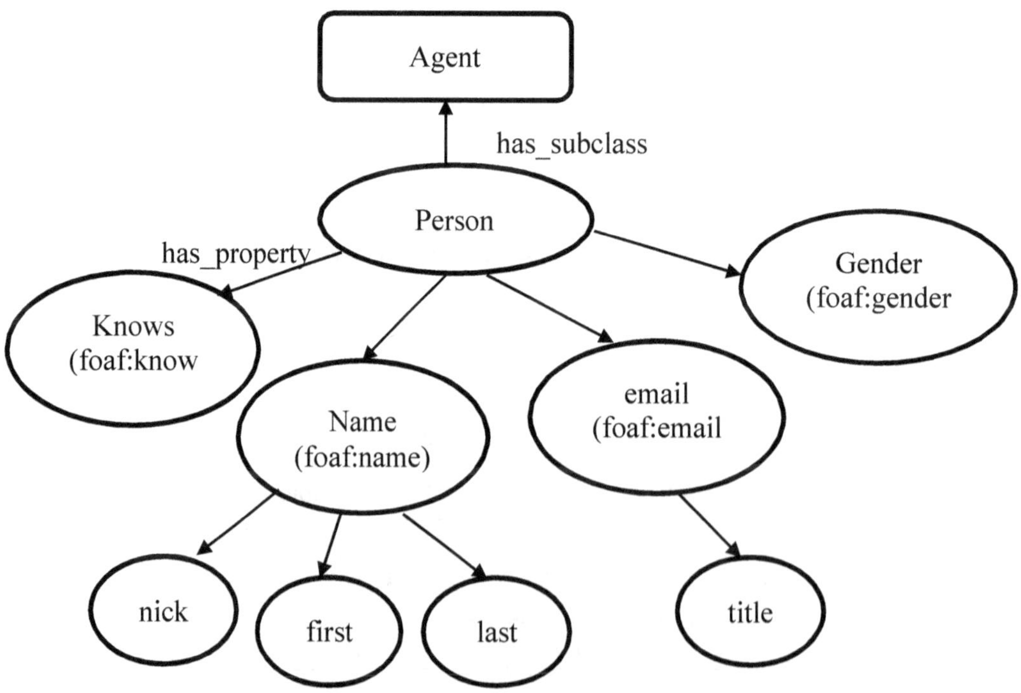

Figure 2.4: FOAF ontology Snippet

2.4.2 Semantically-Interlinked Online Communities (SIOC)

SIOC [14] is a unified model for social and semantic standards. High usage of social sites has led to the birth of various constraints like privacy, lack of interoperability, digital signatures, and security threats. It becomes difficult to query and interlink social data. So, there must be some unified models/vocabularies to handle these issues.

For combining social and semantic paradigms, there was a need to provide a common framework for modeling activities and integration of online community information. This framework was achieved by using SIOC. The code snippet of SIOC is shown in Fig. 2.5.

As ontology is a promising solution to structure information and allows interoperability, the next session describes various ontology development aspects.

```
<rdf:RDF
xmlns:rdf="http://www.w3.org/1999/02/22-rdf-syntax-ns#"
xmlns:rdfs="http://www.w3.org/2000/01/rdf-schema#"
xmlns:foaf="http://xmlns.com/foaf/0.1/"
xmlns:admin="http://webns.net/mvcb/">
<foaf:PersonalProfileDocument rdf:about="">
<foaf:maker rdf:resource="#me"/>
<foaf:primaryTopic rdf:resource="#me"/>
<admin:generatorAgent rdf:resource="http://www.ldodds.com/foaf/foaf-a-matic"/>
<admin:errorReportsTo rdf:resource="mailto:leigh@ldodds.com"/>
</foaf:PersonalProfileDocument>
<foaf:Person rdf:ID="me">
<foaf:name>Usha Yadav</foaf:name>
<foaf:title>Ms</foaf:title>
<foaf:givenname>Usha</foaf:givenname>
<foaf:family_name>Yadav</foaf:family_name>
<foaf:nick>Smily</foaf:nick>
<foaf:mbox_sha1sum>30b2f5faee64d084a0780f724390bff8c0486bf6</foaf:mbox_sha
1sum>
<foaf:knows>
<foaf:Person>
<foaf:name>Neelam</foaf:name>
<foaf:mbox_sha1sum>295863d5ad5b5ea880bde725f16cb21e2d1848fe</foaf:mbox_sh
a1sum>
</foaf:Person></foaf:knows>
<foaf:knows>
<foaf:Person>
```

Figure 2.5: RDF Code Snippet

2.5 ONTOLOGY DEVELOPMENT ASPECTS

Ontology is associated with a wide range of concepts like matching, merging, mapping, engineering, and development. Ontology mapping and merging involves integration, aligning, and reusing of data so that it can be used with existing web applications. Ontology engineering involves the use of automatic tools for managing, mapping, and integrating ontologies to extract precise knowledge from them.

2.5.1 Definitions of Ontology

The ontology can be defined by authors in [17] as *"An ontology is an explicit specification of a conceptualization"*. Although there are several different definitions of ontologies, but this is the most preferred definition among the researchers. The term conceptualization in the definition denotes the representation of concepts, entities that map the real-world understanding of the domain. Ontology also specifies the relationship between these concepts or entities. The definition of ontology had been re-defined by the researcher to highlight the perspective of conceptualization as follows:

"Ontology is a logical theory accounting for the *intended meaning* of a formal vocabulary, i.e., its *ontological commitment* to a particular *conceptualization* of the world. The intended models of a logical language using such a vocabulary are constrained by its ontological commitment. Ontology indirectly reflects this commitment (and the underlying conceptualization) by approximating these intended models."

Ontologies are associated with different languages that are used in the mapping of multiple ontologies. Initially, RDF and XML were developed in which XML specifies the syntax of content rather than its semantics while RDF points to the semantics of data. Over the period of time, more expressive and defined languages came into existence. Some of the most common ontology languages include O*WL (Web Ontology Language)* developed by W3C, *DARPA Agent Markup Language (DAML)* developed by Defense Advanced Research Projects Agency (DARPA), *OIL (Ontology Interface Language)* developed by Europeans, and DAML+OIL.

Example Illustration of OWL specification:

Football and Basketball are sports.

Football is not Cricket.

Football is not Basketball.

```
< owl: Class rdf: about = "#Football">
<owl: disjointWith rdf: resource "#Cricket"/>
<owl: disjointWith rdf: resource = #Basketball"/>
</owl:Class>
<owl: Class rdf: ID = "Football">
<owl: equivalentClass rdf: resource = "Basketball"/>
```

2.5.2 Ontology Expressiveness

There are different types of ontologies based on the power of their expressiveness as shown in Fig. 2.6. Broadly there are two major categories of ontology such as *Lightweight ontologies* and *Heavyweight ontologies* [18]:

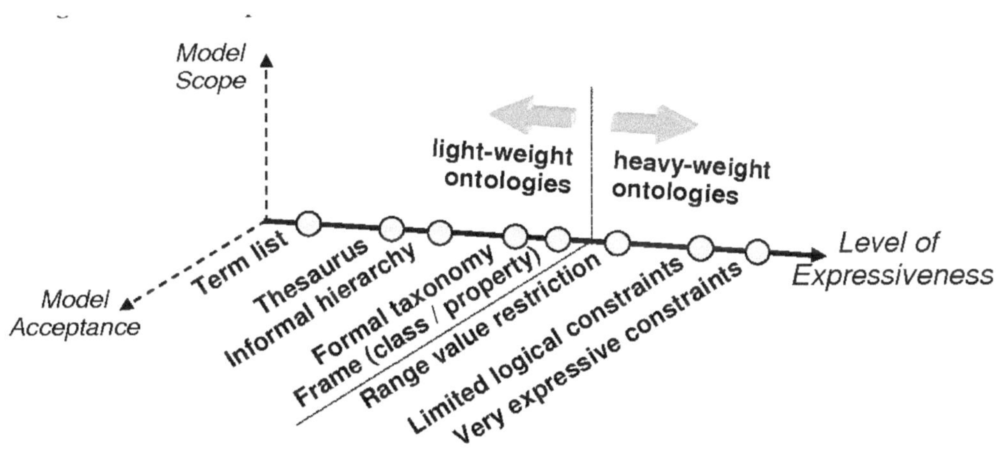

Figure 2.6: Ontology types based on expressiveness

In Fig. 2.6, the *term list* simply denotes the bag of keywords in any domain. The *thesaurus* represents the relationship between the terms of a domain. The concept of generalization and specification in form of hierarchy is defined by the *informal taxonomy*, but no strict restriction had been applied. Superclass may or may not be relatable to the instance of the subclass.

Unlike this, in *formal taxonomy*, there is a strict restriction on inheritance hierarchy. The frame is much comparable with the object-oriented models and the subclass inherit the properties of the superclass. *Range value restriction* characterizes the data type or domain properties. It can further be restricted by *logic constraints*. Very high expressive constraints used the concepts of *first-order predicate logic*.

2.5.3 Importance of lightweight ontologies

Heavyweight ontologies greatly contribute to developing high-end enterprise applications with powerful reasoning capabilities. However, such systems are vulnerable to inconsistencies. Although *lightweight* ontologies can handle inconsistencies but there is not much scope of reasoning in them. Less semantic and low restriction greatly contributes to creating large scalable applications. Considering *lightweight* ontologies for the vast scale of WWW is significant for the practical realization of the Semantic web.

The next section discusses about the ontology engineering which is a tedious task involving the detailed study of the ontology development process, lifecycle, methodology etc.

2.5.4 Activities Involved in Ontology Development

The development of ontology is as complex as measuring the quality of software. It requires each minute detail of activities and tasks from plinth to paramount. Ontology engineers needs to go through all development methodologies and existing design principles for reaching some conclusions. Development-oriented activities are subdivided into *pre-development, development*, and *post-development* processes that occur sequentially while Support oriented activities are conducted in parallel with the development activities [19][20]. The following activities are the backbone of the ontology development process namely: *pre-development, development*, and *post-development* which are defined below.

- **Pre-development Activities:** It specifies the type of application platform to be used for developing ontologies. It also includes the selection of ontology editor tools for defining classes, properties, and their instances. Feasibility study: It checks if a given ontology can be built-in given environment and complies with user requirements.

- **Development Activities:** Various sub-activities are included in the development phase; each of them is described in detail below:
  - Specification phase: This phase consists of activities such as domain vocabulary definition, identifying resources, identifying axioms, identifying relationships, identifying data characteristics, applying constraints, and verification.
  - Conceptualization phase: This phase creates a model in the context of a given domain and presents knowledge at the knowledge level. Several strategies are presented for defining conceptualization viz. *top-down approach* and *bottom-up approach.* Top-down approach begins with a superclass that extends to refine ontology structure. This approach is mostly used in philosophical sciences. The bottom-up approach begins with databases that are sources of multiple data and then do refinement to develop suitable ontology. This process is followed by information extraction (IE) and ontology learning tools like Text-to-Onto [21]
  - Design Phase: This phase proposes the physical structure of the designed ontology that is based on the RDF model. RDF model consists of three triples-Resource, Property, and Value.
  - Formalization phase: This phase produces ontology as output by using ontology tools. It transforms the conceptual model into a formal model that can be re-written in suitable syntax.
  - Implementation phase: It implements formalized ontology with the help of any of semantic languages (OWL, SPARQL) and executed them using some reasoner like Pellet OWL Reasoner.

- **Post-development Activities:** Various sub-activities are included in the post-development process; each of them is described in detail below:
  - Maintenance: Ontologies must be updated from time to time so that the user gets effective and the latest results. It has led to the continuous evolvement of ontologies. Ontology maintenance approaches may be centralized or decentralized.
  - Re-using existing ontologies: Ontologies can be re-used by various applications for formalizing knowledge into an understandable form.

Ontology can re-use other ontology by referencing elements of other ontology in its axioms. The rules or axioms of existing ontologies are adapted to generate new ontology. It is a much easier task rather than developing ontology from scratch.

- **Support Activities:** Various sub-activities are included in the support process; each of them is described in detail below:
    - Knowledge acquisition: This activity gathers knowledge from different sources of information stored in repositories. The multiple sources may include domain expert knowledge, online books, and ontologies.
    - Integration: Combining multiple existing ontologies to generate new ontology is called *integration* of ontologies. The process holds *ontology merging* and *ontology alignment*. *Ontology merging* creates new ontology derived from several ontologies belonging to a similar domain while ontology alignment is used for identifying mapping between source ontologies. Proper documentation is needed to reuse and integrate existing ontologies.
    - Configuration management: It specifies identification, documentation, recording, and reporting of different versions of the ontology. Project management tools and ontology editing environments can be used for performing process configuration management like change request form control, and many more.

The next section describes the possibility of convergence of Social and Semantic Web.

2.6 SOCIAL SEMANTIC WEB FRAMEWORK

Various efforts have been made continuously to achieve extension between Social Web applications and semantic web technologies to develop a system that is error-tolerant and allows formalization of concepts with the use of semantic web technologies. The social applications that make use of semantic annotations are called as *Social Semantic Web applications*.

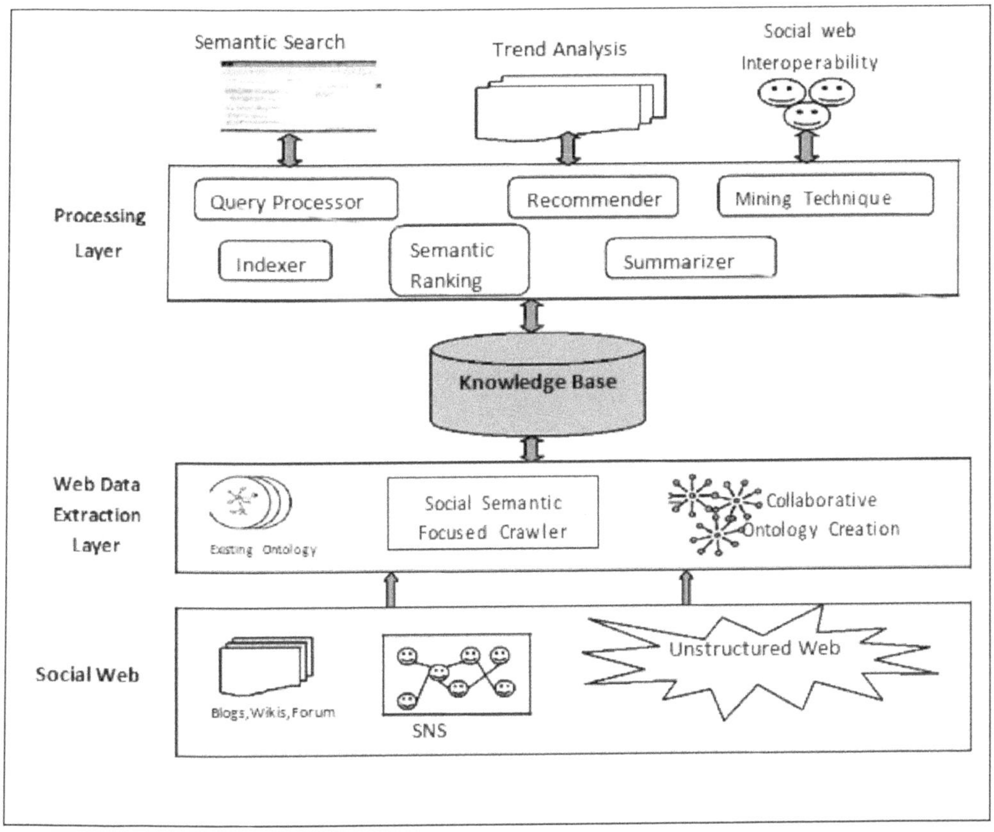

Figure 2.7: Basic Social Semantic Web Framework

The benefits are twofold. On the one hand, it facilitates users sharing and understanding the domain knowledge. On the other hand, applications can use it to provide high-level queries. The crawler collects data sets from the web of data periodically, and the evaluator will rank these data by relevance and quality.

The data that satisfied the criteria will be integrated into the repository. The inference engine supports the evaluator to finish its work, and also perform queries submitted by users. The abstract model for Social Semantic Web framework is shown in Fig. 2.7.

The comprehension of social semantic web framework creates the explicit and rich semantic knowledge which can be utilized in creating new business opportunities. Efficient services like recommendation can be developed, the next section discusses about the categorization of recommendation systems.

2.7 CATEGORIZATION OF RECOMMENDATION SYSTEMS

Recommender System (RS) is a competent tool that assists users by providing a ranked list of items as per their requirements or preferences without being explicitly searching in the system. The main motive of all recommendation systems is to provide the most appropriate items to the right user at right time. Vast researches are going in this field and many different approaches are proposed which take benefit of different types of data and analyzing techniques. The categorization of the recommendation system [22] is shown in Fig. 2.8.

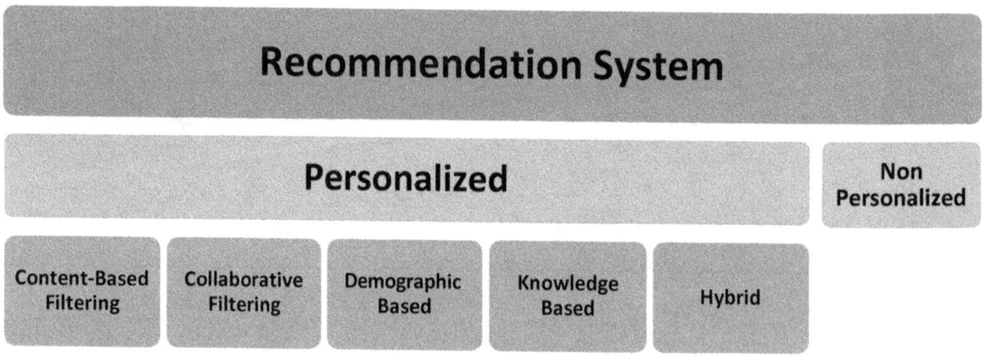

Figure 2.8: Categorization of Recommendation System

In the personalized category of recommendation, the aim is to recommend items to users based on the following:

- User's personalized interest towards an item
- Inspired from the interest of the other users
- Inspired from the user's social network

There are further five different categorizations of personalized recommendation considering a different aspect of recommendation:

- *Content-Based Filtering*: In this category, users are provided with recommendation based on their purchase or interest pattern towards an item. All the items similar to the items searched, purchased, or visited by the users are referred a recommendation. For example, suppose user search for Samsung Galaxy M51 smartphone, then based on the content (the specification) of the phone, other similar and same configuration smartphone from other brands such as MI, OnePlus, Oppo is recommended. In such a case, there is no requirement of data from other users and no issues related to data sparsity and cold start problem.

- *Collaborative Filtering based*: In this category of recommendation, a user is mapped with the other similar users based on their interest and rating towards a set of items. There is a limitation of scalability and cold start problems. It is divided further into two broad categories:
    - *User-based*: In this scenario, different users having similar interests and rating behavior as the target user are considered. The items chosen by similar users are recommended to the target user. For example, suppose the target user and other users have interest in new tech gadgets, so if Amazon echo came into the market and is liked by other users, then this new product will be recommended to the main user.
    - *Item-based*: In this scenario, all the items rated similar to the items like by the user in any particular product category, then those items will be recommended to the user.

- *Demographic based*: In this category, the users are given a recommendation based on the similarity of demographic information such as age, gender, location, employment, etc. The challenge is to retrieve the user's demographic information as it could lead to a breach of privacy and require proper authorization from them.

- *Knowledge-based*: This category of recommendation systems is built for a specific domain. The users have been explicitly asked to provide their preferences and interest. The system is least concerned about the history and mainly uses the knowledge, and the explicit user preference to provide the recommendation. For example, the online platform related to real state housing or renting property comes under this category, where the user specifies the BHK, flooring, amenities, etc.

- *Hybrid Recommendation:* In this category of recommendation, two or more different recommendation approaches can be combined to build hybrid solutions. The limitation of any one system can be dealt with the advantages of the other, resulting in the development of the robust recommendation framework.

The *cold-start problem* is a very famous and potential issue in the recommender systems, although various researches have been done to overcome this challenge. *Cold start problem* split into two categories namely, *New User Cold Start Problem* and *New Item Cold Start Problem*. New user cold-start problem refers to the lack of information about the user's interest or very less ratings provided by the user to the items in the system. *Pure New User Cold Start Problem* refers to the problem when no rating at all is provided by the user in the system. *New item cold-start problem* refers to the scenario when a new item is added to the system and there is a lack of ratings provided to it by the users. This constitutes a problem for the collaborative recommendation algorithm as it largely depends on the item's ratings to provide recommendations. With the increasing e-commerce platforms, huge numbers of new users signing every day or less-active users in almost every application creates a serious issue for the recommendation systems [23].

The next section discusses about the semantic based searching, which is another potential business opportunities created due to the growing semantic web technologies

2.8 OVERVIEW OF SEMANTIC BASED SEARCHING

Traditional search engines are a massive source of retrieving information from the web. The results are being produced by performing *keyword-based* search i.e., it matches user's query keywords with the keywords stored in indexed databases and presents a ranked list of search results to the user. The main drawback of search engines is a lack of relevance and high recall. Consider a query "*Mobile phones with red cover*", this query when entered in traditional search engines produces relevant as well as irrelevant results in relation to terms-*mobile phones, red lotus, flower, and cover*. The traditional search experience does not consider stopping words, auxiliary verbs that reflect the meaning of the given statement. Likewise in the above query, the relation between the *mobile phone* and the *red cover* has lost its significance due to which irrelevant results are produced.

These engines have no inference mechanism to deduce the relationship between semantically similar words.

To reduce this ambiguity and perform an intelligent search, the concept of SW came into existence in 1996 as envisioned by Tim Berners Lee [4]. SW is defined as the collection of information linked in a way so that it can be easily be processed by machines [24]. It is practically not feasible to annotate the entire web content into semantic tags so that current search engines could behave like SSE. So, there is a need to develop a semantic search engine that analyses user queries based on their semantics and produces meaningful results with higher precision and low recall. Researchers have proposed intelligent interfaces to handle user queries using semantic technologies as mentioned below:

- ***Knowledge Base Specific Interface:*** Specific purpose interfaces using domain knowledge base are usually appropriate to use for their simplicity and homogeneity nature. The majority of the web-based form search comes under this category. These interfaces are designed to cater to the most specific and relevant user queries, which are known to the system in advance. The drawbacks of using such systems are the efforts needed for specific interface development and its rigidity due to changes in the schema.

- ***Faceted Browsing***: Faceted browsing technique offers limited facets to users to explore based on the available resources. As this technique does not depend upon the knowledge base, existing SPARQL endpoints require small or no adjustment on top of it. The major limitation of this technique is that it restricts the users with a limited set of queries. For example, it is easier to search for objects specific to class "Student", but it lacks to handle complex queries such as "Student who studies in a school in London", it is because of the fact that restriction "in London" is related to the school not to the class student. Although there are few tools such as Visual SPARQL Query builder [25] which provides ease in generating SPARQL queries, still they are not in reach to common users and usually knowledge developers and engineers are their target users. For using such tools, common users still require an understanding of how SPARQL works and the construct which needs to be used in formulating the queries, and some knowledge of the core schema.

- ***Question Answering (QA):*** Although QA systems allow users to query their questions directly such as Ginseng [26], NLP-Reduce [27], still they need to be confined to a particular domain using models or patterns. The limitation of such a system is that if the user enters a cross-domain query, it could be very difficult for the system to handle such queries and require feedback from the users.

This chapter presented the fundamental concepts and some challenges related to the social and semantic web technologies. The next chapter discusses the research work done in these fields. The literature work in the areas of collaborative ontology and structured data creation, ontology matching systems, recommendation, and semantic search engines is described in detail.

CHAPTER 3

LITERATURE SURVEY

3.1 INTRODUCTION

With the exponential growth in the number of producers of information on the Web, a huge amount of information is getting generated. The lack of rich semantics and requirement of human intervention for analysing web content have aggravated the problem of reaching the specific information. Tim-Berners Lee, creator of WWW had a vision of the Semantic Web, where machines will able to understand the semantics of the data and can overcome various related challenges such as precise information retrieval, interoperability, structured data, recommendation accuracy, etc. According to him, by combining the metadata with the web content, machines would not only present the information rather than would able to understand and process the information on the web pages.

Motivating common users to participate in creating structured data for Semantic Web is the biggest challenge. With the evolution of Web 2.0, ordinary people are able to contribute tremendously to Social Web, using its easy to understand application interface. It can capture mass participation and user-generated content can also be augmented to the existing semantic web. The major challenge is to structure and semantically store data to be processed by machines automatically. In this way, the Social Web and the Semantic Web can complement each other to address the challenges both worlds are facing. The work carried out focuses on the Social Web and Semantic Web Technologies.

Literature survey plays an imperative role in every research work. This chapter describes the work of eminent researchers and highlights the challenges, which require to be addressed. The literature presented in the chapter has been categorized primarily in the following four parts as depicted in Fig. 3.1.

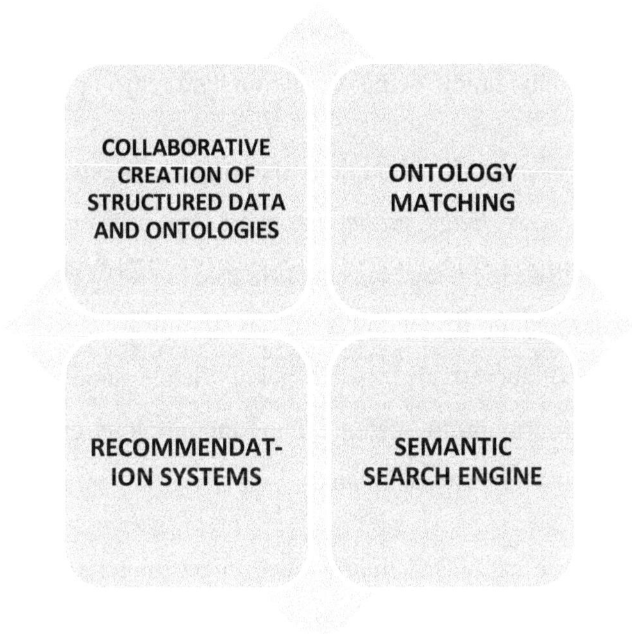

Figure 3.1: Categorization of Literature Work

3.2 COLLABORATIVE CREATION OF STRUCTURED DATA AND ONTOLOGIES

Depending upon the different set of requirements, various approaches and methodologies are proposed and implemented in the literature work done. Several researchers have worked in the field of collaborative creation of structured data and ontologies, some of these works are presented below:

The *myOntology project* [28] uses wikis for community-driven horizontal *lightweight* ontology building by enabling general users to contribute. The *myOntology project* proposed to use the infrastructure and culture of wikis to enable collaborative and community-driven ontology building. It intends to enable general users with little expertise in ontology engineering to contribute. It is mainly targeted at building horizontal *lightweight* ontologies by tapping the wisdom of the community.

Semantic Wikis [29] assist in the collaborative creation of resources by defining properties as wiki links with well-defined semantics. Collaborative knowledge contributed by various users was presented more explicitly and formally thus enhancing the capabilities of wikis. Using simple syntax, navigational links are semantically annotated and further encoded between resource pages which represent the relations between them. Irrespective of degree of formalization and semantic capabilities, semantic wikis have few common features like link annotation, context-aware presentation, improved navigation, semantic search, and reasoning support.

Authors in [30] have presented a methodology that requires creation of ontology using three modules namely *knowledge gathering, modeling of concepts,* and *ontology evaluation.* Web 2.0 allows the social tagging process, Social Web data are annotated and categorized by associating it with tags thus developing folksonomy. Creating and managing these tags collaboratively results in knowledge acquisition. Folksonomy tags are then converted into ontology elements by the ontology engineers and further ontology evaluation procedures are validated.

Researchers in [31] have expressed their views on recent research development in semantic wikis. "*The use of wikis for ontologies*" and "*The use of ontologies for wikis*" are the most used approach for semantic wikis. Many of the researches done over semantic wikis used the first approach in which the wiki acts as the front-end of the collaborative ontology maintenance system.

Semantic Media Wiki [32] is an extension to Media Wiki, which permits semantic data to be encoded within wiki pages. Extended wiki syntax helps in encoding the semantic data into wiki text. Every article corresponds to exactly one ontological element (class or property). Every annotation in the article makes statements about this element. The links between the semantic wiki pages are referred to as *Relations*. Finally, this is converted into formal ontology. In paper [33], researchers have developed a system to support the primary work of ontology development between ontology developers collaboratively, without the need for domain experts to be present.

Folksonimized Ontology (FO) proposed by [34], uses three *3E steps* technique namely *Extraction, Enrichment, and Evolution.* A new blended approach is presented which allows the semantic capability of folksonomies used by ontologies and vice versa. Visual review and visual enhancement tools help in implementing and testing the completed system.

Researchers in [35] have proposed a novel approach for supporting concurrent ontology development framework to enable experts from a different group to simultaneously edit ontology, *Concurrent Versioning* is used which is a standard model in software development. To overcome the challenge of resolution and conflict detection, the researchers take semantic and the structure of the ontology versioning into account, followed by reconciling with precisely defined standards. A system, named *ContentCVS* was developed by a researcher which proved to be computationally efficient and useful.

Another interesting approach to take advantage of review given by customers for any product in online shopping was taken into consideration to develop cross domains ontology [36]. The idea is to develop domain ontologies based on the user reviews and in turn, benefit them with relevant information quickly. Many users generally compare products that span multiple domains, this arises the need for ontology alignment among multiple domains and to form a cross-domain ontology. In this work, Natural Language Processing (NLP) approaches have been used to construct domain ontology. A novel ontology alignment approach has also been proposed to handle cross-domain product comparison and purchase decisions.

Detailed and systematic survey of all the tools related to ontology development, the Web 2.0 tools, was carried out by researchers in [37]. They focused on the requirement of the user in virtual learning environments (VLEs) and provided them with a review of the system depending upon the preferred activities and the learning style. The work was funded by EU 7FP and the results were implemented under iTEC pan-European research and development project to design future classrooms.

Authors in [38] explored the researches based on combining UML and ontology. Both UML and ontologies were used for representing knowledge with varied functionalities. The work provided extensive study comprehending both the domains with theoretical as well as practical perspectives.

Researchers in [39], developed a generic ontology model for representing the questionnaire domain so that the reasoning over the survey report could be automatically done by machines rather than humans. With the growth of smart mobile devices, it is much easier to gather the deep insight of the respondents on the subject under research which leads to significant growth in the amount of retrieved information from a large number of respondents. The proposed approach may become applicable for a personalized environment and other decision support systems.

3.2.1 Ontology Development Languages

Various languages have always been desired by professionals for developing ontologies. Following are the types of ontology languages used in the Semantic Web.

LOOM [40]**:** It is one of the knowledge representation languages which is based on description logics and rules to build concepts automatically.

SHOE [41]**:** It is used to extract relevant information from web documents. It also combines knowledge representation data and ontological features.

OML [42]**:** It stands for *Ontology Markup Language* that is treated as an extension of SHOE.

XOL [43]**:** It stands for *Ontology Exchange Language* that is based on XML and used for the development of ontologies in any tool.

DAML+OIL [44]**:** DAML stands for *DARPA Agent Markup Language* and OIL stands for *Ontology Interchange Language*. It is used for achieving semantic interoperability among various resources.

CycL [45]**:** It is one of the formal languages that use predicate logic to define concepts in the domain. It comes under the category of generic ontologies.

The detailed comparisons between various ontology development tools are shown in Table 3.1.

3.2.2 Ontology Development Tools

Most of the existing ontology development systems are very complicated and lack in motivating the different expertise of users to contribute to developing ontologies. They are deficient in providing easy to use interfaces for a non-technical common user, making it difficult for them to understand the system and sharing their perspective for domain representation. Ontology development tools mainly provide a solitary environment and involve the domain expert in the initial stages of the ontology engineering phase, thus impede the complete development process. The detailed comparison between various ontology development tools is shown in Table 3.2.

Table 3.1: Comparison among Ontology Development Languages

Features	LOOM	SHOE	OML	XOL	DAML+OIL
Concept documentation	Yes	No	Yes	No	Yes
Instance attributes	Yes	Yes	Yes	yes	Yes
Class attributes	Yes	No	Yes	yes	Yes
n-ary relations	Yes	Yes	Yes	No	No
Cardinality constraints	Yes	No	No	No	Yes
Concept instances	Yes	Yes	Yes	yes	Yes

3.3 ONTOLOGY MATCHING SYSTEMS

Different architectures have been proposed for ontology matching systems. These are divided into various categories based on the size of ontologies, approach used, the number of matchers used etc. In this study, large scale ontology matching systems have been presented along with the other ontology matching system based on various approaches.

3.3.1 Large Scale Ontology Matching Systems

Most of these methods have three main stages:

- (i) Partitioning the large ontology to several sub-ontologies.
- (ii) Applying the matching method to each pair of sub-ontologies.
- (iii) Combining the results.

The main features and the methods of the first stage of partitioning the large ontology to several sub-ontologies are discussed. This approach resembles the technique of divide and conquers, in which the goal of matching the large-scale ontology is broken down into sub-goals of matching small or sub ontologies and results are combined at the end. First of all, the entities of the input ontology need to be clustered using different clustering techniques. Various researchers [46, 47] have opted for the Agglomerative

Hierarchical Clustering category to cluster all the entities of input ontology by implementing ROCK and SCAN algorithm.

Table 3.2: Comparison among various Ontology Development Tools

Ontology Development Tool	Open Source	Import Format	Export Format	Language	Availability	Storage	Technique Used/ Description
OntoEdit [48]	No	RDFS, F-Logic, DAML + OIL	RDB	Java	Free	Yes	Comprehensive use of inference, flexible plug-in framework
Graffoo [49]	Yes	OWL2, Turtle, RDF/XML	OWL/XML	-	Free	Yes	Graphical framework to develop SPAR ontologies
UBOT [50]	-	UML, XML	DAML +OIL	Java	Free	No	NLP based, maps UML stereotypes to DAML-specific elements
OWLGrED [51]	No	OWL, UML, RDF/ XML	OWL, UML, RDF/ XML	-	Free	Yes	Based on UML class diagram and allow operability with Protégé
Anzo [52]	No	XML, RDF, XLS	XML, RDF, XLS	-	Paid	Yes	Used with excel, two rule engines.
WebOnto [53]	No	OCML	GXL, RDF, OIL	Java	Free	Yes (HTML Model)	Generating instance editing form from class automatically
Top Braid Composer [54]	No	RDF, OWL, XHTML, Microdata	Convert RDF Graphs, RDF, OWL	Eclipse (Java)	Paid	Yes	Commercial tool, Jena base,
Swoop [55]	No	OWL, XML, RDF, Text	RDF, OIL, DAML	-	Free	Yes (HTML Model)	Creating, editing, debugging ontologies
Dogma Studio [56]	No	OWL, RDF, DAML, OIL	OWL, RDF, DAML, OIL	Dotnet	Paid	No	To allow non-IT experts to contribute in creating ontologies
WebODE [57]	Yes	XML, RDF, XCARIN, OWL	OIL, DAML, OIL, Flogic	Prolog, Java	Free	-	Scalable, Extensible, Integrated workbench, allows interoperability with other systems
Collaborative Protégé [58]	-	RDF, RDFS, DAML, OIL	XML, OWL, Clips	Java	Free	Yes (JDBC)	Collaborative environment, work on different formats and suitable for large ontologies as well.
TODE [59]	No	RDF, RDBMS, OWLLite, N-3, N-Triple	RDF, RDBMS, OWLLite, N-Triple, N-3	Dotnet	Free	Yes	Easy web environment, reasoning, visualization and inference

Once the cluster formation is done, the entities lie in the same cluster set are strongly related with each other, while the entities present in the different cluster are weakly related to each other. Therefore, it can be assumed that the different clusters of sub-ontologies represent different and autonomous sub-domain of knowledge.

In the second stage, the main concern is to lower the run-time of finding the alignments between two input ontologies. The alignment process is executed between entities of pairs of sub-ontologies. Only the highly relevant pair of sub-ontologies will be processed further to the matching process to avoid exhaustive pair-wise comparisons. These methods can be found in Falcon-AO [60] and COMA++[61], LOMPT [62].

A block (sub-ontology) formed in the first stage is used and a concept of selecting candidate block was proposed to find mappings between their entities [63]. Various similarity measures were proposed at block level by assuming that the two blocks may share a large number of concepts and terminology to represent entities if they express the same or nearby topics. The similarity between the blocks can be computed using two methods. The idea behind the first method is that the similarity between two blocks is more is the anchors discovered between them is more. The pair of entities having a high similarity value is called an anchor [47]. Another method to find the similarity in blocks is to find the similarity between their block documents. A block document contains information such as the name and label of all the entities present in it. Various researches such as Lily [64], TaxoMap [65], Anchor-Prompt [66], AnchorFlood [67], are based on these methods only.

The novel method based on filter and verification for matching large ontologies has been proposed in [68]. The *filter phase* reduces the heterogeneous nature of the input ontologies and further the reduced ontologies were matched in the verification phase. OAEI dataset has been used for evaluating the proposed approach and it proves to be successful in improving the efficiency and the accuracy of the system.

In [69], the proposed hybrid approach is based on a parallel and distributed environment along with the combination of efficient matching strategies. Initially, the input ontologies are decomposed into resource-based subsets. In the next phase, ontology clusters are created using the entity's ranking and centroid selection. In the last phase, similar cluster identification was done using Latent Semantic indexing, and finally using various efficient matches, matchable entities are identified. In [70], the researchers overcome the limitation of local optimal solution of using Evolutionary Algorithm for matching a large number of concepts in sensor ontology matching system. At first, a novel similarity measure for matching identical sensor concept is constructed. Secondly, the authors have proposed a hybrid algorithm that benefits by reducing the premature convergence and enhancing its speed. It combines the Compact Evolutionary Algorithm for global search and the TABU search algorithm for local search and the system proves to be efficient in discovering alignments.

In [71], researchers have restricted their model to the biomedical domain. Input ontology is divided into sub-tasks and matching of sub-tasks is carried out using a fully automated machine learning-based model. The machine learning model is trained using the knowledge base created by crawling the external sources in the biomedical domain and without human intervention. Initially, input ontology indexing and loading are done, followed by input ontology partitioning using a partitioning algorithm. Thereafter local matching learning module is computed using knowledge base and local training set feature selection. At last, alignments generated as output are evaluated using reference alignment.

3.3.2 Systems Based on Other Approaches

In the ontology engineering and development process, ontology authoring is a crucial task. Understanding of the authoring pattern by ontology engineers is essential for the development of ontology engineering tools. According to the user's expertise, the perspective of the task, location, and supervision varies with the different settings of ontology authoring. In [72], it is proved that the different authoring setting addresses the range of expertise, task type, and location impact, they also revealed the common core workflows among all of them. In [73], an inference inspector plug-in is proposed and it is validated that this plug-in improves the correctness and the speed in understanding authoring action.

To facilitate semantic interoperability in any domain, entities in upper ontology needs to be integrated. Integration is a very tedious task and requires human interventions despite the emergence of many automated methods. In [74] authors have asked the experts to fill web survey for the travel domain by classifying 46 entities. It is evident from their study that there is a high probability for the experts to classify entities inconsistently. Consider the importance of the task, it was recommended that the methodology for manual integration should be improved. In [75], aspect-based semi-automated ontology builder is implemented for semantic analysis (SOBA). Various efforts have been made to improve the efficiency and the effectiveness of knowledge and aspect-based sentiment analysis. The performance of the proposed model is evaluated by comparing it with the Two-Stage Hybrid Model (TSHM). Although SOBA lacks in improving the effectiveness of TSHM, but it reduces the human intervention in building ontology by 50%.

Researchers in [76] focus on finding data-driven approach to handle the increasing amount of data in the healthcare domain to fully automate its tasks. The proposed model suggested the conversion of healthcare data into an equivalent HL7 FHIR structure. It focuses on developing healthcare ontologies and storing them using the triple store. The concepts, relationships, and axioms from the triple store are given as input to identify semantic similarity using Retina API [77] and Levenshtein distance [78] is used to calculating the syntactic similarity among concepts and finally, the results are aggregated. Finally, the quality of the proposed mechanism is evaluating through Non dominated Sorting Genetic Algorithm (NSGA-III) as well as using alignment API and proves to provide new opportunities in healthcare sector.

In most ontology matching research, entity or concept mapping has been given more importance rather than analyzing the structural relationships between them. In [79] researchers studied the finding alignments using structural similarity. Initially, MSI (Inheritance Similarity Method) based on the concept is used as a similarity method which includes inheritance relation for computing similarity. Secondly, the relationship between siblings is included to enhance the similarity value between the entities using MSS (Siblings Similarity Method). Researchers in [80] targeted in achieving the subsumption relation alignment as well. The COMPOSE framework is proposed which consists of three processes. The first process is ontology profiling which determines the terminological, structural, and lexical analysis. The second process is matcher selection and configuration which describes various matching algorithms such as string-based, structure-based and lexical matcher. In the third phase sequential, parallel, and hybrid matcher combinations are applied. The detailed comparison of some large-scale ontology matching system is represented in Table 3.3.

Table 3.3: Comparison of Large-scale ontology matching systems

Publication	Dataset	Linguistic similarity measure	Data Structure	Parallel Matching	Search Space/ Time Reduction	Scalable	Technique Used
Overview of YAM++ (not) Yet Another Matcher for ontology alignment task [81]	OAEI 2012 and OAEI 2013	Multi linguistic matcher	Indexes, Graph based	No	Yes	Yes	Structural information is encoded into bitmap and disk-based ontology matching approach is used. To store temporary data, disk-based mechanism is applied.
LOMPT: An efficient and scalable ontology matching algorithm [62]	Mouse anatomy and NCI Anatomy	SI-SUB	Structure based, hash table	No	Yes	Yes	A novel scalable matching algorithm and new neighbour based structural proximity is proposed.
COGOM: COgnitive Theory Based Ontology Matching System[82]	OAEI 2015.	Tversky psychological model of similarity	Graph based	No	Yes	Yes	Cognitive units of knowledge are used to modelled the concepts of ontology
PSOM2—partitioning-based scalable ontology matching using MapReduce [83]	OAEI 2013	EI-Sub	Hash table	Yes	Yes	Yes	New partitioning-based scalable ontology matching system, new light-weight linguistic matcher (EI-sub) and MapReduce-based EI-sub were used.
Matching large ontologies: A divide-and-conquer approach [47]	OAEI 2007,	I-Sub	Structure based	No	Yes	No	structure-based partitioning algorithm, block mappings, two powerful matchers, V-DOC and GMO, are employed
Using Compact Evolutionary Tabu Search	OAEI 2014, 2016 and 2018	Sensor concept similarity measure	Indexes	No	Yes	No	Evolutionary Tabu Search algorithm, new optimal model of

algorithm for matching sensor ontologies [70]							sensor ontology matching, Compact Evolutionary Tabu Search algorithm (CETS) is presented
Ontology Alignment using Stable Matching [79]	OAEI 2017	Inheritance similarity method	Graph Based	No	No	No	Adopted two alignment methods: Method of Similarity of Inheritance and Method of Sibling Similarity
Partitioning and Local Matching Learning of Large Biomedical Ontologies [71]	OAEI, 2017	cross-searching the input ontologies with the available external biomedical knowledge bases	Structure Based	No	Yes	No	Partitioning approach outperforms existing techniques, Local matching while using a specific machine learning model
Aggregating the syntactic and semantic similarity of healthcare data towards their transformati on to HL7 FHIR through ontology matching [76]	Medication and Laboratory based	syntactic and semantic similarities , Levenshtei n distance	Indexes	No	No	No	Interoperability through the transformation of healthcare data into the corresponding HL7 FHIR structure, Levenshtein distance and their semantic fingerprints are calculated
Hybrid Large-Scale Ontology Matching Strategy on Big Data Environment [69]	Conference Dataset, Human and mouse Anatomy	Latent Semantic indexing	Structural based	Yes	Yes	Yes	A new hybrid ontology matching approach that benefits on one hand from the opportunities offered by parallel platforms, and on the other hand from ontology matching techniques

In the next section, new approaches to handle the limitation of recommendation engine based on ontology, LOD, Social network, and data mining are presented along with the tabular comparisons.

3.4 RECOMMENDATION SYSTEMS

Recommender System (RS) is a competent tool that assists users by providing a ranked list of items as per their requirements or preferences without being explicitly searching in the system. This system has proved to be an important tool to recommend items, thereby personalizing the applications for various domains such as tourism, marketing, movies, songs, hotels & restaurants, news, forecasting theories and many more. There are many famous recommendation systems provided by top e-commerce applications such as Flipkart, Amazon prime videos, Makemytrip, etc.

3.4.1 Based on Cold Start Problem

With the increasing e-commerce platforms, a huge number of new users signing every day or less-active users in almost every application creates a serious issue for the recommendation systems [84]. Another major issue is the *new item cold Start Problem* which refers to the newly added item in any particular system which has very less or no rating provided by the user. So in this scenario, analyzing the item and referring it to the user can be a tedious task [85]. New item cold start problem is also called the *early-rater problem* in various works of literature [86].

In recent literature, many hybrid approaches have been proposed to overcome the problem of new user cold-start such as cross-domain collaborative filtering using matrix factorization models [87], Learning latent factor representation for videos based on modeling the emotional connection between user and item [88], enhanced content-based algorithm using social networking [89], combining social sub-community division and ontology decision model [90], using social network textual information to model user interest and item [91].

Researchers have proposed the solution for *cold start problem* by exploiting blog textual data and labeling them as per the user's opinion, and then constructed a user-item rating matrix for collaborative filtering and improving recommendations [92]. Authors in [93] improved [94] by presenting a concept called *Proximity-Significance-*

Singularity which improves the disadvantages of Pearson correlation coefficient and cosine similarity [95] to improve the *new user cold start* problem.

3.4.2 Based on Linked Open Data

Utilizing the power of connected and structured linked data in the recommendation system holds a lot of research potential. The Linked Open Data (LOD) cloud is an enormous set of RDF statements interconnected together forming a cross-domain ontology graph and wrapper many domains, such as companies, people, geographical locations, movies, music, books, etc. DBpedia, as one of the largest LOD is known to be the "*typical entry point*" to these data [96]. The RDF mapping of Wikipedia is commonly considered as the *nucleus* of the emerging *Web of Data*. As DBpedia sets a standard to define properties and classes representing different domain and providing an enormous amount of machine-readable data, major research is going on to investigate how recommender systems can be made beneficial with this overabundance of data [87] and how Linked Data about items can be used for collaborative filtering algorithm [97].

In most of the latest literature, authors have exploited DBpedia majorly to define or modify various similarity measures using its properties gathered from LOD [98][99]. Social network platforms like Facebook had been used to gather user's music preferences and using DBpedia for calculating similarities between various music items and building a personalized playlist for users [100]. *Limited content analysis* is the core issue where Linked Open Data is significantly playing a major role and many researchers are taking advantage of using it. Researchers have developed an application named *TasteWeights* , it is a kind of recommender system in which user's preferences for music genre is extracted from Facebook and then DBpedia is exploited using SPARQL query end-point to find all the music played by new artist belonging to the same genre which the active user liked and then recommending the same to other users [101].

Various matrix factorization models were evaluated for collaborative filtering for cross-domain by using the LOD, which acts as a connector to analyze the items like by users in different domains. The metadata extracted from the LOD helps in generating the relationship between the items that belong to a different domain. But this approach has some limitations, as it can rely only on those domains which share information with other domain. If both source and the target domains are closed domains, it would not be possible to share information and hence semantic linking between the items would not be exposed [87]. Table 3.4, shows the technique used and the limitation of some of the related works.

Table 3.4: Technique and Limitations of various Recommendation Systems

S. No.	Publication	Technique Used	Achievement	Limitations
1	An application of fuzzy geographically clustering for solving the cold-start problem in recommender systems [102]	Data like user demographic information, their opinion, social tags are used to determine the best neighbours for the new user	Analogous users are more accurately determined	Very less user's demographic information is considered
2	Semantics-aware Recommender Systems exploiting Linked Open Data and graph-based features [103]	LOD based features, Random Forests, Naïve Bayes and Logistic Regression.	Accuracy of recommendation framework is improved	Similarity degree between users is not considered, Sparsity is ignored
3	A recommender system based on collaborative filtering using ontology and dimensionality reduction techniques [104]	EM clustering for clustering and non-incremental SVD for dimensionality reduction), Ontology Based Similarity,	Solve two main draw-backs of recommender systems, sparsity and scalability, using dimensionality reduction and ontology techniques.	User's demographic or its browsing information has not been considered
4	A new user similarity model to improve the accuracy of collaborative filtering [93]	Determining the analogous users using new similarity technique clustering algorithms, decision trees	Enhancement in the similarity degrees between users. No requirement for additional data.	Needs consideration in choosing the optimal number of groups and the splitting criteria
5	Addressing the New User Cold-Start Problem in Recommender Systems Using Ordered Weighted Averaging Operator [87]	• Optimistic exponential type of ordered weighted averaging (OWA) operator is applied • Fusion of CF and demographic and fusion of CF and CBF classifiers have been used	Improvement in performance of hybrid recommender system under "new user cold start" problem	Missing values are not handled

3.4.3 Other Approaches

Researchers have tried to improve the hybrid recommendation system for the movie domain based on demographic and collaborative filtering based approach. Their strategy categorizes the genres of movies based on demographic attributes, e.g., user age (child, teenager, or adult), student (yes or no), have children (yes or no), and gender (female or male) [105].

Researchers have developed a recommendation algorithm to offer the best suitable Cloud Platform as a Service (PaaS) for application developers to carry out web application management and development. Their experimental analysis shows their work deals with the problem of scalability [106]. It could be extended in the future using various semantic models.

Researchers have also developed the system based on the semantic web technologies and modeled all the information based on graph language which is Ontology Web Language 2 (OWL 2). This recommender system comes under the hybrid category combining various approaches like combined content-based, context-aware and CF. Experimental evaluation was done using Movie Lens data set and results are shown using F1 measures such as precision and recall [107].

Recommendation systems are widely adopted in the education sector as well. A system for recommending e-learning resources to the learners using an ontology and Sequential Pattern Mining (SPM) was proposed which comes under a hybrid knowledge-based recommender system. The authors use ontology to model various learning methods and learning resources and used SPM to find more about user's sequential learning patterns [108]. A complete framework was put forward using various web mining techniques and ontologies based on different domains to overcome major issues like cold start problems, sparsity, and scalability. MovieLens dataset was evaluated using various precision metrics [109].

Authors in [110] carried out a systematic literature review of research work carried in the recent past on mitigating the cold start problem using social networks and collaborative filtering for providing recommendations. Analysis of research done over the period; it is found that the researcher increases have focused on mitigating the cold start problem using social network. The comparison based on what evaluation parameters have been used by the researchers is shown in Table 3.5 and the detailed comparison among various recommendation systems dealing with user cold start problem is presented in Table 3.5

Table 3.5: Comparison based on different Evaluation Parameters

Publication	Evaluation Parameters						
	Precision	**Recall**	**F1-measure**	**MAE**	**MMR**	**Coverage**	**Other**
Addressing the user cold start with cross-domain collaborative filtering: exploiting item metadata in matrix factorization [87]	Yes	No	No	No	Yes	Yes	Yes
Latent factor representations for cold-start video recommendation [88]	No	No	No	No	Yes	No	Yes
Using Linked Data to Build Open, Collaborative Recommender Systems [97]	Yes	Yes	No	No	No	No	No
An Effective Recommender Algorithm for Cold-Start Problem in Academic Social Networks [89]	Yes	Yes	Yes	No	No	No	No
A Method to Solve Cold-Start Problem in Recommendation System based on Social Network Sub-community and Ontology Decision Model [90]	No	No	No	Yes	No	No	No
Exploring Social Network Information for Solving Cold Start in Product Recommendation [91]	No	No	No	No	Yes	No	Yes
Using semantic web to reduce the cold-start problems in recommendation systems [111]	No	No	No	Yes	No	Yes	No

Table 3.6: Detailed Comparison among related research works

Publication	Dataset	Similarity Measure	Domain	Social Network	Ontology Used	LOD	Technique Used
Addressing the user cold start with cross-domain collaborative filtering: exploiting item metadata in matrix factorization [87]	Facebook	Other	Book, Movies, Music (Cross Domain)	Facebook	No	DBpedia	Cross domain collaborative filtering using matrix factorization models
Latent factor representations for cold-start video recommendation [88]	Video Emotion, Amazon Product	No	Videos (Domain Independent)	No	No	No	Learning latent factor representation for videos based on modelling the emotional connection between user and item
Using Linked Data to Build Open, Collaborative Recommender Systems [97]	Smart Radio	binary cosine similarity	Music	No	No	DBpedia and Myspace	Used Linked Data about items for collaborative filtering algorithm
An Effective Recommender Algorithm for Cold-Start Problem in Academic Social Networks [89]	Created MyExpert App	Other	Academic Item	Academic social network	No	No	Enhanced content-based algorithm using social networking
A Method to Solve Cold-Start Problem in Recommendation System based on Social Network Sub-community and Ontology Decision Model [90]	MovieLens	Pearson similarity	Videos	No information	Taxanomy	No	Combining social sub-community division and ontology decision model
Exploring Social Network Information for Solving Cold Start in Product Recommendation [91]	Douban Website	Other	Books	Douban Website	No	No	Used social network textual information to model user interest and item
Using semantic web to reduce the cold-start problems in recommendation systems [111]	MovieLens	Composed Similarity, Jaccard, Jaro Winkler	Movie	No	Yes	No	Used semantic web structure and ontology

The next section addresses the research work done in improvising the traditional search engine along and developing a framework for intelligent semantic search engine which caters to the requirement of Web 3.0.

3.5 SEMANTIC SEARCH ENGINE

Several studies that have been conducted to build Semantic Search Engine (SSE), some of them explained are as follows:

Researchers in [112] proposed the conceptual architecture of SSE that uses KB for deriving inferences. This base is being created from the mapping of RDBMS. But the architecture does not include any method to retrieve data from KB. Authors in [113] devised a framework for domain-specific ontology based search engine that focuses on agricultural information about the state of West Bengal. It produces relevant results by mapping classes and instances. But this framework is unable to retrieve relevant results from heterogeneous formats of data.

Authors in [114] proposed domain specific ontology based search engine that focuses on transport services. It includes the use of Case-Based Reasoning algorithm to design KB and then applies the concept of threshold to rank the given results. This approach could not work well due to a lack of annotated data in the context of transport service.

Researchers in [115] designed prototypes for multiple domains including books, medicine, mobiles that stores their RDF content from web pages into a repository. But the model failed to create semantic annotations of RDF content into OWL format. OWL is a stronger language than RDF and conveys inherent meaning better.

Authors in [113] proposed a semantic search framework that produces exact search results by performing mapping between classes and instances with the help of RDF codes. This system is specifically developed for the agriculture sector of West Bengal which provides all the information related to the agriculture of that state. Authors in [116] proposed the framework of a semantic search engine consisting of a user interface to automatically suggest the query based on the ontology. Query optimizer further allows users to tag pre-defined ontology classes or attributes. The documents are indexed using the traditional method of indexing, a new ranking approach had also been suggested and the results are filtered using the resulting optimizer.

It is very challenging for the common user to explore RDF based Linked Data or knowledge base effectively. Also, it is not expected for the user to be well versed in writing SPARQL or to know about the underlying ontology structure. Authors in [117] proposed Semantic Focused Crawler to overcome the mentioned limitations. It is graph-based interface for querying using Subject-Predicate-Object format. The auto-complete feature of query builder assists users in choosing the domain ontology related entities without requiring them to have prior knowledge about ontology or SPARQL.

In various scenarios, users' queries may span to more than one domain which bringing a necessity for developing a cross-domain ontology for better search results or recommendations. In [36], the online reviews provided by the users are analyzed using various natural language processing for developing domain ontologies. Further, a new alignment technique is devised to form cross ontology by aligning the various domain ontologies.

A novel systematic method is proposed to understand natural language questions rather than using semantic parsers. Large numbers of low budget binary templates were created automatically. Efficient indexing was used to facilitate better searching over template decomposition. Two-level disambiguation strategies were designed and performed namely, 'entity level ambiguity' and 'structure level ambiguity'. Researchers in [118] proposed a framework which assists users in translating question in Natural Language into a structured query for specific domain knowledge-based system. The new graph structure, vocabulary, and semantic query graph have been defined to handle the complexity of compounded questions. The subgraph in the knowledge base has been identified based on the query expansion and its semantic graph generation. The subgraph generated is directly converted into structure query language.

Authors in [119], Proposed OSCAR, the Open Citations RDF Search Application, provides a user-friendly interface by hiding the complexity of writing SPARQL query by the common user. It provides access to any RDF triple store with easy to use SPARQL endpoint. Researchers in [120] identified the fragment of first-order logic that captures the underlying structure of the user query by formulating the faceted search interface. The complexity while answering such queries is well studied for RDF / OWL formats. An efficient algorithm for interface generation and updating was also proposed. The system was also tested for scalability with relevant results.

Authors in [121], extended the natural language pattern of user query by assigning a node known as 'Query Focus' for further matching it semantically. To find out the top diversified 'k' matches with the 'query focus', an efficient technique was proposed, thereby querying the knowledge graph by user query in natural language. Various research allowed users to ask a query in natural language with domain restricted vocabulary [122],[123]. Researchers in [124] proposed SQUALL structure to take user query as input and it is similar to natural language. The query has been directly mapped to the SPARQL based upon semantic and syntactic analysis without requiring a resource mapping process.

Authors in [125] proposed a Semantic Supported Information Retrieval System (SIRS), which is ontology-based and the input query is processed using a Probabilistic Latent Semantic Indexing (PLSI) algorithm. This work also concentrates on providing a personalized web search using *Multi-Criteria Particle Swarm Optimisation* (MCPSO) for handling the personal interest of the user. Traditional content-based web page recommendation systems had not utilized the power of semantic knowledge in discovering the patterns and recommendations. Also, authors in [126] proposed using semantic knowledge in all phases of data mining. Sequential Pattern mining algorithm, *CloSpan* was used to create frequent sequential patterns over semantic space. A semantically enriched pattern was generated, further, in offline mode, it is provided to the web page recommendation process for better results.

To improve the quality of search results, web databases need to be enriched and a semantic knowledge base should be created. In [127] framework to rank web pages was proposed known as ONTOPARK, which is based on ontology. In this work, the Vector Space Model has been combined with ontology for Information Retrieval. In this framework, RDF knowledge base was created by annotating the RDF files semantically for each query. In [128] three layer architecture known aa SRD-CP was proposed. In the first layer, the document domain was decided based by constructing semantic tree pattern based on RDF. The second layer handles the processing of complex queries using constrained application protocol and HTTP protocol. The third layer uses the generated SPT to include the word co-occurrence with the help of it association frequency. Apriori algorithm was used to find the association between the documents on the web

Human lacks in refining through large web page results retrieved by the traditional search engine for a specific query instead, machines can able to process the required information efficiently. Machines lack in understanding the underline structure and also the context of the user query, which requires users to brainstorm within a large set of results to find the desired one. The work had been done to rank the web pages based on their context sensitivity. Domain related ontology was used to generate the ranking factor for web pages [129]. The data properties on a web page were analyzed concerning the domain ontology, and the higher is the number of data properties inside the web document, the higher would be its ranking factor value. Authors in [130] worked on retrieving the web documents while enabling the effortless integration of data from multiple sources and also on reducing inconsistencies. An efficient web search engine framework was proposed to accurately fulfill the user requirements by enabling the multiple data sources integration during retrieval of search results web pages.

Comparative analysis of the related research works is shown in Table 3.7.

The next section describes the research carried out in the area of convergence of Social and Semantic web towards creating the robust Social Semantic Web applications are discussed.

3.6 SOCIAL SEMANTIC WEB

Social Web is growing enormously as it made it easy for people to publish online. Published information should be semantically annotated and structured to be useful for information sharing. Semantic Web annotates data syntactically as well as semantically thus making it in machine-understandable format. So, these two aspects can be aggregated to form SSW.

Table 3.7: Pros and Cons of related Search Engine Systems

S.No.	Title	Technique	Pros	Cons
1.	A Domain specific ontology based semantic search engine [113]	A semantic search engine framework has been proposed that produces relevant results by using mapping technique between classes and instances with the help of RDF codes.	(a) Uses ontology to maintain semantic relationships among classes and instances rather than using NLP. (b) Values of property can be computed from RDF codes and displayed to user	No ranking of results is being done.
2.	New framework for semantic search engine [116]	The components include user-interface, query optimizer and processor, ranking and indexing.	(a) Query optimizer scans keywords and matches them with words stored in ontology database.	(a) No updating of ontology database. (b) User interface is not connected to any semantic framework.
3.	OntoSearch: an ontology search engine [131]	The proposed OntoSearch system perform keyword based search by finding RDF files (ontology) and compares keywords with contents of RDF files.	(a) Combines Google search results with RDF and present them in hierarchical fashion. (b) OntoSearch acts as visualization tool and can be linked to other web ontology editor tools	(a) Synonym problem is not well addressed in this version of tool
4.	Semantic Information Retrieval using Ontology in University Domain [132]	It extracts knowledge from given ontology and puts these results in Google search API to form refined query.	(a) Uses WordNet API for generation of semantically similar words. (b) Matches terms used in user query with designed ontology to produce refined query.	(a) Does not evaluate Google results. (b) It builds ontology manually related to university domain
5.	A Semantic Search Engine for Answering Domain Specific User queries [133]	The proposed search engine components include user-interface, query processor, knowledge base. Mapper and ranking.	(a) Uses Mapper to represent semantic results into textual format. (b) Query processor scans keywords and matches them with words stored in ontology database.	(a) No comparison and evaluation of IR performance. (b) Does not evaluate Google results

Although millions of users contribute to Social Web but the data generated is unstructured and lacks semantic standards. The adoption of semantic web technologies can enforce the structuring of data and provide interoperability among various Social Web applications. Therefore, Semantic and Social Web can complement each other by overcoming the challenges faced by both the worlds

The Social and Semantic Web is a mixture of multi-disciplinary information that is evolving with powerful speed as a medium of learning in an open environment. In fact, the results produced may be irrelevant depending on the user's query which makes it difficult to initiate the learning process. So, there is a need for post-processing of search results so that semantically relevant results are available to the user [134].

Authors in [135] explained that the interoperability and portability of social data are some of the major bottlenecks of social network applications like Facebook, Twitter, Flicker, and many more. To represent and integrate social information explicitly and efficiently, it is mandatory to enrich social information with the power of semantics

Various efforts have been made continuously to achieve extension between social web applications and semantic web technologies. It is required to develop a system that is error-tolerant and allows formalization of concepts with the use of semantic web technologies. The social applications that make use of semantic annotations are called *Social semantic web* applications. The combination of Social and Semantic Web also allows informal annotations in the form of tags that connects with RDF or other semantic web languages.

Several articles have been published that described the benefits of the Social and Semantic web [136]. Authors in [13] and [7] points out that folksonomies can potentially bridge the gap between the Social and the Semantic Web. They also represent a medium for sharing information online, collective intelligence instead of observations from a panel of experts.

Researchers in [137] stated that it requires drawing of two fields to measure strength. Various investigations have been done regarding the evolution of the Social and Semantic web in past years. Topics in this area include the development of ontologies for tagging, the extraction of ontologies from social network graphs [138] and folksonomies, collaborative ontology evolution [139], tag similarity measures [140], etc.

Ranking relevant pages semantically is one of the methods of information retrieval and ranking that helps in focusing on resource content rather than finding sources of data in a given environment [141]. Authors in [142] devised a framework for performing semantic search and ranking of sources in the Social Bookmark system (SBS) to compute resource relevance.

The realization of the semantic web to its full potential is highly dependent on mass participation. The creation of easy-to-understand and useful applications is required to motivate ordinary people to contribute to the evolution of the semantic web.

In the subsequent chapters, main contributions to overcome the limitations and challenges addressed in this chapter are discussed in detail.

3.7 SUMMARY

This chapter covers the complete literature required as pre-requisite before working on the social semantic web applications. The literature survey has been done for problem identification in areas such as current Web 2.0, collaborative ontology development, semantic web technologies, recommendation systems and semantic search techniques. It is summarized below:

- Limited Data integration among the social web applications
- Developing ontologies are time consuming process and involves only the ontology engineers and domain experts in deciding the domain representations.
- Different organizations store and model their data in different formats and hence does not allow users to access the integrated information.
- Recommendation systems are inefficient and provide low accuracy in dealing with less active or in-active users
- Large number of search results retrieval makes it difficult for user to get the desired information.
- Lack of user expertise in writing queries to get the precise search results from the existing structured data hub.

The subsequent chapters describe in detail the contribution of the research to overcome the challenge identified in the available literature.

CHAPTER 4

EASYONTO: A COLLABORATIVE TOOL FOR STRUCTURED DATA CREATION AND LIGHTWEIGHT ONTOLOGY DEVELOPMENT

4.1 INTRODUCTION

With the evolution of Web 2.0, there is an exponential growth in the number of people producing unstructured information on the Web. This has resulted in ambiguities and irregularities which makes it difficult to process and understand the information. The lack of rich semantics and the requirement of humans to intervene in analyzing web content has aggravated the problem of reaching the specific information. With the advancement of the semantic web, various tools are created but most of them build only for expert level ontology engineers.

Ontologies proved to be a necessity for supporting knowledge management including interoperability, retrieval, storing, and sharing of data. It is considered as the main pillar of the semantic web [143]. Ontology development is a tedious task, various tools for ontology creation, editing, merging, alignment, maintenance tools had been developed over the past many years. Different functionality, plug-ins were provided for different levels of user. Some of them designed graphical user interfaces suitable only for ontology developers or for users having technical expertise.

4.2 REQUIREMENT FOR LIGHTWEIGHT ONTOLOGIES

With Web 2.0, social web applications allow users to collaboratively create, reuse and share information, resulting in the establishment of common consensus and understanding. Ordinary people are able to contribute tremendously to the Social Web, using its easy to understand application interface. It can capture mass participation and the user's generated content is growing exponentially. But the major challenge is to structure and semantically store that data so that machines can process them automatically. Ontology development can overcome this challenge. Some of the requirements and limitations of developing lightweight ontologies are discussed below:

- Ontology should include perspectives of different users, rather than involving only the ontology engineers and few experts. Therefore, ontology development should involve mass participants to take into account the perspective of common users and should be a collaboration process [28].

- Also, for faster development, ontology engineering should be a collaborative process. There is a requirement to create easy to use, simple, and collaborative ontology development system for the common users to expedite the ontology engineering process.
- In this era, different requirements need ontologies to model different types of data. In lack of such scenarios, interoperability and sharing will not be feasible. If the system allows common specifications, then information from varied sources could be integrated and easily shared on different platforms.
- With the help of social web applications, it would be easier to attract mass participation for collaboration and contribution towards ontology development. Although it would be challenging to create easy to understand social web application and motivate user for mass participation.
- Due to high expressiveness, heavyweight ontologies greatly contribute to developing high-end enterprise applications with powerful reasoning capabilities. However, such systems are vulnerable to inconsistencies. Although lightweight ontologies can handle inconsistencies but lacks in reasoning.
- Less semantic and low restriction greatly contributes to creating large scalable applications. Considering lightweight ontologies for the vast scale of WWW is significant for the practical realization of the Semantic Web.
- Most of the existing ontology development systems are very complicated in nature and lacks in motivating the different expertise of users to contribute in developing ontologies. Ontology development tools mainly provide the solitary environment and involve the domain expert in the initial stages of the ontology engineering phase, thus slow down the complete development process. Non-technical common users consider it difficult to understand the system and sharing their perspective for domain representation.

Keeping these points in consideration, "EasyOnto" system is proposed and implemented which allows the users to easily understand the system and develop lightweight ontologies. The proposed system creates a collaborative working environment and does not involve the expert in the initial stages, thereby expediting the process of ontology development.

4.3 PROPOSED LIGHTWEIGHT ONTOLOGY DEVELOPMENT SYSTEM

The proposed system allows users to collaboratively develop lightweight ontologies for any domain of interest. The system is intended to provide the common users, who are not ontology engineers, an interface to also allow them to contribute their consensus towards ontology construction. As shown in Fig. 4.1, the system is designed for all expertise of users. The simpler and easier to use system is majorly divided into the following phases:

1. Domain Selection
2. Adding Class/Relation/Instance
3. Superclass and Subclass mapping
4. Class and Relation mapping
5. Class, Relation and its instance mapping
6. Database Creation
7. Domain Expert Validation
8. Formal Light Weight Ontology Development

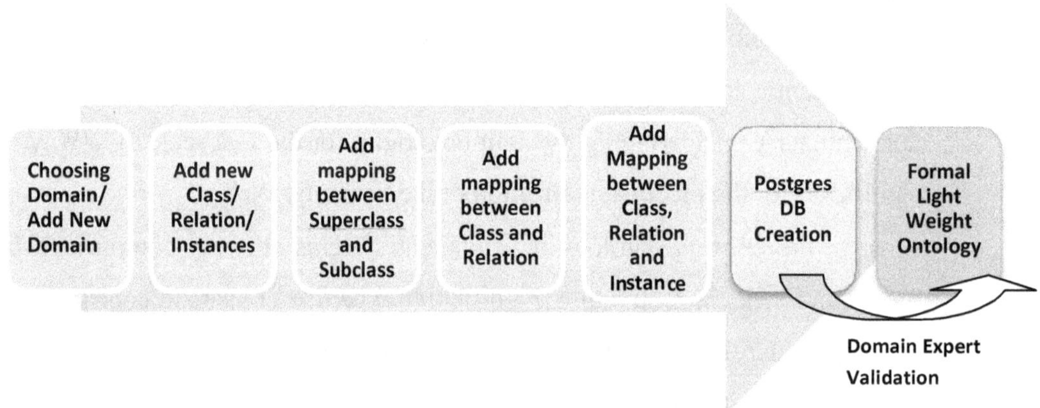

Figure 4.1: Process for collaborative Light Weight Ontology Development

4.3.1 Phase 1: User Registration and Domain Selection

Firstly the users need to register on the proposed system and "Sign In" through the login page as shown in Fig. 4.2. Depending on the interest or knowledge of the users in any particular domain, the users can choose from the domain list already available in the system's database and proceed further. The users can also able to add a new domain by choosing the option *Add Domain* which adds the domain in *PostgreSQL 9.3 Database Management System* (DBMS) [144] at the backend.

Example illustration:

As shown in Fig. 4.3, some domains like *Movie, Animal, Vehicle, Animal, and Travel* have already been added to the system for easeness of domain selection. In this work, the *Movie* domain is chosen to demonstrate the complete system and all the experimentation has also been done on this domain. Users can decide from the list of the available domain and click on the *Select* button to move further.

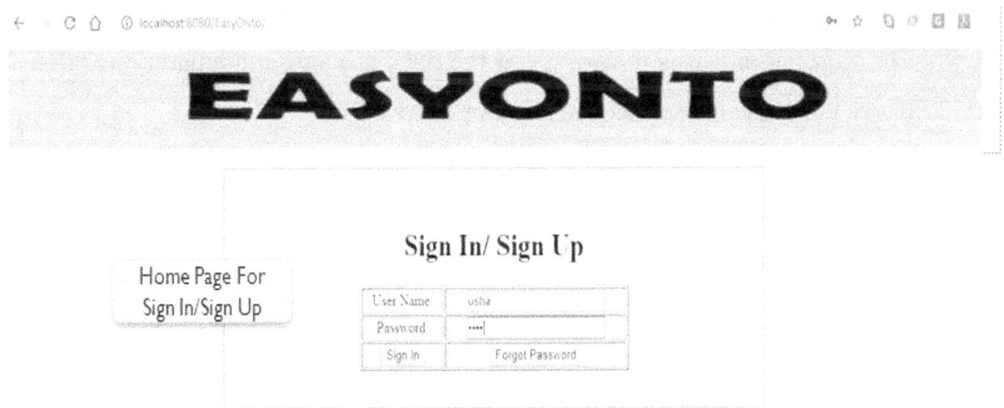

Figure 4.2: Sign In/Sign Up for EasyOnto

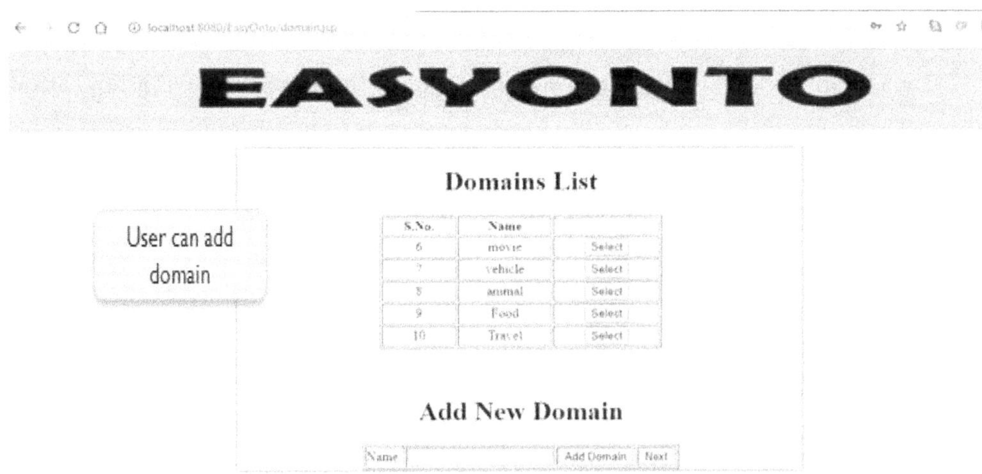

Figure 4.3: Domain Selection Page

4.3.2 Phase 2: Add Class/Relation/Instance

In this phase, the users can insert values for ontology class, relation or instance of a selected domain. The following steps describe its working in more details:

- On choosing the appropriate option from the tabs such as *Add Class, Add Relation* and *Add Instance*, the entire list of the available entities present in class, relation, or instance is shown to the users.
- If the users are satisfied with the values of entities present and have nothing more to contribute in these categories, there is an option to move further in system, by choosing the *Next* button.
- Otherwise, users have options to add a new class, relation, or instance by inserting the value in the text box provided and click on the *Add* button.
- The *Add* button saves the values to the database and immediately updates the entity in the available class, relation or instance list.
- Similarly, users can add new value to the relations or to the instance.
- On completion of this task, users have the option to proceed further by clicking on the *Next* button.

Example illustration:

(a) ***Add Class***: In any ontology, *Class* represents the category or the concept of a particular domain. In this example of the *Movie* domain, the class such as *Director, Person, Actor, Genre*, etc. are added to the system by inserting its value in the textbox and clicking on *Add Class* button as shown in Fig. 4.4(a).

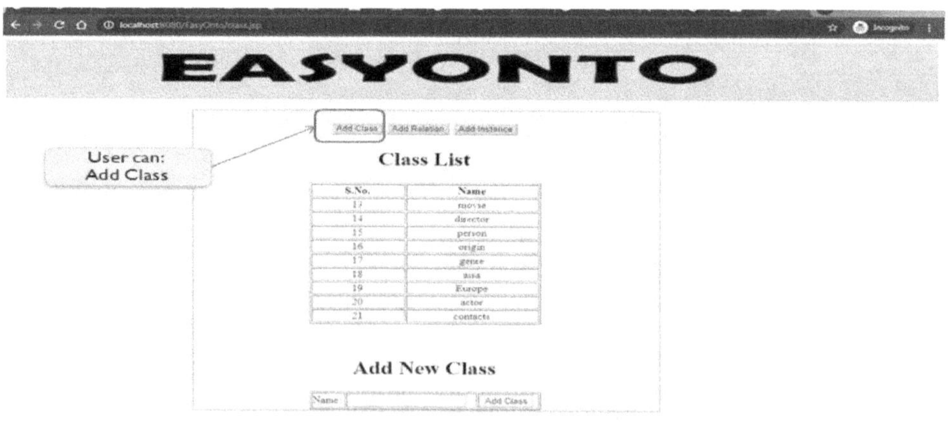

Figure 4.4(a): Represents *Add Class* Feature

(b) ***Add Relation***: *Relationship* in ontology is represented by properties or attributes related to the chosen domain. For the *Movie* ontology, relations such as *ReleaseDate, hasGenre, title, runtime, directedBy*, etc. are entered in the system by clicking on the *Add relation* button, as shown in Fig. 4.4(b

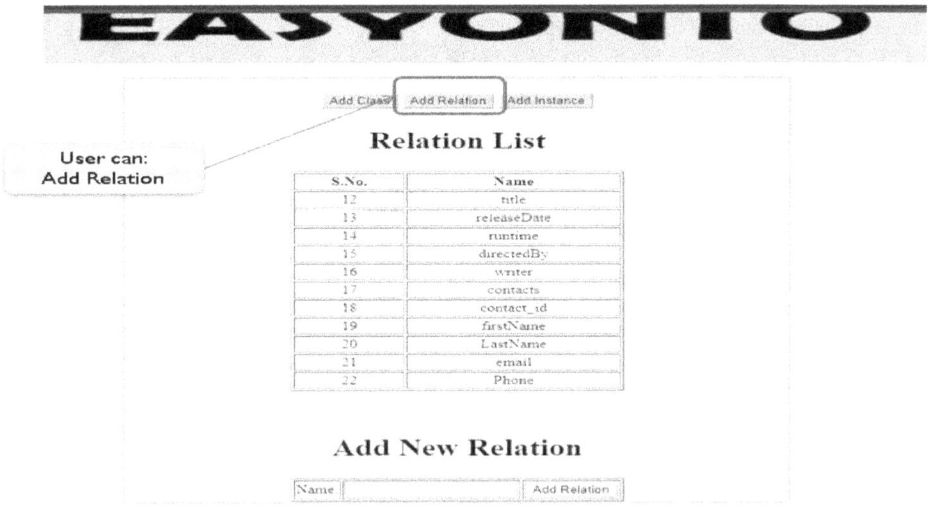

Figure 4.4(b): Represents *Add Relation* Feature

(c) ***Add Instance***: *Instance* represents any value which can be text, number, picture, and video corresponding to the domain. In this example, instances such as *Inception, Harry Potter, Fiction, Comedy, Sanjay Leela Bansali*, etc are added, by clicking on *Add instance* button, as shown in Fig. 4.4(c).

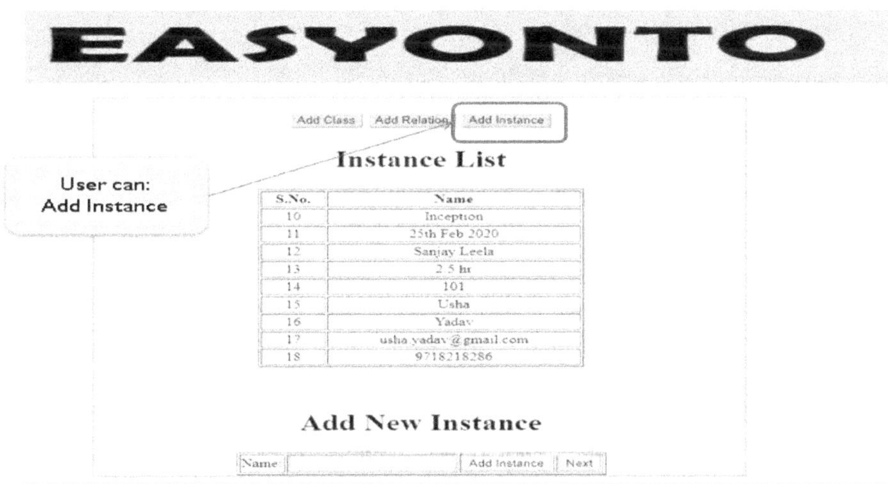

Figure 4.4(c): Represents *Add Instance* Feature

4.3.3 Phase 3: Superclass and Subclass Mapping

In this phase, users have the option to decide the mapping between the classes. The user can choose a class as a superclass and mapped it to another class as its subclass as shown in Fig. 4.5. The following steps describe its working in more details:

- On clicking tab, *Add Subclass Mapping*, the entire list of the available superclass and subclass mappings is shown to the users.
- If the users are satisfied with the mapping done and have nothing more to contribute in these categories, there is an option to move further in the system, by choosing the *Next* button.
- Otherwise, users have options to add new superclass and subclass mapping, by click on the *Subclass Mapping Form*.
- All the classes added by the users in the system are shown in the drop-down list besides the label *Superclass* and *Subclass*.
- Users are required to choose the class from the drop-down list which represents superclass and other class as its subclass to define the mapping between both the classes.
- The mapping is saved to the database on clicking on the *Save* button and also immediately updates the mapping shown in the available mapping list.

Example illustration:

In this example, the *Person* class is chosen from the drop-down menu as a superclass and *Director* class is chosen as a subclass, and the mapping is saved in the system by clicking the *Save* button. Similarly, the *Person* class is also chosen as the superclass of *Actor* class and *Origin* as the superclass of *Asia* class as shown in Fig. 4.5.

4.3.4 Phase 4: Class and Relation Mapping

In this phase, the classes are mapped to their relevant properties/relations as shown in Fig. 4.6. Each property/relation has a domain and range which describes the relation. The domain represents the class that particular relation is being linked to and its range will define the data type for that relation value. The following steps describe its working in more details:

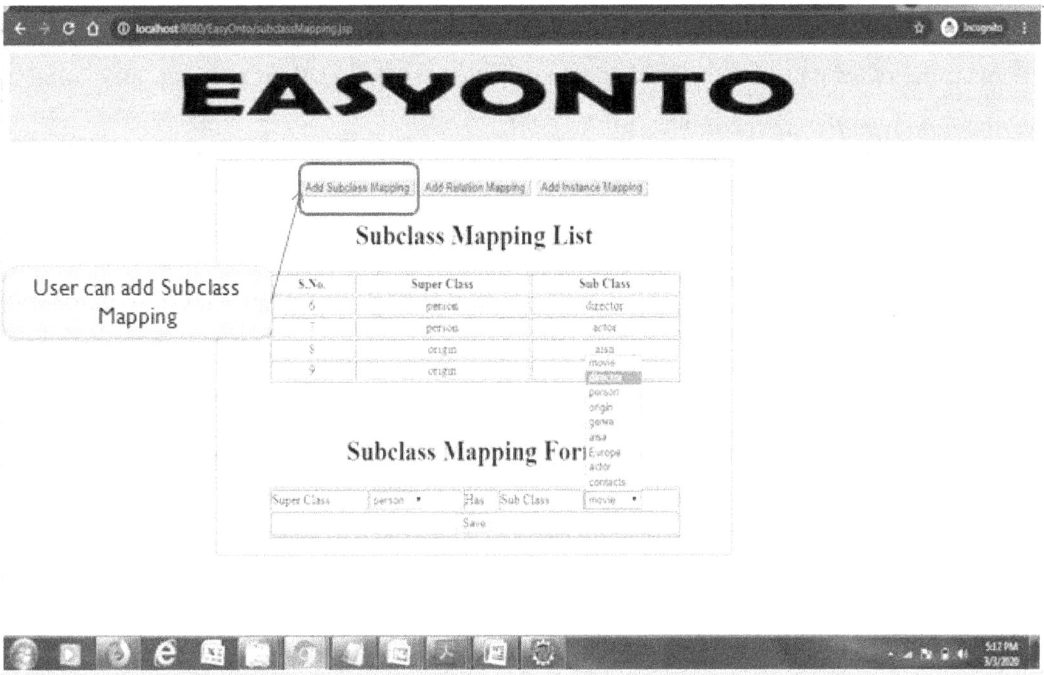

Figure 4.5: Representing Subclass and Superclass Mapping Feature

- On clicking tab, *Add Relation Mapping*, the entire list of the available class with their relation mappings is shown to the users.
- If the users are satisfied with the mapping done and have nothing more to contribute in these categories, there is an option to move further in the system, by choosing the *Next* button.
- Otherwise, users have options to add new relation mapping, by using the *Relation Mapping Form.*
- All the classes added by the users in the system are shown in the drop-down list besides the label *Class* and all the relations entered by the users in the system are shown in the drop-down list besides label *Relations.*
- Users are required to choose the class from the drop-down list and its corresponding relation to define the mapping.
- Users are also required to specify the range of that relation, by specifying its value in the textbox provided.
- The mapping is saved to the database on clicking on the *Submit to create table* button and it also updates the mapping shown in the available mapping list.

This creates a new table for each unique class in the database. The table created will have the *class* name as the *table* name, all its *relations* as their *column,* and *range* as the *data type for each column.*

Example illustration:

In this example of M*ovie* ontology, as shown in Fig. 4.6, class M*ovie* is mapped to relations such as *title, releaseDate, runtime, directedBy* and their range is specified as *Varchar, Date, Time, Varchar* respectively. On clicking the "Submit to create" button, a table with the name "Movie" is created in the database with the following column names:

TABLE: Movie
COLUMNS: title (Varchar)
releaseDate (Date)
runtime (Time)
directedBy (Varchar)

Similarly, a table is created for class "Contacts".

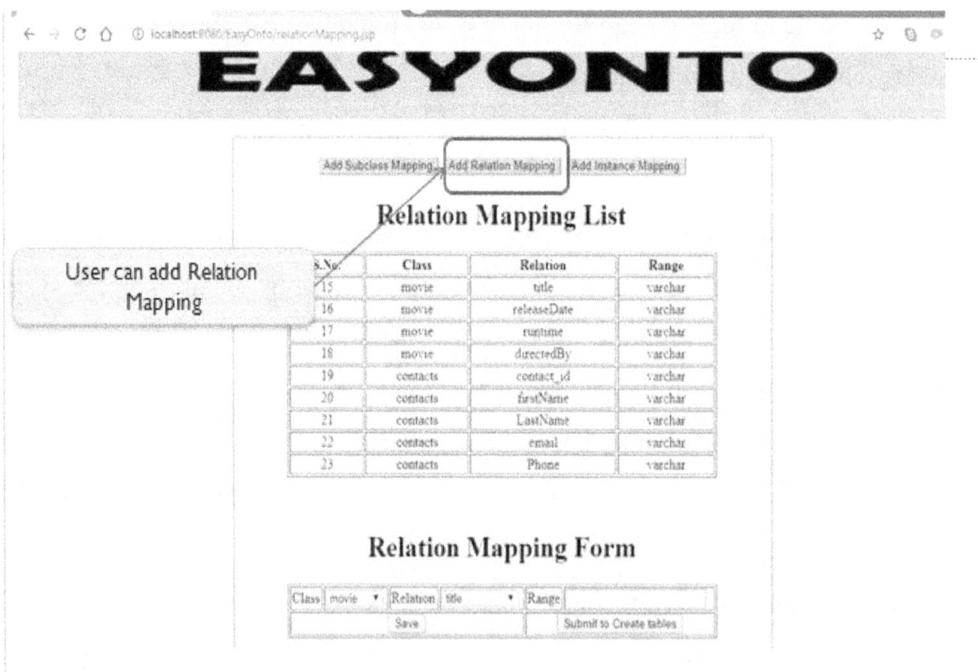

Figure 4.6: Representing Class and Relation Mapping Feature

4.3.5 Phase 5: Class, Relation and Instance Mapping

In this phase, the instance values corresponding to each of the properties/attributes of a class are mapped as shown in Fig. 4.7. The following steps describe its working in more details:

- On clicking tab, *Add Instance Mapping*, the entire list of the available instances mapped with the relation/property of a class is shown to the users.
- If the users are satisfied with the mapping done and have nothing more to contribute in these categories, there is an option to move further in the system, by choosing the *Next* button.
- Otherwise, users have options to add new instance mapping, by using the *Instance Mapping Form*.
- All the classes added by the users in the system are shown in the drop-down list besides the label *Class*
- When the users choose the class from the drop-down list, only the relations correspond to that class are shown to the users in the drop-down list besides label *Relations*.
- Users are required to choose the relations one at a time and correspondingly specify the instance value from the drop-down list to create mapping and click on *Save* button. This will save instance mappings and they are shown on the interface.
- On completion of the mapping between the relation and the instance, users are required to click on *Submit to Insert Records* button.

In the previous phase, the structure of the table corresponding to the classes is created in the database. This phase inserts the *new row* in a *table* in the database that corresponds to the class selected from the drop-down list. The *relations* represent the *columns* of the table and their corresponding instance represents the rows in a table.

Example Illustration:

As shown in Fig. 4.7, class *Movie* is mapped to relations such as *title, releaseDate, runtime, directedBy*. So, if the user selects class *Movie* and its relation as *title*, the instance as *Inception*, this represents an instance mapping. The following instancesare mapped in the database in this example:

TABLE: Movie

COLUMNS: title (Varchar) = Inception

releaseDate (Date) = 25th Feb, 2020

runtime (Time) = 2.5 hr

directedBy (Varchar) = Sanjay Leela

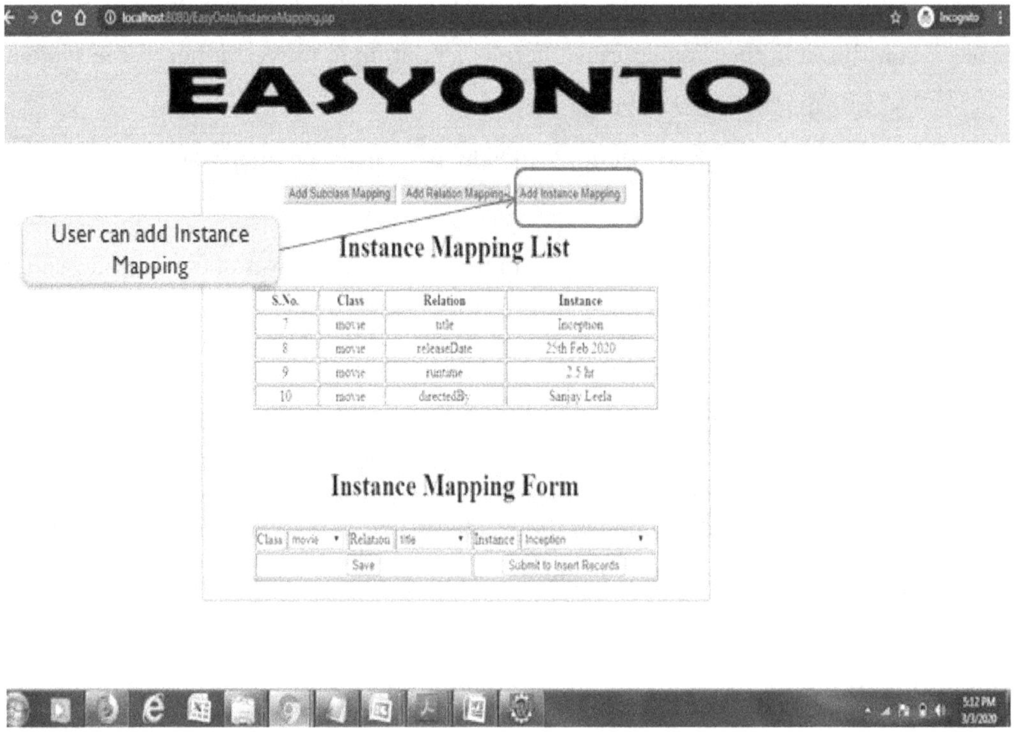

Figure 4.7: Representing Class, Relation, and instance Mapping Feature

Once all the phases are completed and the database has all the entities and the mappings between them, then the platform is ready to be validated and refined by the domain experts. The domain experts review all the entities and the mapping created among them. Once the model is validated by the domain expert, it is ready to be converted into a formal lightweight ontology using a database to ontology conversion tool.

The next section describes the database used by the system and how it stores the entities and the mappings between them.

4.4 POSTGRESQL DATABASE CREATION

All the added classes, relations, instances, followed by all the mappings done in the proposed system are stored in the *PostgreSQL 9.3* DBMS. The few snapshots are shown in Fig. 4.8 and Fig. 4.9.

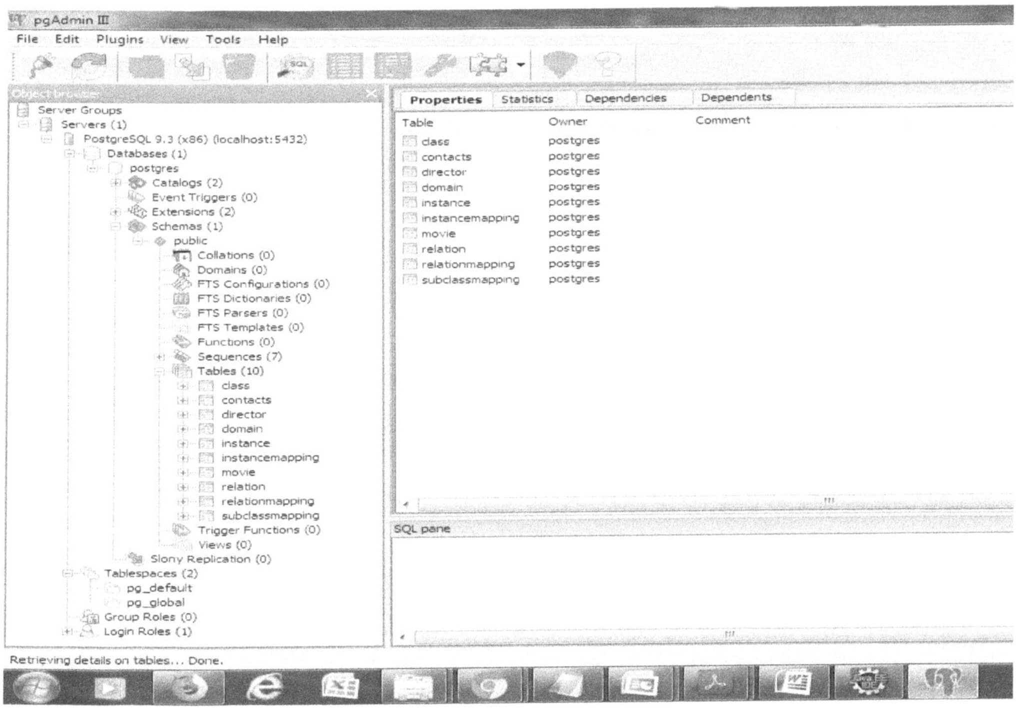

Figure 4.8: Snapshot of *PostgreSQL* showing the tables created

Fig. 4.8 shows the different tables created in the database corresponding to each phase of the *EasyOnto* system such as *Class* table, *Relation* table, *Instance* table which store the entities corresponding to the class, relation, and instance of ontology respectively. Similarly, *subclassmapping* table is created to save the superclass and subclass mappings. The *movie* table, *domain* table, *contact* table, etc. are created and updated during relation and instance mapping phases.

The entries stored during the *Relation Mapping* phase are shown in Fig. 4.9. A separate table is created for each unique entry in the class column of the *relationship mapping* table. As shown in Fig. 4.9, the unique value in the class column is *movie* and *contacts*. Therefore, the *movie* table has four columns namely *title, releaseDate, runtime, directedBy,* and the *contacts* table has five columns namely *contact_id, firstName, LastName, email, Phone*.

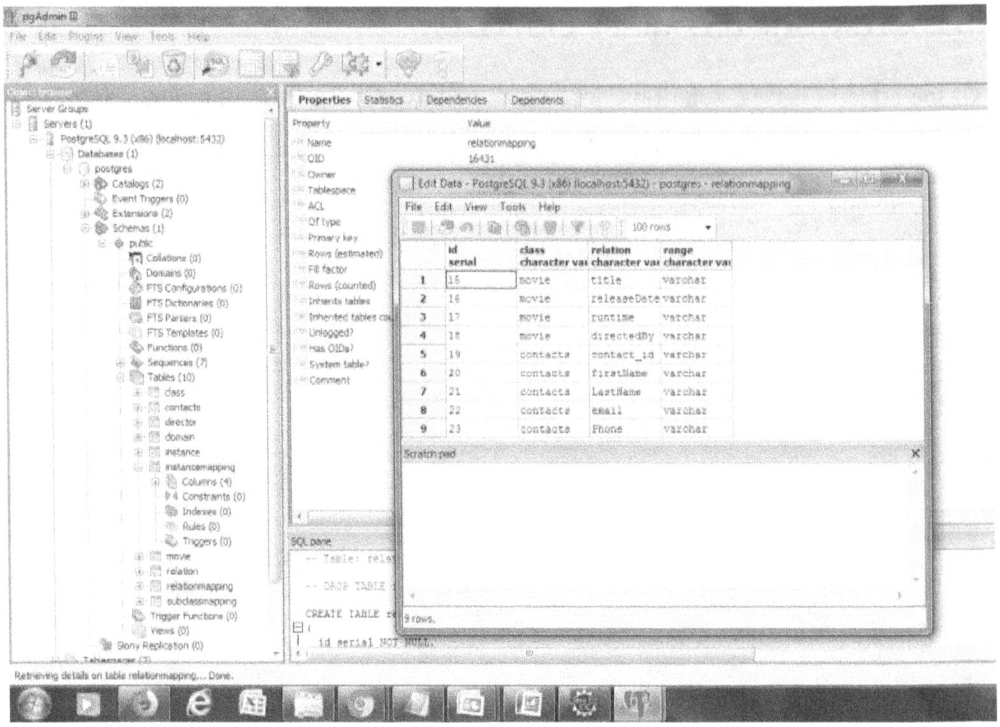

Figure 4.9: Snapshot of *PostgreSQL* showing *Relation Mapping* table

All the data generated by the proposed system is stored and maintained by the *PostgreSQL* DBMS system and also needs to be validated. The next section describes the onology validation by the expert.

4.5 ONTOLOGY VALIDATION BY DOMAIN EXPERTS

The common users contribute in developing the ontologies by following all the phases of EasyOnto system and the information is stored in the database.

The domain experts are chosen based on their experience and expertise in the domain and the panel of domain experts validate the ontology at the backend. The validation phase will require domain experts to follow the *Ontology Content Evaluation* [145] method based on its consistency, completeness, conciseness, expandability, sensitiveness. The explanation of Ontology Content Evaluation is out of the scope of this work.

Once the informal ontology data in the database system is validated by the domain expert, it is converted into the formal lightweight ontology by using the existing database to ontology conversion tools. The next section describes the conversion process.

4.6 CONVERSION OF INFORMAL TO FORMAL ONTOLOGY

Once the domain knowledge is recorded in the database, and it's been validated by a domain expert at the backend, formal lightweight ontology could be generated. There are various existing tools for converting relational databases to OWL/RDF. In this work, the *DB2OWL* [146] tool has been used to formally create lightweight ontologies. The snippet of the generated ontology written in OWL or RDF is shown in Fig. 4.10.

```
@prefix rdf: <http://www.w3.org/1999/02/22-rdf-syntax-ns#pd> .
@prefix rdfs: <http://www.w3.org/2000/01/rdf-schema#> .
@prefix xsd: <http://www.w3.org/2001/XMLSchema#> .
@prefix prd: <http://localhost:8890/rdfv_demo/schemas/movie#> .
@prefix prdf: <http://localhost:8890/rdfv_demo/schemas/Person#> .

pd:Product a rdfs:Class ;
 rdfs:label "Movie" ;
 rdfs:comment "Deals with bollywood movie" .

pd:product_id a rdf:Property ;
 rdfs:domain prd:movie ;
 rdfs:range xsd:string ;
 rdfs:label "movie_title" .

pd:product_description a rdf:Property;
 rdfs:domain prd:movie ;
 rdfs:range xsd:date ;
 rdfs:label "release_date" .

pd:product_category a rdf:Property ;
 rdfs:domain prd:movie ;
 rdfs:range prdc:Person  ;
rdfs:label "has_director" .
pd:product_format a rdf:Property ;
rdfs:domain prd:movie ;
 rdfs:range prdf:Person ;


 rdfs:label "has_actor" .
```

Figure 4.10: Snippet of generated OWL File

The lightweight ontology generated includes the consensus of different users and has been developed by the collaborative contribution from the common users. The next section describes the comparative analysis between the proposed *EasyOnto* system and the existing ontology development system *Protege* [147].

4.7 EXPERIMENTAL SETUP

In this section, the comparison between the EasyOnto and the Protege tool is done based on various features. The details about the experiment setup arranged and the result analysis are explained further.

4.7.1 System Requirements

The proposed system EasyOnto was developed using Java and IDE Eclipse-jee-photon-R-win32-x86_64, with Apache Tomcat 8.0 server, and used *PostgreSQL 9.3(x86)* as DBMS for the backend. The usability of the proposed system and its comparative analysis with the Protege was evaluated using a survey conducted through Google Forms. The questionnaire was designed and constructed for users from different educational institutions. A brief introduction about the ontologies was given to the respondents and they had been asked to perform the small task on both *EasyOnto* and *Protege* systems, and accordingly provide a rating as per their experiences.

4.7.2 Subject Population

Approximately 70% of the respondents were students, 25% were faculties and 5% others, they had a background in technology, management, Fashion textile. Respondents had no prior knowledge about the ontology or more specifically about the Protege.

4.7.3 Survey Questionnaire

A questionnaire was split into two sections, on the first sections, the questionnaire for the comparative analysis for both the system, Protege, and Easyonto was shown. The next sections presented the questions to individually rate the proposed system, EasyOnto.

The comparative analysis of both the ontology development tool was measured on a relative scale. The snippet of the survey for this comparison is shown in Fig. 4.11(a-b). The *7 point scale* was chosen to allow respondents to show their preference on either side of the scale. The *7 scale points* are namely, *Strongly Prefer Protege, Prefer Protege, Slightly Prefer Protege, No Preference, Slightly Prefer EasyOnto, Prefer EasyOnto, Strongly Prefer EasyOnto.* The respondents can also choose *No Preference* to show no interest in either system. The questionnaire on this comparison mainly focused on *usability, graphical interface, learning capabilities, and error handling.*

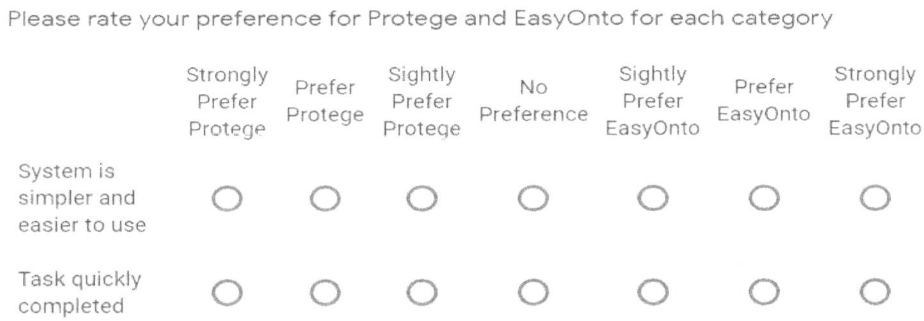
Please rate your preference for Protege and EasyOnto for each category

	Strongly Prefer Protege	Prefer Protege	Sightly Prefer Protege	No Preference	Sightly Prefer EasyOnto	Prefer EasyOnto	Strongly Prefer EasyOnto
System is simpler and easier to use	○	○	○	○	○	○	○
Task quickly completed	○	○	○	○	○	○	○

Figure 4.11(a): Snippet of Comparison Questionnaire

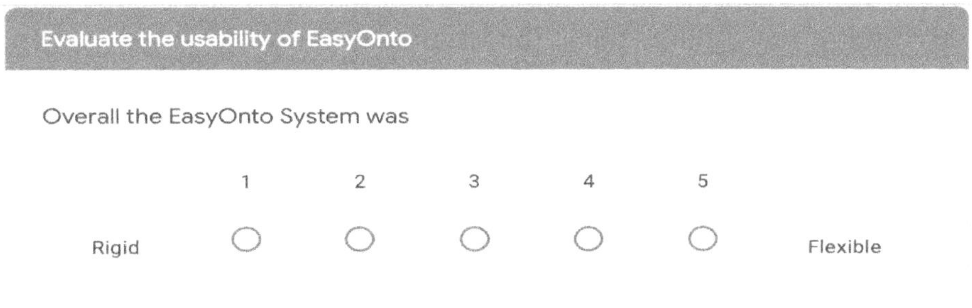
Evaluate the usability of EasyOnto

Overall the EasyOnto System was

	1	2	3	4	5	
Rigid	○	○	○	○	○	Flexible

Figure 4.11(b): Snippet of Comparison Questionnaire

A separate questionnaire was also framed for the proposed *EasyOnto* system. The ratings given by respondents were measured on a scale between *1-5*, where *1* is considered as the *negative response* and *5* being the *highly positive* response. If the response received is *3* on the scale, it indicates that the respondents do not incline towards any direction. The questionnaire mainly focused on *usability, task completion, understanding mappings, speed, and handling user-generated mistakes.*

4.7.4 Results and Discussions

The conclusions drawn from the survey conducted are discussed in this section and Fig. 4.12(a-c) and Fig. 4.13(a-j) present the result analysis related to each question.

(a) Comparative Analysis between EasyOnto and Protege

According to the first section of the questionnaire with nine different categories framed for the comparative analysis between the two ontology development systems namely *Protege* and *EasyOnto*, its response analysis is presented in Fig. 4.12(a-c)

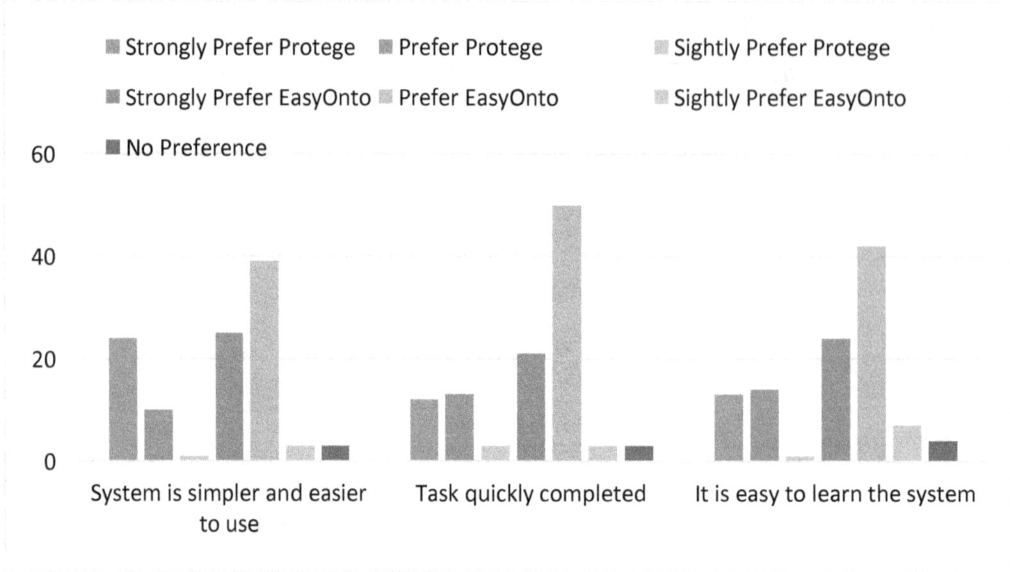

Figure 4.12 (a): Comparative result of EasyOnto and Protege

It is observed from the comparative analysis shown in Fig. 4.12 (a), that in the category *System is simpler and easier to use*, 40% of the respondents prefer EasyOnto as compared to only 10% of respondents prefer *Protege* which implies that the common user had found proposed system as simple and easily understandable. *EasyOnto* also outperforms in the categories of *Task quickly completed* and *It is easy to learn the system* with more than 50% of the respondent agreeing to it. This implies that the users with different expertise were able to understand the system well and performed the complete task with much ease. This is significant in developing lightweight ontologies.

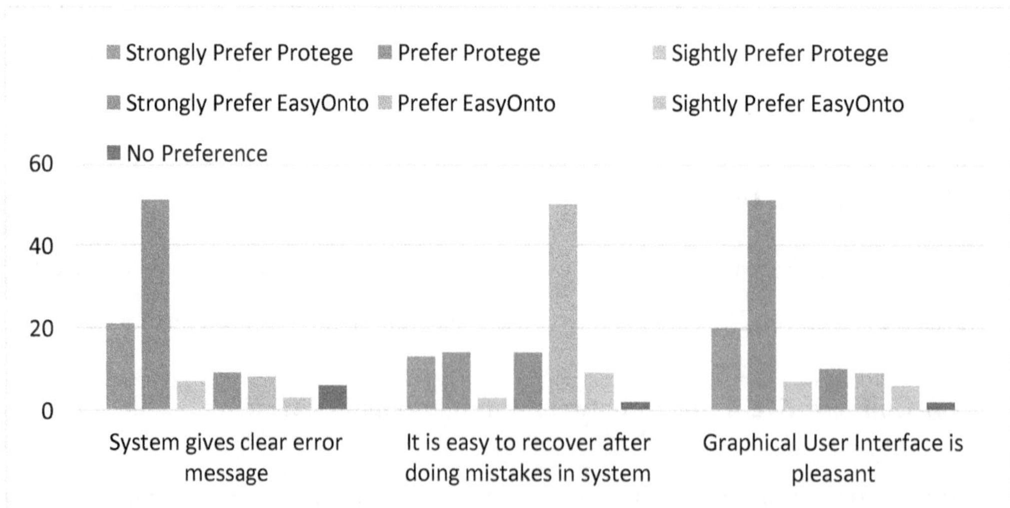

Figure 4.12 (b): Comparative result of EasyOnto and Protégé

It is observed from the comparative analysis shown in Fig. 4.12 (b), that the *EasyOnto* needs improvement in giving a *clear error message* to the users, as more respondents prefer *Protege* for this category. But more than 50% of respondents still prefer *EasyOnto*, when it comes to recovering from the mistakes done in the system. It can also be observed that the users prefer *Protege* for its *pleasant graphical user interface* and *EasyOnto* needs to improvise in giving a more professional look to the system.

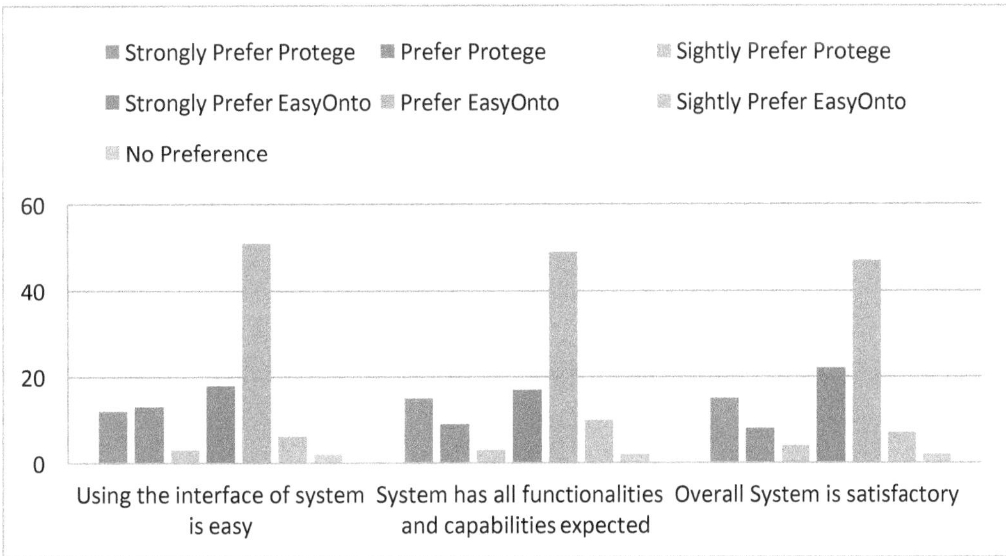

Figure 4.12 (c): Comparative result of EasyOnto and Protégé

It is observed from the comparative analysis shown in Fig. 4.12(c), that for the significant features such as *Using the interface of the system is easy, System has all functionalities and capabilities expected* and *the overall satisfaction, EasyOnto* outperform the *Protege* with more than 50% of the respondent preferring it.

(b) Evaluation of EasyOnto System

According to the survey results shown in Fig. 4.13 (a-j), EasyOnto was positively scored for 8 questions out of 10 questions, a few of which are significant for creating lightweight ontologies by users of different expertise.

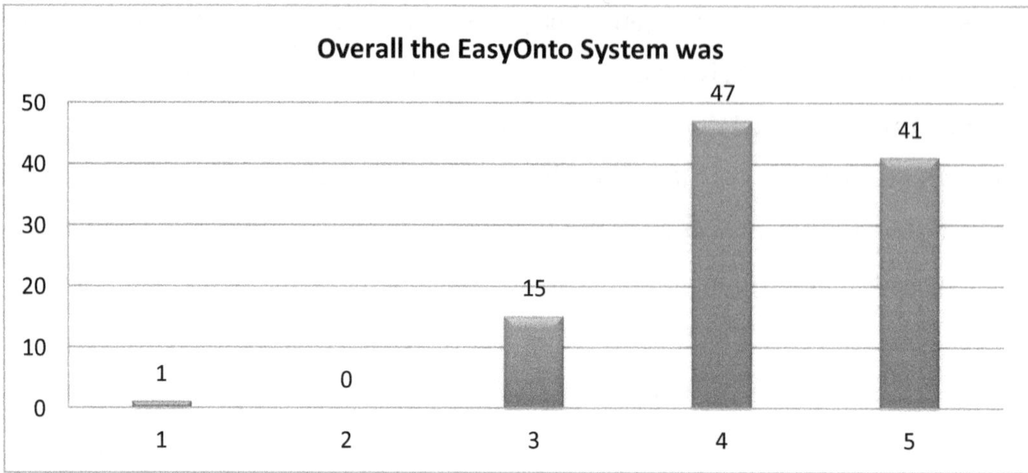

Figure 4.13 (a): Shows responses to survey question about EasyOnto: "Overall EasyOnto System was?"

In Fig. 4.13(a), *1* in scale corresponds to *Rigid* and *5* correspond to F*lexible*. It is observed that 84% of respondents gave *positive response* to *EasyOnto* for being a flexible system.

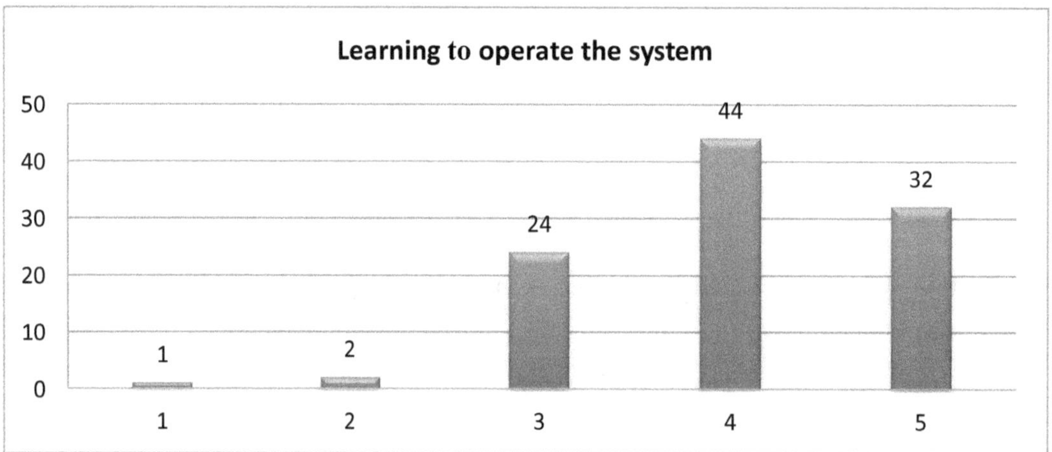

Figure 4.13 (b): Shows responses to survey question about EasyOnto: "Learning to operate the system?"

In Fig. 4.13(b), *1* in scale corresponds to *Tough* and *5* corresponds to *Easy*. In the opinion of 80% of respondents, *EasyOnto* allows users to easily operate on the system.

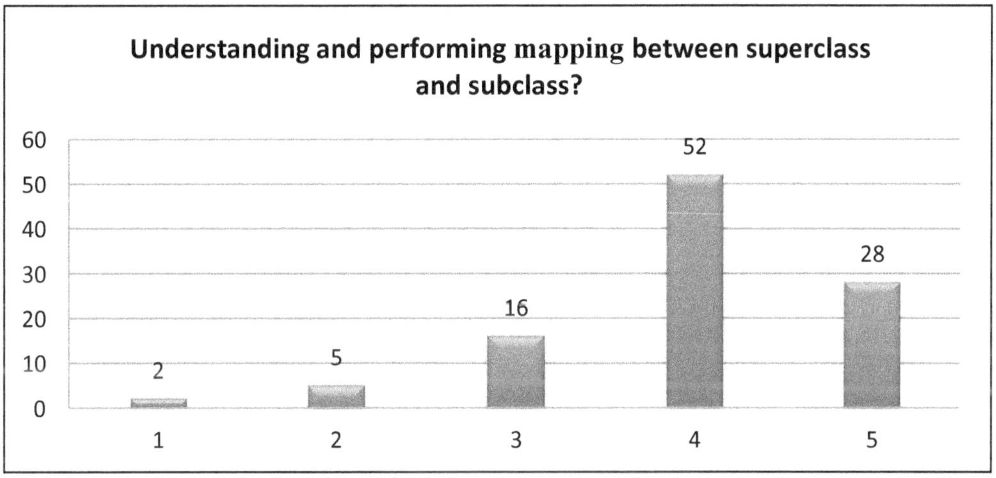

Figure 4.13 (c): Shows responses to survey question about EasyOnto: "Understanding and performing relation mapping specifying domain and range?"

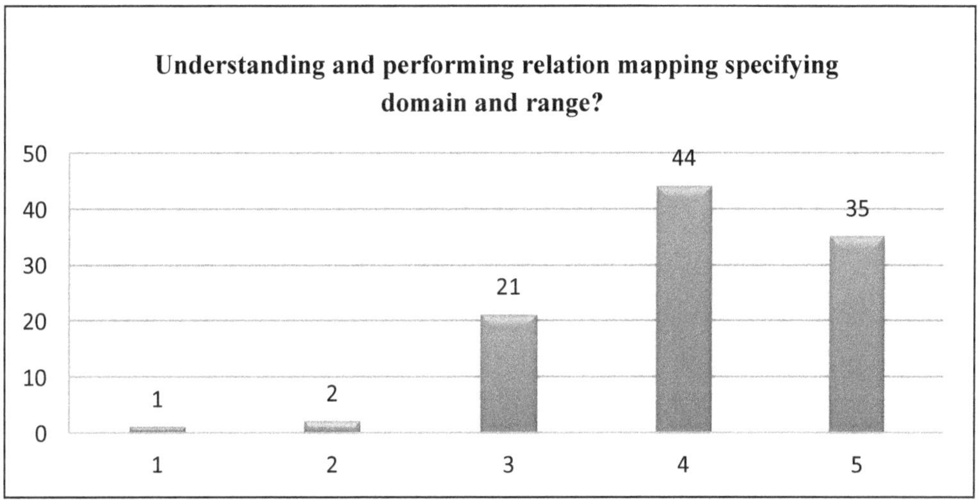

Figure 4.13 (d): Shows responses to survey question about EasyOnto: "Understanding and performing relation mapping specifying domain and range??"

In Fig. 4.13(c,d,e), *1* in scale corresponds to *Difficult* and *5* corresponds to *Easy*. It is observed that around 80% of respondents felt that in *EasyOnto*, it is easier to do the following tasks:

- Understand and perform the mapping between the superclass and subclass
- Understand and perform relation mapping specifying domain and range
- Mapping each instance to its corresponding class and attribute/relatio

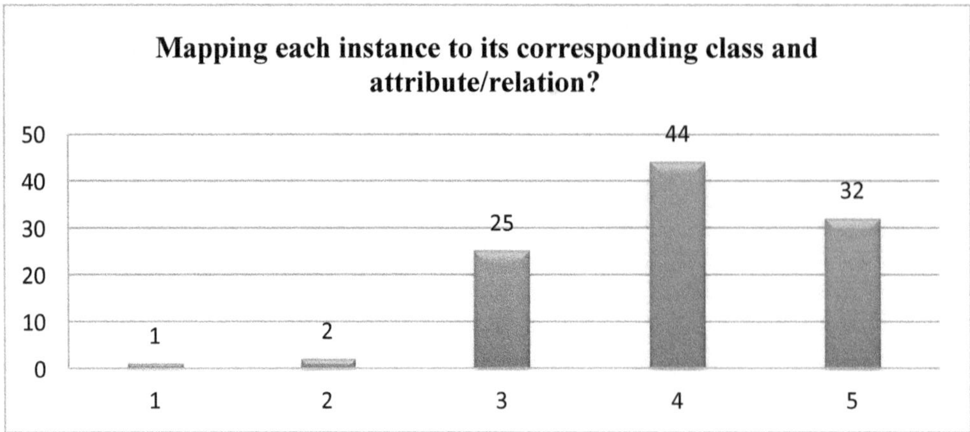

Figure 4.13 (e): Shows responses to survey question about EasyOnto: "Mapping each instance to its corresponding class and attribute/relation?"

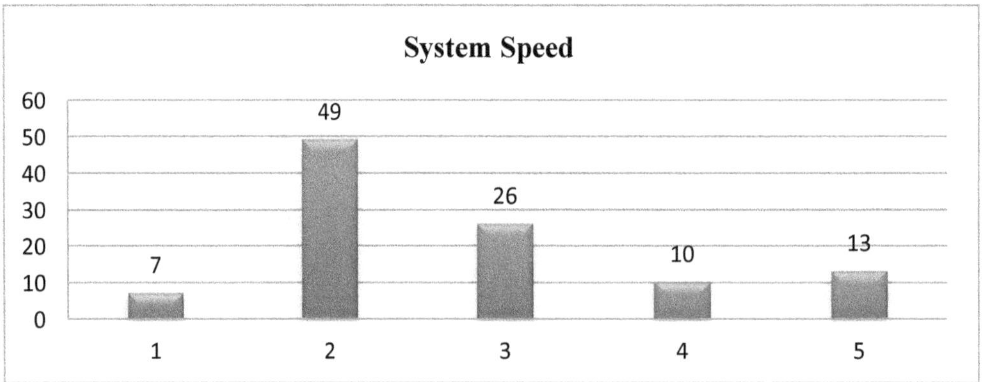

Figure 4.13 (f): Shows responses to survey question about EasyOnto: "System speed?"

It is depicted in Fig. 4.13 (f,g), that on average 46.5% of respondents observed that EasyOnto has some issues related to the system speed and its ability to notify errors to the users, which needs to be improvisations.

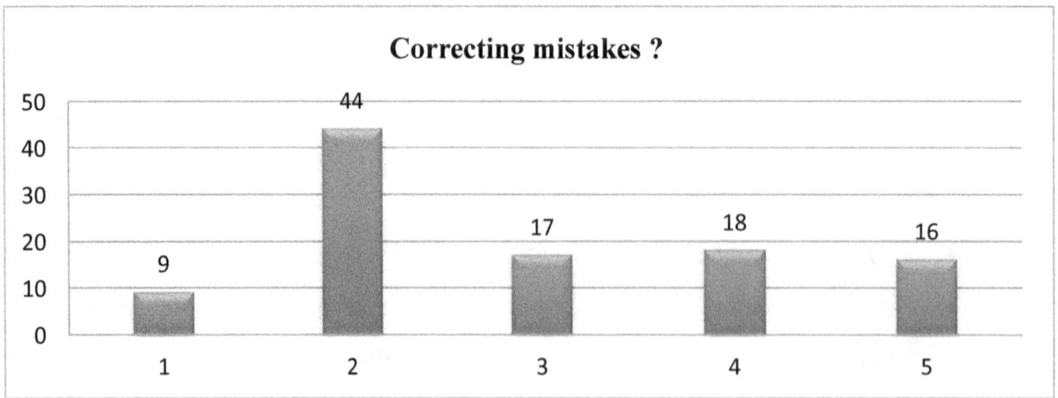

Figure 4.13 (g): Shows responses to survey question about EasyOnto: "Correcting mistakes?"

In Fig. 4.13 (h & i), *1* in scale corresponds to *Reliable,* and *5* corresponds to *Unreliable*. In the opinion of 72% of respondents, *EasyOnto* is a reliable system and in Fig. 4.13(h), it is observed that 83% of respondents agreed that the proposed system is designed for different expertise of users.

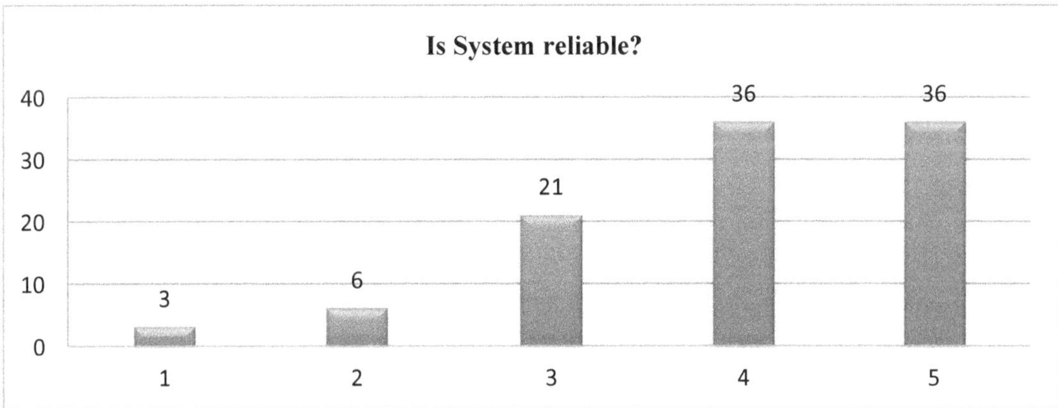

Figure 4.13 (h): Shows responses to survey question about EasyOnto: "Is system Reliable?"

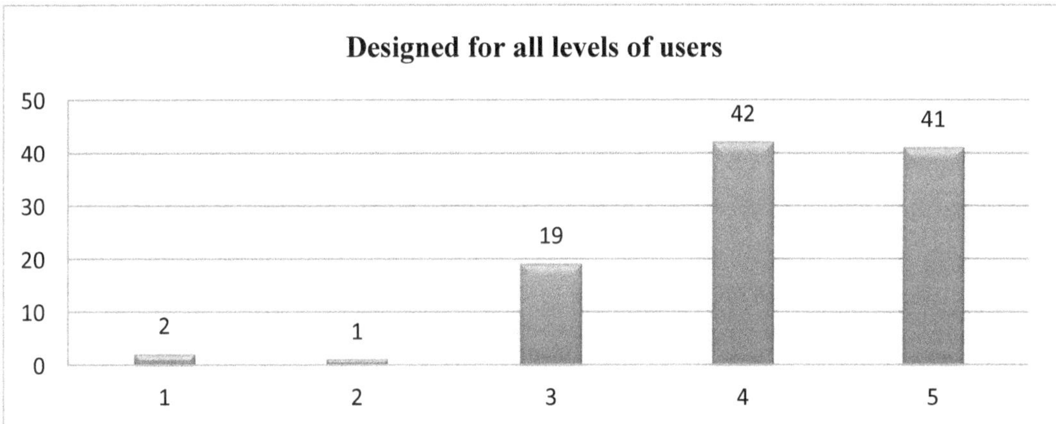

Figure 4.13 (i): Shows responses to survey question about EasyOnto: "Designed for all levels of users?

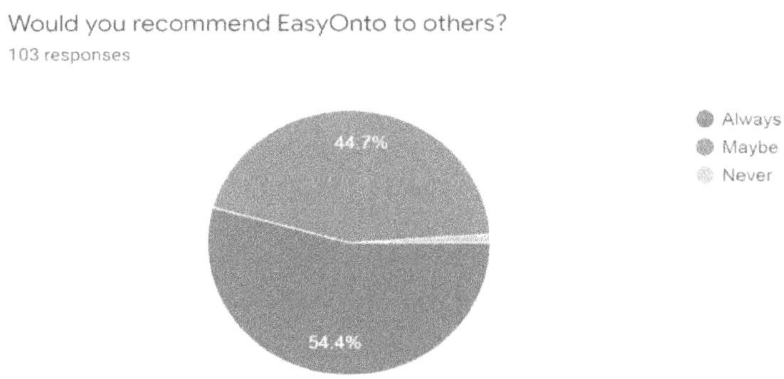

Figure 4.13 (j): Pie chart depicting responses to survey question about EasyOnto: "Would you recommend EasyOnto to others?"

It is observed in Fig. 4.13(j), that in the opinion of 54.4% of respondents, *EasyOnto* is a well preferable lightweight ontology development system for users with different expertise and would like to recommend it to other users. The system has all the capabilities and functionalities for any naïve user to easily understand the system to create ontologies related to any domain. The system is overall satisfactory and allows the collaborative creation of structured data.

4.8 SUMMARY

In this work, a system, *EasyOnto* was developed to allow common users to collaboratively create lightweight ontologies. The domain representation through ontologies should include the consensus of different people rather than only the ontology engineers. The proposed ontology development system is designed for different expertise of users by providing easy to use interface. Mass participation in *EasyOnto* system accelerates the process of the ontology acquisition phase and eliminates the need of involving domain experts in the initial stages of ontology construction. The experts at the backend validate and refine the informal ontology created in the database, before converting it into formal ontology. Overall, 54.4% of respondents were sure to recommend the proposed *EasyOnto* to other common users to contribute in creating ontologies and structured data. The results of the proposed approach suggest that *EasyOnto* is a step taken in the right direction in terms of lightweight ontology construction.

Large numbers of ontologies are created for the same domain catering to the requirements of different businesses. Therefore, an efficient ontology matching technique is required to align these ontologies and allow data integration. The next chapter describes the proposed ontology matching framework for efficient matching ontologies using multilevel partitioning concepts.

CHAPTER 5

MPP-MLO: MULTILEVEL PARALLEL PARTITIONING FOR EFFICIENTLY MATCHING LARGE ONTOLOGIES

5.1 INTRODUCTION

In this data age, ontologies are gaining lots of consideration in Computer Science, especially in the field of Semantic Web technologies. Sharing of information and integration among various applications in the organization is only possible due to the efforts put in developing the semantic web by W3C. Ontology is a new way to represent knowledge. The growing usage of the Semantic Web has resulted in an increasing number, size, and heterogeneity of ontologies on the web. The efficient ontology matching technique is required to handle heterogeneity problems.

Several challenges outlined in the field of ontology matching systems have been discussed in the latest researches. One of the most challenging issues in ontology matching systems is *large scale ontology matching*. The main reason for such an issue is that the terminological and conceptual level of large scale ontologies is very heterogeneous in nature. Furthermore, the resource requirement is another major challenge. Exploring large scale ontologies require large search space to uncover correspondences. Also, at each computational stage, there is a high requirement for main memory to store and process temporary results. Therefore, the effectiveness and efficiency of any large scale ontology matching system will strongly get impacted by the mentioned factors.

In this research work, a partition-based ontology matching system is proposed, which deals with parallel partitioning of the ontologies at multiple levels. At the first level, the root based ontology partitioning is proposed to produce sub-ontologies. Thereafter, matchable sub-ontologies pairs are created using an efficient linguistic matcher (IEI-Sub) to uncover anchors and then based on maximum similarity value, pairs are created. However, a distributed and parallel approach of MapReduce based IEI-sub process has been proposed to efficiently handle the anchor discovery process which is highly time-consuming process. In second level partitioning, an efficient approach is proposed to form non overlapping clusters using entity score and membership function. Finally, clusters are given as input in the ontology matching system to discover final alignments.

5.2 PRELIMINARIES FOR ONTOLOGY MATCHING

An Ontology is a formal, explicit specification of a shared conceptualization [148]. The basic definition of the ontology according to the graph model of RDF [149, 150] is used in this work.

Definition 1 (Ontology): Ontology is termed as a graph **!** =(",$\mathcal{R}$,$\mathcal{L}$) which is a directed labeled graph. "={$\%_1$,…,$\%_n$} is a set of classes or properties representing the concepts of an ontology where *n* is the number of nodes that defines concepts. $\mathcal{R}$={$\&_1$,…,$\&_m$} denotes the set of direct edges representing all the relationship between the concepts in ontology **!**, where *m* is the number of edges defines the relationship. $\&_k \in \mathcal{R}$ represents a directed relationship between two adjacent concepts $\%_{i,j}$∈" i.e. $\&_k$= ($\%_i$, $\%_j$). $\mathcal{L}=\{\ell_1,\ldots,\ell_m\}$ denotes a set of labels that show the name of each concept in graph node.

Definition 2 (Entity): Classes and properties in the ontology are consistently called entities where *e* signifies an entity and *E* signifies entity set. An ontology having more than a thousand entities is termed as *large ontology*.

Definition 3 (Ontology Matching): Let *O, O'* be the two input ontologies. Matching ontology *O* with *O'* discover the set of alignments $A=\{a_1, a_2, \ldots, a_n\}$ where each a_i $(1, 2, \ldots, n)$ has 5-tuple: (id_1, d, d', u, v). In tuple, id_1 denotes a unique identifier; *d* represents an entity in **!**, and *d'* represents an entity in **!'**; *u* denotes an equivalence, generalization or specialization or disjointness relations between *d* and *d'* and finally *v* shows the similarity between *d* and *d'* in the range [0, 1].

Definition 4: The goal of the partitioning algorithm is to create a separate set of clusters $(_{1,2},\ldots,(_n$ of entities (E), such that all the entities in one cluster would have high cohesion while the coupling between the two clusters $(_i$ and $(_j$ would be low. Eq. (5.1) and Eq. (5.2) show that no two clusters have shared concepts and the main ontology is the union of all the clusters.

∀($_1$…j and i,j= 1,2,…,* ,*- .≠/, (.∩(/=0 (5.1)

($_1$∪($_2$∪…($_n$=**!** (5.2)

These ontologies definitions have been followed through this work and the next section describes in detail the proposed *large scale ontology* matching system.

5.3 PROPOSED FRAMEWORK FOR LARGE SCALE ONTOLOGY MATCHING

The proposed framework *MPP-MLO* (Multilevel Parallel Partitioning for Efficiently Matching Large Ontologies) is described in Fig. 5.1.

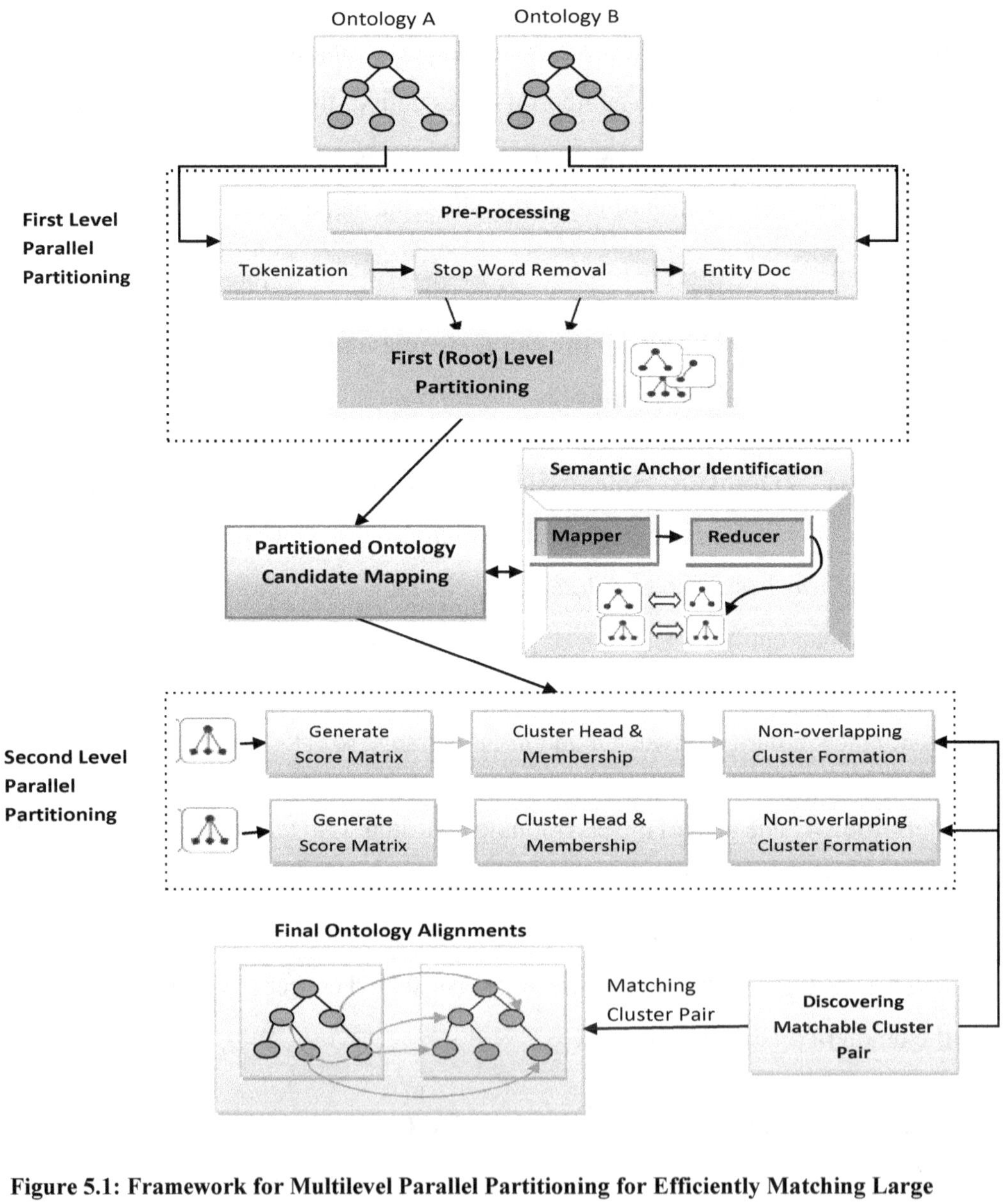

Figure 5.1: Framework for Multilevel Parallel Partitioning for Efficiently Matching Large Ontologies

The system is composed of four phases namely *First Level Partitioning, Partitioned Ontology Candidate Mapping, Second Level partitioning, and Final Alignments Discovery.*

Step 1: First Level Partitioning

In first level partitioning, initially the input ontologies are parsed and pre-processing such as tokenization, stop word removal, and stemming of comments/labels are done. Also, each entity's document is prepared consisting of *structural connection, linguistic description, and closeness centrality.* All the entities which are directly connected to the root concept in input ontologies are partitioned into several sub-ontologies. The computed sub-ontologies should always satisfy the condition given in *Definition 4*.

Step 2: Partitioned Ontology Candidate Mapping

In this module, sub-ontologies generated from step 1, are analyzed to find anchors among entities using proposed MapReduce based IEI-Sub method. As this module consumes high computational time, therefore, MapReduce framework of Big Data technologies has been used. Further, matchable sub-ontology pairs are formed based on the maximum number of anchors found.

Step 3: Second Level partitioning

In second level partitioning, each matchable sub-ontology pairs are further partitioned in parallel into number of *clusters*. Each entity present in sub-ontology pair is assigned some score calculated using *Entity Score function* based on entity's document as described in step 1. Then, the *cluster heads* are determined based on high rank score and chosen *d* distance apart from each other. The remaining entities in the *clusters* are placed under different *cluster heads* based on membership function, *forming non-overlaping clusters*. The *matchable cluster pairs* are formed based on the maximum number of anchors found between *clusters*, applying the same process by which *matchable sub-ontology pairs* are formed, as explained in step 2.

Step 4: Final Alignment Discovery

In this module, the matchable cluster pairs are given as an input to an already proven ontology matcher for further alignments discovery.

The next section described in detail the processing of first level portioning of two input ontologies.

5.4 FIRST LEVEL PARTITIONING

In this module two ontologies are given as input and the pre-processing is applied.The *entity document* creation is also created for each entity present in the ontologies followed by the root level partitioning. The detailed process is explained below:

5.4.1 Pre-processing

In this step, *tokenization, stop word removal*, and *stemming* are done on the label, comments, and name of an entity. After this, the document for each entity of the input ontologies is formed based on their *structural connection, linguistic description, and degree centrality* as described below:

a) ***Structural Connection***

Structural connection SC*(e,d)* of an entity $e \in E$, *(E* denotes entity set) is defined as in Eq. (5.3):

$$SC(e,d) = \{subClass(e,d) \cup superClass(e,d)\} \quad (5.3)$$

where subClass(*e,d*) denotes the subclass or children of entity *e* within *d* levels. The superClass(*e,d*) denotes the superClass or the parents of entity *e* within *d* hierarchical level in the ontology.

b) ***Linguistic Description***

Linguistic description contains all the human-readable information such as name, comments or labels provided to that entity of input ontologies.

c) ***Closeness centrality***

Closeness centrality is the measure that reflects the significance of node most nearer to all other nodes present in the graph. In Eq. (5.4) the cost of reaching all the nodes from one node is calculated. The *distance (i,j)* denotes the function to calculate the shortest path between the node *i* and *j* in the graph, where $j \in V$, *V* is a set of vertices in the graph.

$$C(i) = 1/\sum_{j} distance(i,j) \quad (5.4)$$

5.4.2 Root Level Partitioning

In all the previous work done [47, 151, 152] for ontology matching using the partitioning technique, the main concern is the memory and the computation time consumed. Every entity is compared to all other entities in the same ontology either to calculate their *intra similarity measures* or requires *in-partitioning process*. For calculating *intra similarity measures*, the similarity between entities present in input ontologies are calculated based on their neighborhood. However, in *partitioning process*, each entity present in ontology is assumed to be a *cluster*, and then based on the similarity value among them, clusters are merged. In this work, *root level partitioning* is been proposed that is efficient and less time consuming process. The entities directly connected to the root node in the input ontologies is partitioned from root level to create sub-ontologies. The entities present in sub-ontologies created are more similar to each other than the entities present in another sub-ontologies.

Scenario 1 (Considering traditional partitioning method)

- Suppose, there are two input ontologies that contains 1500 entities and 2000 2000 entities respectively. The same partitioning process is applied to both the input ontologies in parallel.
- In the process of partitioning, initially every 1500 entities would be assumed to be an individual cluster and during the process, they will be merged to form final partitions. For merging the entities of input ontology, intra similarity measure is computed, in which each entity will be compared with every other entity in the ontology. It means each entity will be compared to other 1499 entities and 1999 entities of two input ontologies respectively . This procedure itself requires high computation and thus increases time and space complexity.
- On completion of the partitioning procedure, the ontology is partitioned into *clusters* and further processing is required to find the best matchable cluster pair for finding alignments. However, the size of clusters created is still considered to be very high for any exisiting efficient ontology matching system to process without having memory and time computation constraints.

Scenario 2 (Considering Root Level Partitioning):

- Consider the same example of input ontologies containing 1500 entities and 2000 entities. Suppose there are 30 entities and 40 entities that are directly connected with the root node of input ontologies respectively.
- So, without using much computation to find intra similarity and further applying complex partitioning technique, the input ontologies can be easily partitioned at the first level to form sub-ontologies.

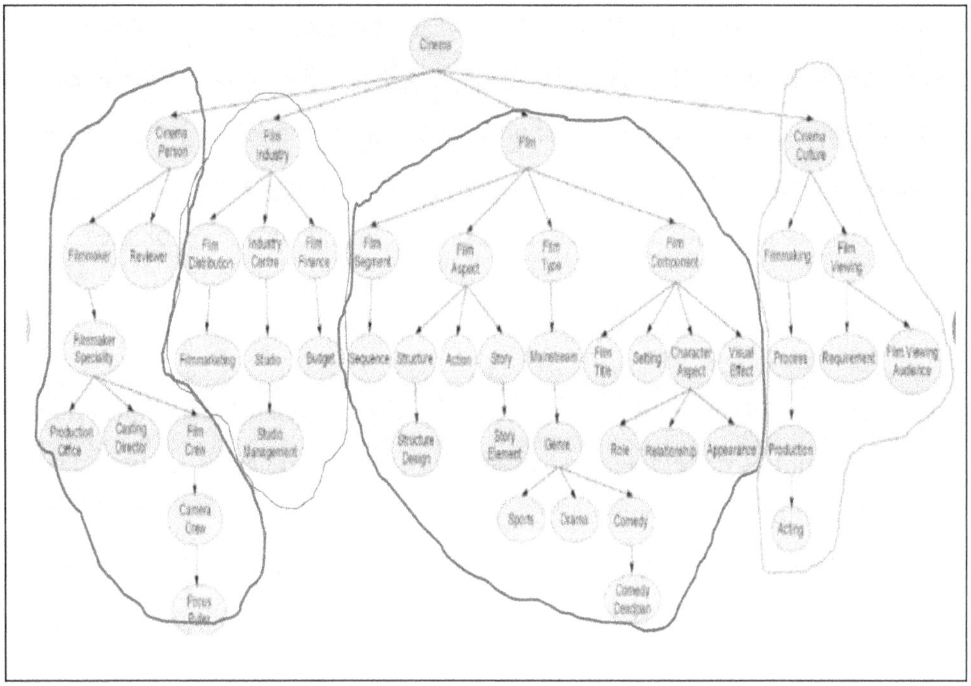

Figure 5.2: Sample Root Level Partitioning using Cinema Ontology

- As shown in Fig. , the sample ontology is partitioned into 4 sub-ontologies by applying root level partitioning. The entities connected directly to the root node are partitioned to form sub-ontologies.
- So, instead of $n*(n-1)$ or $m*(m-1)$ computation where n and m entities of input ontology 1 and input ontology 2 respectively, the root level partitioning would require linear computation time, thus reduces computational complexity to a great extent. The first level partitioning process is computationally efficient and the sub-ontologies created are further partitioned using second level partitioning to form clusters.

- The size of clusters created after two levels of partitioning is appropriate for any exisiting efficient ontology matching system to process without having memory and time computation constraints.

Example Illustration:

- Consider a tree view of two sample input ontologies as shown in Fig. 5.3. The proposed first-level partition is done by partitioning all the entities which are directly connected to the root node, which is "Thing".
- So, in input ontology 1, the root level partitioning is applied to the entities Product, DVD, Book, Pocket, and Article as these entities are directly connected to the root node, and all the entities connected from them will be placed in the same group known as *sub-ontologies*. The sub-ontologies generated are shown in Fig. 5.4.
- Similarly, in Ontology 2, the root level portioning is applied to the entities Monograph, Essay, Pocket as these entities are directly attached to the root node and all the connected entities to be placed in the same *sub-ontologies*, as shown in Fig. 5.4.

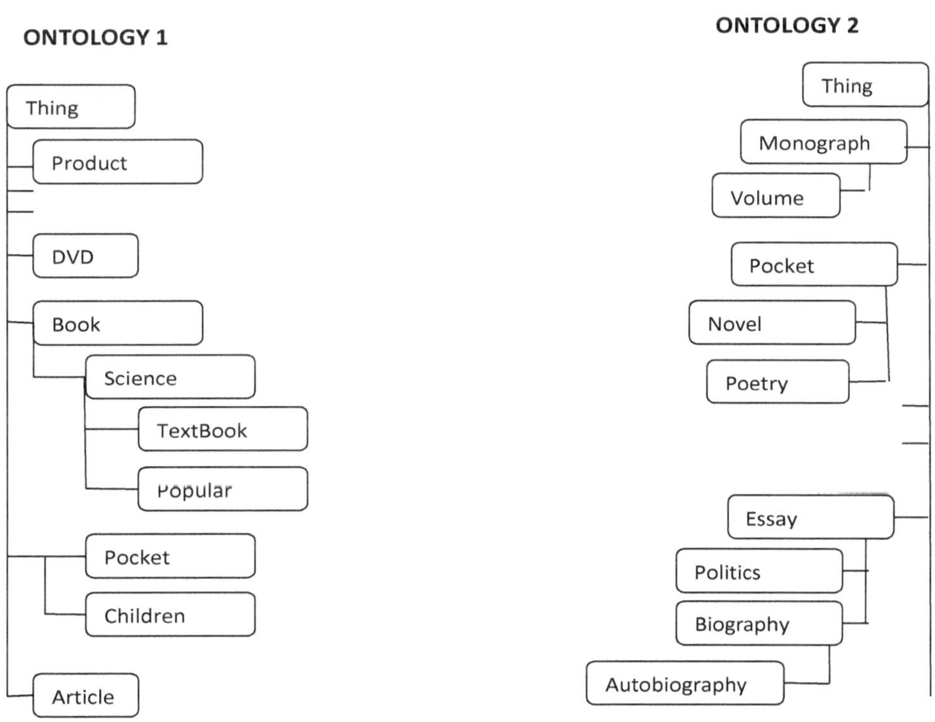

Figure 5.3: Tree view of two sample input ontologies

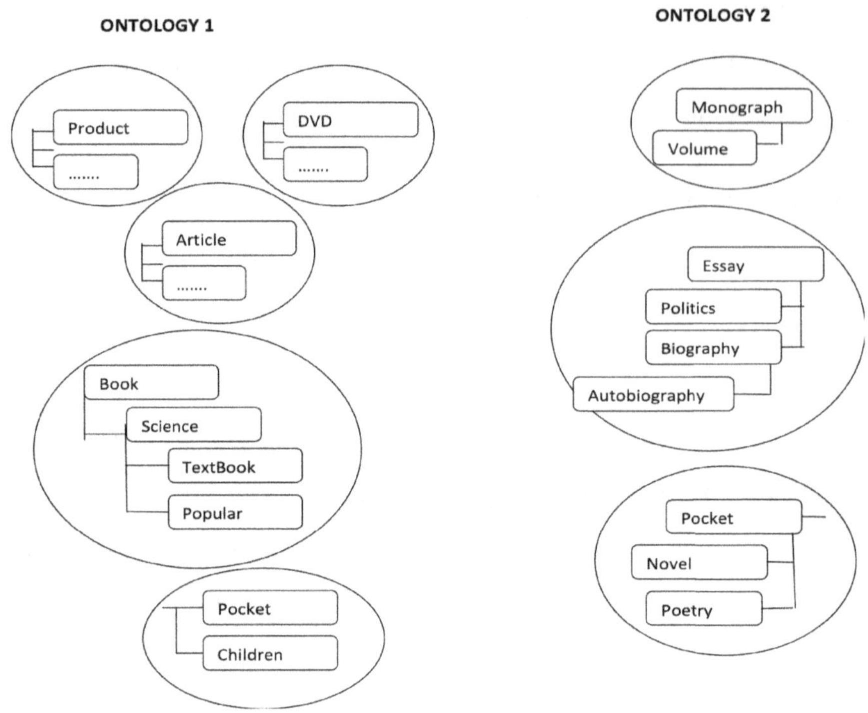

Figure 5.4: Sub-Ontologies after First Level Partitioning

Once the input ontologies are partitioned into sub-ontologies using the root level partitioning technique, the similarity is computed between the sub-ontologies called as *candidate mapping*. The next section described this process in detail.

5.5 PARTITIONED ONTOLOGY CANDIDATE MAPPING

This module is divided into two parts, one is to uncover anchor using MapReduce based IEI-Sub (Improved EI-Sub [83]) matcher, and the other module is to find matchable sub-ontology pair.

5.5.1 Uncovering Anchor using IEI-Sub

Entity pairs showing high linguistic similarity are known as *anchors*. Each sub-ontology of input ontology *O* is matched with each sub-ontology of other input ontology *O'* for uncovering anchors. Entities in the sub-ontologies showing maximum anchor similarity become matchable sub-ontology pairs for further alignment discovery. Without partitioning, the Cartesian product of all entities of the two large input ontologies needs to be processed for finding alignment [153]. Using partitioning only a section of sub-ontology pair needs to be processed for the same, this helps in saving major computational time and space. However, in this module of anchor uncovering the computation time for *n* and *m* entities of input ontologies *O & O'* would be high, as it will require *n*m* comparisons.

In this system, efficient linguistic matcher IEI-Sub is proposed which is derived from EI-Sub [152] and the wrinkle [154]. There are three linguistic matchers designed especially for *partition based ontology* matching system such as I-Sub [155] and SI-Sub [62] and EI-Sub [152], the first two take commonality and the difference between the string into account and the last one focuses only on the commonality between strings, as proven by [155] that "difference should play a less important role on the computation of the overall similarity".

The proposed function in Eq. (5.5) and Eq. (5.6), finds the commonality between string and used *correction coefficient p* for the improvement of similarity results. It recursively finds the common substring and then removes the common part and again starts with the leftover part.

$$1.E_{FGHH} = \frac{\mathbf{I} * \sum_{S} KLM(FGHHGMNOPQMR)}{KLM(L_T)UKLM(L_V)} \tag{5.5}$$

$$IEI\text{-}Sub(e1,e2) = 1.E_{FGHH} + (E + *) * < * (1 - 1.E_{FGHH}) \tag{5.6}$$

where

- e_1 and $e_2$are the entities in the sub-ontology *SO* and *SO'*respectively
- *m* and *n* are the length of the common prefix (start of the string) and the length of common suffix (end of the string) up to a maximum value of four characters respectively
- *p* is a constant scaling factor to improve results, whose value is 0.1.

Example illustration:

In this example, the similarity between the two entities is calculated using the proposed IEI-Sub method.

1. **Entity 1= Booknumber, Entity 2= Booknum**

   In this, common strings are "Booknum" which is 7 characters long and common prefix is common characters from the beginning of string. But a maximum of four characters can be taken into account. So, the value of m= 4 and common suffix is common characters from the end of string, which is 0 in this case, so, the value of n=0. Therefore, as per the Eq. (5.5) and Eq. (5.6).

$Sim_{comm.}$= 2*7/(10+7) = 0.82

IEI-Sub(e_1,e_2) = 0.82+(4+0)*(0.1)*(1-0.82) = 0.892

Finally, the similarity values between the given entities based on IEI-Sub is 0.892.

2. **Entity 1= hasActorName, Entity 2= hasArtistName**

   In this example, common strings are "hasA" and "Name" so, the total common string is 8 character and common prefix is "hasA" which is 4 characters long, therefore value of m=4 and the common suffix is "Name" which is 4 characters long, the value of n=4. Therefore, as per the Eq. (5.5) and Eq. (5.6).

   $Sim_{comm.}$= 2*8/(12+13) = 0.64

   IEI-sub(e_1,e_2) = 0.64+(4+4)*(0.1)*(1-0.64) = 0.92

   As observed, *hadActorName* and *hasArtistName* is almost similar, yet their similarity value using commonality showing in Eq.(5.5) is just 0.64, but when using the scaling factor *m* and *n*, the results are improved, depicting the right similarity value, which is 0.92.

The similarity value is compared with a threshold value, if similarity value is greater than a threshold value, two entities are be called as *anchor*. It has been reported by Ontology Alignment Evaluation Initiative (OAEI) 2007 [156] that 50% of the total alignment can be generated using efficient linguistic matcher.

5.5.2 MapReduce based IEI-Sub

The proposed first level partitioning has decreased the computational time required for anchor discovery significantly, as the anchor discovery is only required within the sub-ontologies generated after first level partitioning. So, instead of comparing complete n*m entities present in two input ontologies, the system needs to compare only *a*b* entities in sub-ontologies candidate pair, where *a,b* are the entities in sub-ontology 1 and sub-ontology 2 and $a*b<n*m$. Even though the IEI-Sub matcher is computationally efficient, the anchor identification process still takes lots of computation time.

The advancement of Big data technology, which provides an efficient solution to deal with high computation time and storage problems can prove to be very beneficial for finding anchors at this stage. So, in this module, *HADOOP 2.7.3* platform [157] is used which works on the MapReduce framework. IEI-Sub matcher is modulated as per the *mapper* and *reducer* function for computation in distributed and parallel environment to find anchors.

Fig. 5.5 shows the proposed method based on the MapReduce technique and Algorithm 5.1, 5.2 and 5.3 describe the *Key Generation, Mapper,* and *Reducer* algorithm respectively. The process of MapReduce framework is described below:

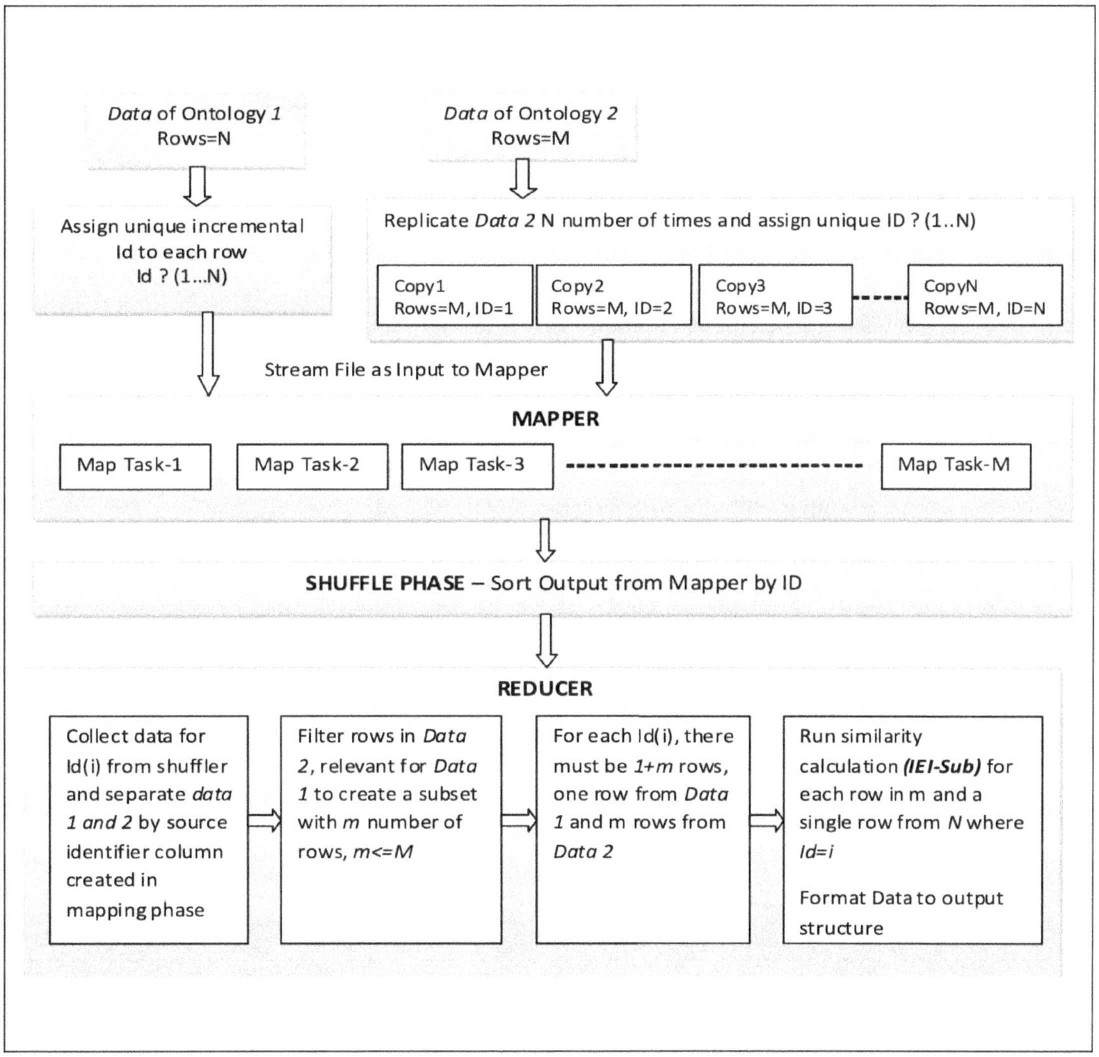

Figure 5.5: MapReduce Framework for Uncovering Anchor

Step 1: Input to MapReduce Framework

The input given to MapReduce framework is sub-ontology 1 named as *Data1* and sub-ontology 2 named as *Data2* which consisting of all the entities with their names, label, and comments and represented by *N* and *M* rows respectively.

Step 2: Key Generation

In *Data1*, the unique incremental values are assigned to each record, where *Id* ϵ *(1..N)* and this streaming file is given as input to the Mapper. On the other hand, in *Data2*, it has been replicated *N* times, each copy having *M* records and similarly, this streaming file is given as an input to the Reducer. The algorithm for key generation is presented in Algorithm 5.1.

Algorithm : Key Generation

Input : Sub_Ontology1 as A, sub_Ontology2 as B
Output : Unique key assigned to each row of datsets

1. declare empty datafile C
2. for each row in datafile A
   - 2.1 assign incremental numeric key as Id
   - 2.2 append ID to data row // unique incremental values are assigned //
   - 2.3 append field datasource with value "A" to each row //additional datafield to identify data source //
3. for I in {1,N}, where N = number of rows in datafile A:
   - 3.1 assign ID column with value i
   - 3.2 for each row in datafile B
     - 3.2.1 append Id to data row
     - 3.2.2 append field datasource with value "B" to each row
     - 3.2.3 append generated row to datafile C

Algorithm 5.1 : Key Generation in MapReduce Framework

Step 3: Mapper Phase

In the Mapper phase, the mapper will use the *"Id"* as a key and will convert inputs from two different files to a common output structure, preserving all columns and appending additional column to identify source data (*Data1/Data2*). The mapper phase emits <Key,Value> pair, where the key is the {Id} and the value is the tuple {name, label, comment, datasource}. The algorithm for mapper phase is presented in Algorithm 5.2.

Algorithm : Mapper

Input : Id, Value
Output : [name, label, comments, datasource])
for each Id:
1.1 get columns from datafile A
1.2 get colums from datafile B
1.3 create a commom structure to include values from both A and B
1.4 Emit (Id, [name, label, comments, datasource]) // additional column is appended to identify source data (*Data1/Data2*) //

Algorithm 5.2 : Mapper Phase of MapReduce Framework

Step 4: Sort and Shuffle Phase

The output generated by the mapper is given as input to the 'Sort and Shuffle' Phase. This phase sorts the output by *"Id"* and this file will be given to the Reducer phase as an input.

Step 5: Reducer Phase

In Reducer Phase, data is collected for *Id(i)* and data is separated from (*Data1/Data2*) by source identifier column created in the mapper phase. Rows in *Data2* relevant for *Data1* are filtered to create a subset with *a* number of rows, where $a<M$. For each *Id(i)*, there must be *1+a* rows, one row from *Data1* and '*a'* rows from *Data2*. Similarity measure (IEI-Sub) is executed for each row in *'a'* and a single row from N where (*Id=i*). The algorithm for reducer phase is presented in Algorithm 5.3.

Step 6: Output Generation

The linguistic similarity using label, comment, and name between the entity pair is calculated at the reducer level. The output produced from this framework is <Id,RESULT> which corresponds to <Key-Value> Pair. The *Id* is the *key* that represents distinct entity pair identity and the *RESULT* is the *value* that represents the similarity among the entity pair.

The similarity value assigned to the entity pair is the highest linguistic similarity value calculated between the entity pair using their label, comment, and the local name. Only the entity pair having a similarity value higher than the given threshold value qualifies as the anchor, whereas the remaining entities are simply ignored.

Algorithm : Reducer

Input : [Id,Values]
Output : [Id,RESULT] // The *Id* is the *key* that represents distinct entity pairidentity and the *RESULT* is the *value* that represents the similarity among the entity pair //

```
1. Initiate variable PREV_ID to null
2. Declare array ARR
3. Def calculate(ARR):
   3.1 split ARR to variables, NAME, LABEL, COMMENTS, DATASOURCE
   3.2 separate rows from datasource A and B
   3.3 filter B for all relevant sub classes for A
   3.4 for each item in B:
       3.4.1   calculate similarity with A and assign to variable RESULT
       3.4.2   Emit (Id,RESULT)
4. For each row in streaming input:
   4.1 get ID from row
   4.2 if PREV_ID is null or PREV_ID=ID:
           4.2.1.1 append Values to ARR
       else:
           4.2.1.2 call function calculate(ARR)
           4.2.1.3 empty ARR
           4.2.1.4 set PREV_ID = ID
```

Algorithm 5.3 : Reducer Phase of MapReduce Framework

The MapReduce framework calculates the similarity values between the entities from the sub-ontologies. In the next section, these values are utilized to identify matachable sub-ontology pairs.

5.5.3 Identification of Matchable Sub Ontology Pairs

The anchors discovered in the previous section were used to find the matchable sub-ontologies pair. If the two sub-ontologies share a maximum number of anchors, then these two sub-ontologies are identified as matchable sub-ontology pair. Linguistic similarity implies the possibility of discovering more number of alignments. Therefore, if two sub-ontologies share a high linguistic similarity, it means there is a high probability of finding more alignments between them. Fig. 5.6 shows the sample matchable sub-ontology pair linked with an arrow.

The detailed process of formation of matchable sub-ontology pairs is explained below and its algorithm is presented in Algorithm 5.4.

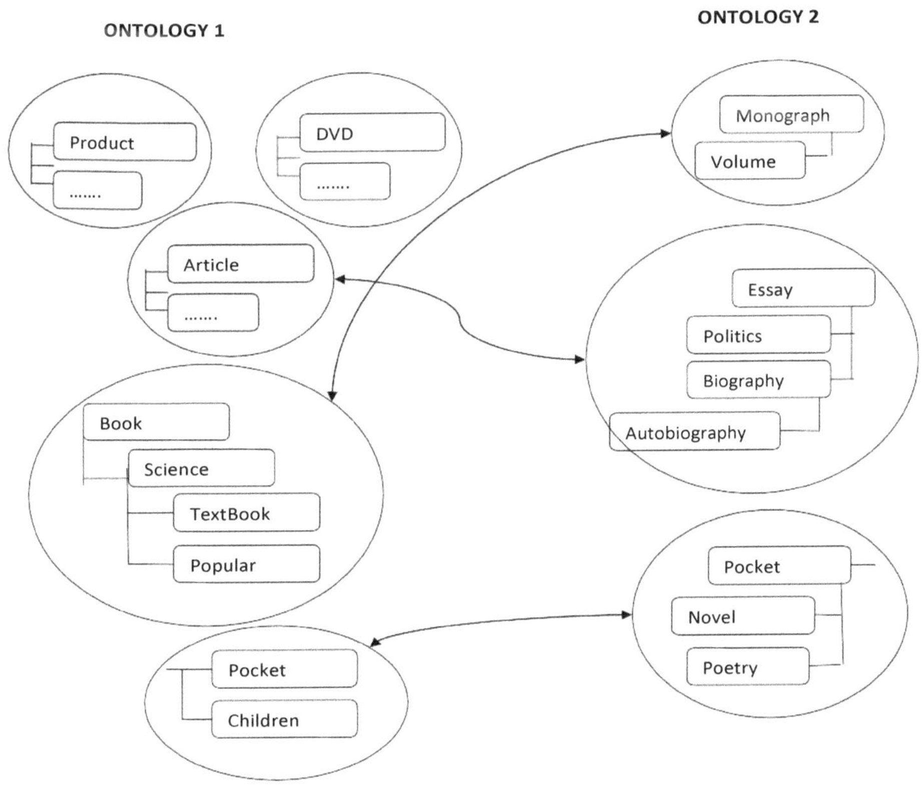

Figure 5.6: Matchable Sub-ontology Pair

- Let SO_1 and SO_2 represent two input ontologies, SO_1 represents the set of sub-ontologies generated after first level partitioning of input ontology $O1$, ns_1 is the number of sub-ontologies in SO_1.
- Similarly, SO_2 represents the set of sub-ontologies generated after the first level partitioning of input ontology $O2$, ns_2 is the number of sub-ontologies in SO_2.
- The equation defined in Eq. (5.7) shows the mathematical expression based on which matchable sub ontologies have been identified which is the ratio between the anchors shared between two sub ontologies to the total number of anchors present in them.

$$So\_sim(sc1_i,sc2_j)=\frac{\sum_{ScT}^{\grave{}aT}\sum_{bcT}^{\grave{}aV} \text{I*YMFZGP([\textbackslash]\^{},[\textbackslash I\_)}}{\sum_{efT_d ghi_T} \text{YMFZGP(NF]}_d\text{,NFI}_b\text{)} U \sum_{efV_d ghi_V} \text{YMFZGP(NF]}_S\text{,NFI}_d\text{)}} \quad (5.7)$$

- The function *anchor* $(sc1_i, sc2_j)$ computes the total number of anchors between the sub-ontology $sc1_i$ *and* $sc2_j$ where $sc1_i \in SO_1$ and $sc2_j \in SO_2$.
- The threshold value, α[0,1] is also set to describe the criteria for minimum similarity. If the sub-ontology pair similarity values are greater than the threshold value, then only they will be called a matchable sub-ontology pair. Due to the discovery of matchable sub-ontology pair, further alignment computation would decrease greatly.

Algorithm: Matchable SubOntology Pair

Input: Set of two SubOntologies SO_1 and SO_1, ns_1 is the number of sub-ontologies in SO_1, ns_2 is the number of sub-ontologies in SO_2
Output: Set of Matchable subontology pair , MS

```
α=0.75,i=1,j=1
//calculating the share anchor between two sub-ontology pair (sc1i, sc2j)
    for each i in range(0,ns1)
            for each j in range(0,ns2)
              shared_anchor+= ,*?hp=(sc1i, sc2j)
  end

//total number of anchor between two sub-ontology pair
       for each 7?1qr1s]
            tot1+= ,*?hp=(7?1q, 7?2D)
       end
      for each ,*?hp=(7?1q, 7?2D)
            tot2+= ,*?hp=(7?1Q, 7?2q)
       end

//Calculating similarity between two sub ontology pair
   For each subontology in SO1
        For each sub-ontology in SO2
             So_sim(sc1i, sc2j) = NZYPLt_YMFZGP / 0G0]U0G0I
             If ((So_sim(sc1i, sc2j)>α)
                  MS= MS U (sc1i, sc2j)
         end
   end
```

Algorithm 5.4: Matchable Sub-Ontology Pair Algorithm

The next section describes the processing of second level partitioning and it is applied only to the matchable sub-ontology pairs identified in this section. The remaining sub-ontologies from both the input ontologies are ignored due to the lack of similarity discovered among them.

5.6 SECOND LEVEL ONTOLOGY PARTITIONING

The matchable sub-ontology pairs are identified from the process of partitioned ontology candidate mapping as discussed in Section 5.5. These matchable sub-ontology pairs are provided as input to the second level partitioning to discover the final alignments as shown in Fig. 5.7.

In this module, the second level partitioning of matchable sub-ontology pairs is done in parallel, thus reducing the computation time of cluster formation. Therefore, the matchable sub-ontology pair $sc1_i$ *and* $sc2_j$ where $sc1_i \in SO_1$ *and* $sc2_j \in SO_2$ respectively is done in parallel to create a set of clusters $(_{1,2},\ldots,(_n$ for each sub-ontology.
where,

- $sc1_i$ *and* $sc2_j$ are the matchable sub-ontology from input ontology O_1 and O_2 respectively,
- SO_1 *and* SO_2 are the set of sub-ontologies from input ontology O_1 *and* O_2 respectively, and $(_{1,2},\ldots,(_n$ represents the clusters created.

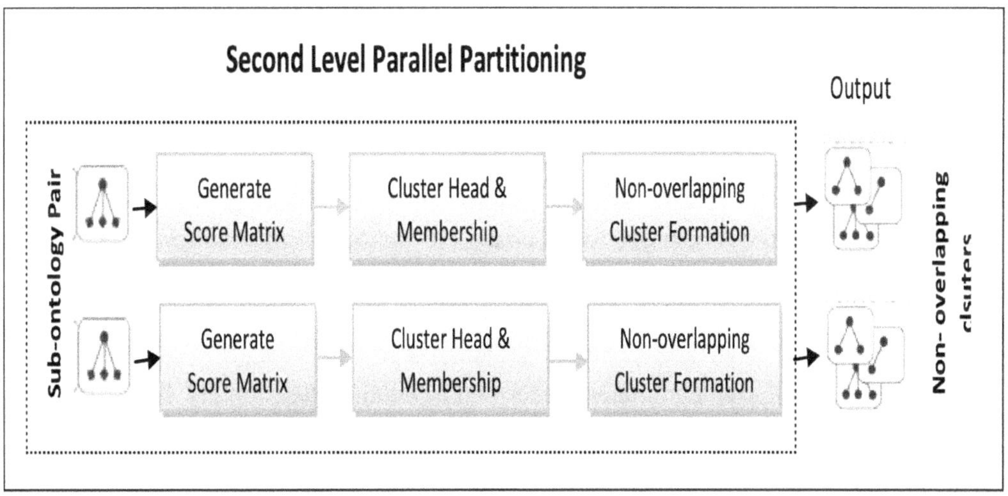

Figure 5.7: Second Level Partitioning Process

The complete process for second level ontology partitioning to generate non-overalapping clusters from the input sub-ontologies pair is described in detail in the following subsections and the algorithm is described in Algorithm 5.5.

Algorithm: Second Level Partitioning

Input: Set of entities E in sub-ontology after first level partitioning, n number of optimal partitions
Output: Set of Clusters X

STEP 1: Calculating each entity score using ranking function

Entity_RankScore= Structural Connection SC(ei,d) + Closeness Centrality CC(ei)

STEP 2: Determining *'n'* cluster head:Entities having highest RankScore is determined as Cluster head with'd' distance apart.

STEP 3: All each cluster is assigned under one cluster head, and all its direct sub classes or children are placed in the cluster.

STEP 4: Each leftover entity is compared with Cluster head based on membership function and entity sharing maximum similarity value with the cluster head, is assigned to that particular cluster.

v3E93=7h.<w8*?A.p*(3Q, 2xQ) = y * 12 (3Q, 2xQ)+ z * {1 (3Q, 2xQ)+ | * 11(3Q, 2xQ)

STEP 5: Return set of Clusters

Algorithm 5.5: Second Level Partitioning Algorithm

5.6.1 Entity Score Calculation

All the entities in the ontologies are scored based on the entity itself and its neighbors. More is the score of the entity, more important is the entity and more chances to be chosen as cluster head. Score calculation function should be computationally efficient and effective. The entity's document has already been created corresponding to each entity during the pre-processing phase, it contains information about *structural connection, linguistic description,* and *degree centrality* parameters as described in Section 5.4.1. The score calculation function calculates the score of each entity based on the following two parameters described in detail in Section 5.4.1.

- structural connection
- closeness centrality

The entity having more surrounding nodes implies more structural connection and assigned more score. Similarly, high is the closeness centrality, high is the score of the entity. Score calculation function then calculates the score of each entity based on the given two parameters as shown in Eq. (5.8).

$$\text{Entity}_{\text{Å}\backslash\text{ÇÉÑ}} = SC(e, d) + CC(e) \tag{5.8}$$

where *SC(e,d)* is the structural connection and *CC(e)* is the closeness centrality as described in Eq. (5.3) and Eq. (5.4).

5.6.2 Determining Cluster Head (CH)

Once the score of each entity is computed by entity score functions, the next task is to select the *cluster head.* The cluster head is chosen based on the *entity score* calculated for each entity using Eq. (5.8). The node with the highest entity score is chosen as the *cluster head.* The cluster head should be evenly distributed in the sub-ontologies, which means the entities representing the cluster head should be placed some distance apart.

In ontology, the number of nodes defines concepts, and the set of direct edges representing all the relationships between the concepts in ontology as described in Definition (1). Each edge between the concepts is counted as *one distance unit.*

Example Illustration:

As shown in Fig. 5.8 , the sample ontology structure, the distance between Node C and Node A1 is 1, as they are connected with one vertex. The distance between Node C and Node A5, is the number of edges traversed to reach Node A5 from Node C, which is two edges. Therefore, Node C and Node A5 are 2 distances apart.

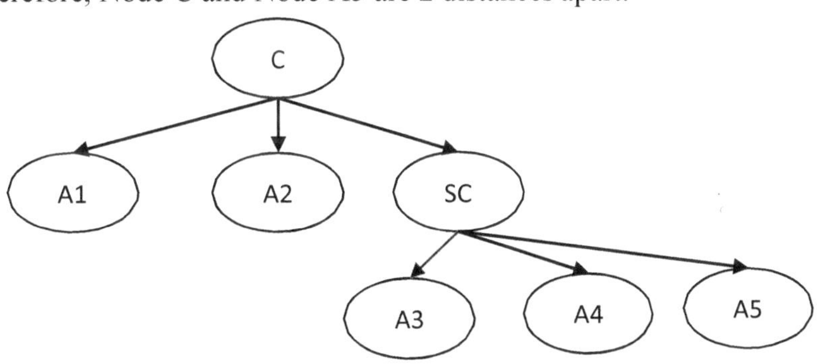

Figure 5.8: Sample Ontology

If the cluster heads are assigned randomly, this would create a problem of uneven distribution of the cluster head in the given ontology. To overcome this limitation, a minimum of *d* distance should be kept between two chosen entities as *cluster head.* The appropriate value of *d* could be computed using the trial and error process [158].

5.6.3 Non-overlapping Cluster Creation

In this section, the process of assigning entities in the sub-ontologies to the cluster head is described.

After determining the cluster heads, all their direct subclasses or child nodes are assigned to them to create non-overlapping clusters. As per Definition (4), two clusters that do not have shared concepts and its main ontology represents the union of all the clusters is called *non-overlapping clusters.*

Example Illustration:

As shown in Fig. 5.8, suppose Node SC is chosen as *Cluster head*, then all its direct child node such as A3, A4, and A5 are assigned to the Node SC to form a cluster. Finally, the cluster contains the node SC, A3, A4, and A5 with Node SC as the cluster head.

The proposed technique is computationally efficient as it reduces the computation required in performing comparisons and calculating the membership function for the direct child nodes. However, some entities are left in the sub-ontologies which have not been assigned to any cluster.

Therefore, a *membership function* is proposed which computes the leftover entity's membership with each cluster head and assigned the right cluster to them. The next section explains in detail the membership function and assignment of remaining entities to the clusters.

5.6.4 Membership Function

At this stage, the direct children of the cluster heads have already been placed in clusters. The next task is to build a *membership function* that can correctly categorize entity $e_i \in E$ to the cluster X_i.

- First, all the remaining entities are assigned a variable *assign* whose default value is *false*.

- Each entity would be placed only in one of the clusters which result in non-overlapping clusters. Instead of comparing the leftover entities to all the other entities in the cluster, they will only be compared to the cluster heads.
- The similarity value between the entity and each cluster head is calculated using the membership function. The entity showing maximum similarity value with the cluster head is assigned to that particular cluster and and the value of the "assign" variable would be changed to "true".

The membership function in Eq. (5.9) considers the combination of three parameters to calculate overall similarity, such as *structural connection, naming similarity, and semantic similarity*

- The *structural connection* described in section 5.4.1, measures the neighborhood similarity between entity and cluster head. More the number common neighbors, more is the similarity value between entity and cluster head.
- The *naming similarity* measures the similarity between the label or name of the entity and cluster heads. Authors in [159] proved that the name of nodes is the most dominant feature. For this purpose, the *Levenshtein distance* [160] is being used which is also called *string edit distance*.
- The *semantic similarity* measures the semantic relation shared between the entity such as hyponym, hypernym, synonyms etc.

The membership function between the entity e_i and *Cluster Head* (CH_j) as follows:

v3E93=7h.<w8*?A.p* (3, 2x)= y * 12 (3, 2x)+ z * {1 (3, 2x)+ | * 11 3, 2x) (5.9)

where

- α,β,γ are constants and denote the importance given to each parameter and $\alpha+\beta+\gamma=1$, $SC(e_i,CH_j)$, represents the structural connection between entity and cluster head,
- $NS(e_i,CH_j)$, represents the naming similarity between entity and cluster head,
- $SS(e_i,CH_j)$ represents the semantic similarity between entity and cluster head

The set of matchable cluster pairs are created in this section using second level partitioning process, the next section describes the process of finding alignments between them that allows the matching between the two input ontologies.

5.7 FINAL ALIGNMENT DISCOVERY

In this section, best matchable cluster pair is found by candidate mapping process and finally matchable cluster pairs are given as input to proven ontology matching systemfor finding final alignments. The process is shown in Fig. 5.9 and the detailes description is presented below:

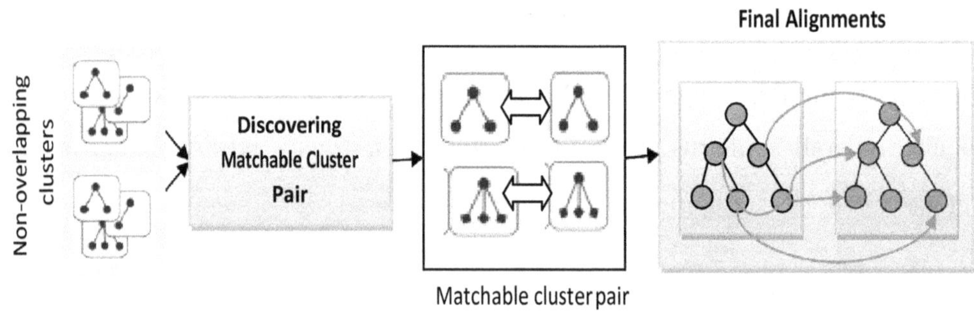

Figure 5.9: Process of final alignment discovery

- In this phase, the same procedure is applied to find the candidate mapping between the clusters as done for finding the candidate mapping between the sub-ontology pairs, details described in Section 5.5.

- However, the high linguistic similarities values among the entity sets are already computed using IEI-sub method and the MapReduce framework to find the achors. Therefore, only the matchable cluster pairs are required to be discovered following the same as technique as described in Section 5.5.3.

- The size of the matchable cluster pair created after two level of partitioning is suitable for matching and finding alignments by proven ontology matcher without having the constraints of computational time and space.

- All the matchable cluster pairs generated as the output will pass on to the powerful linguistic matcher VDoc [161] and structural matcher GMO matcher [162] for final alignment discovery as followed by researchers in [47, 152].

The alignments between the two input ontologies has been discovered following the multilevel partitioning approach. The next section discusses about the efficieny and the performance of the proposed system with the existing systems using number of experiments and the comparative result analysis is presented.

5.8 EXPERIMENTAL RESULTS

To prove the efficiency and the scalability of this proposed multilevel ontology matching system, different ontologies of varying sizes are taken into account.

Dataset Description : The small ontology pair datasets such as Toursim AB and Russia 12 [163], used for partitioning. Another large scale ontology pair is taken into account such as FMA–NCI, NCI–SNOMED (40%), FMA–SNOMED (40%) [164] can be downloaded from OAEI (Ontology Alignment Evaluation Initiative) along with the reference alignments. The other details related to number of class is shown in Table 5.1.

Table 5.1 : Details of Datasets Used

S. No.	Ontology Pair	No.of Classes	No. of Classes
1.	Russia1-Russia2	Russia1 = 151	Russia2 = 162
2.	TourismA–TourismB	TourismA = 340	TourismB = 474
3.	FMA–NCI	FMA = 78,989	NCI = 66,724
4.	FMA–SNOMED (40%)	FMA = 78,989	SNOMED (40%) = 122,464
5.	NCI–SNOMED (40%)	NCI = 66,724	SNOMED (40%) = 122,464

The enormous computation is required to match these three large pair of ontologies depending upon the number of *matchers* used, the more the number of *matchers* required in matching the ontologies pair, the more would be the computation required. The experimental results are analyzed based on various performance measures such as *F-measure, execution time with partitioning and without partitioning, anchor identification, IEI-Sub matcher,* and *the experiment on precision, recall, and f-measure.*

5.8.1 Execution time with Partitioning and Without Partitioning

This experiment demonstrated the requirement for the partitioning the large ontology in ontology matching systems. The proposed system is transformed to find the alignment between the input ontologies without partitioning. As shown in Fig. 5.10 and Fig. 5.11, MPP-MLO has proved to be more efficient with partitioning as compared to without partitioning, although the accuracy of the system is slightly compromised because the Cartesian product comparisons of all the entities are not done in the case of

MPP-MLO with partitioning. The computation required in MPP-MLO without partitioning is very high as compared to MPP-MLO with partitioning.

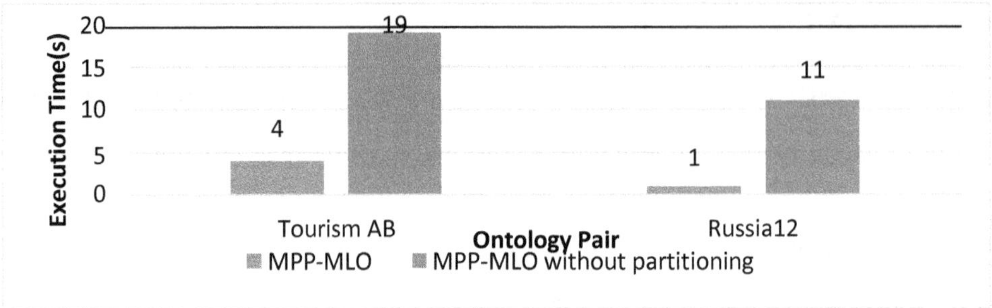

Figure 5.10: Execution time of MPP-MLO with partitioning and MPP-MLO without partitioning

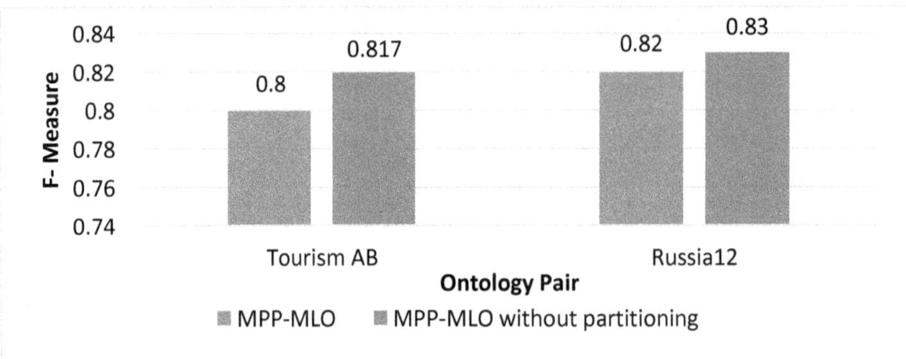

Figure 5.11: F-measure of MPP-MLO with partitioning and MPP-MLO without partitioning

5.8.2 Comparision of Similarity Measures

In Table 5.2, the execution time required for discovering the anchors among the entities pair based on IEI-Sub measure from proposed approach, EI-Sub from *PSOM2* [83],I-Sub from *Falcon* [63], and SI-Sub measure from *LOMPT* [62] are compared and shown.

Table 5.2: Execution time comparison for anchor identification of Falcon, LOMPT, PSOM2, and MPP-MLO

	FMA–NCI	FMA–SNOMED (40%)	NCI–SNOMED (40%)
Falcon I-Sub	44,214	148,392	106,448
LOMPT SI-Sub	35,623	117,267	84,413
PSOM2 EI-Sub	39,919	125,192	90,118
MPP-MLO IEI-Sub	39,515	124,784	89,798

Although the execution time taken by IEI-Sub is almost the same as that of EI-Sub, and on average, it is reduced by 13.4% as compared to the execution time taken by I-Sub. It can be clearly inferred that the SI-Sub execution time is less than IEI-Sub as the latter used very naïve similarity but in additional experiments, it is shown that this method is less effective as compared to others. The matchable cluster pair and the matchable sub-ontology pair are identified only based on anchors discovered which further helps in finding the final alignment set. Therefore, choosing the right matchable cluster pair is the crucial task for the overall ontology matching system.

5.8.3 Execution Time for Anchor Identification

In this experiment, anchor discovery is done on three large ontologies done using IEI-Sub over a different number of nodes in the *Hadoop environment* and the results are compared. The results are shown in Fig. 5.12 (a,b,c), it can be observed that there is almost 51.5% reduction in execution time for FMA–NCI and in case of NCI–SNOMED (40%) and FMA– SNOMED (40%) there is a reduction of 57.5% and 54.8% in execution time respectively.

This proves that MPP-MLO achieves a reduction in execution time and hence more scalable as compared to other existing ontology matching systems.

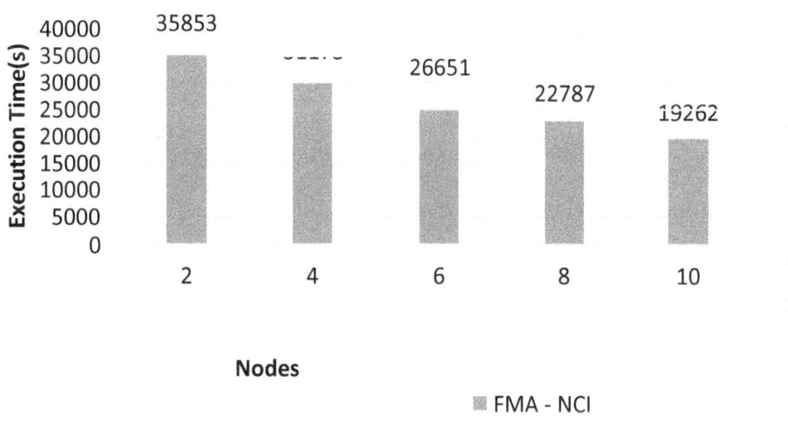

Figure 5.12 (a): Execution time for anchor identification using MapReduce based IEI-Sub for FMA–NCI

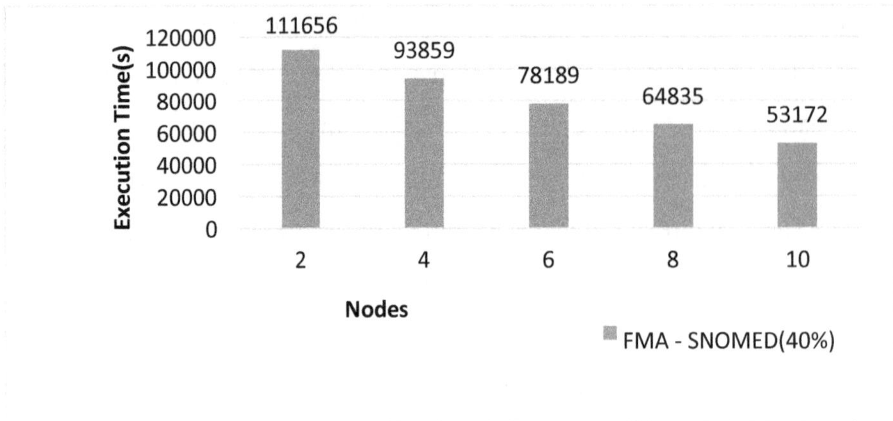

Figure 5.12 (b): Execution time for anchor identification using MapReduce based IEI-Sub for FMA–SNOMED (40%)

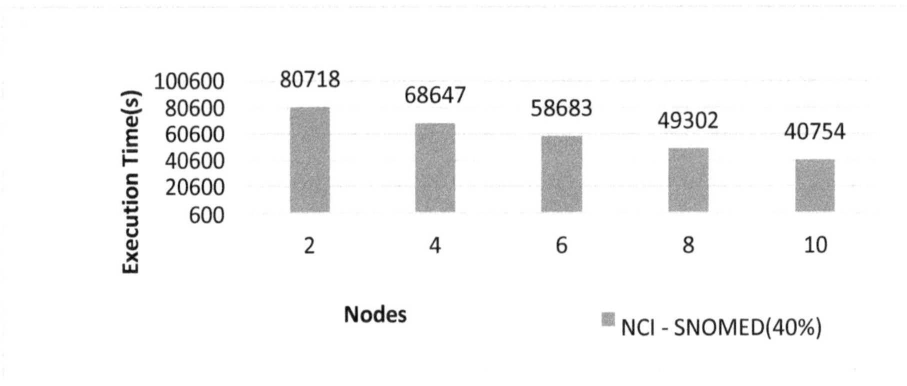

Figure 5.12 (c): Execution time for anchor identification using MapReduce based IEI-Sub for NCI-SNOMED (40%)

5.8.4 Comparision of Performance Measures

The main motive of proposing the ontology matching system, MPP-MLO is to achieve high accuracy, better efficiency, and scalability while matching different ontologies. FMA–SNOMED (40%), FMA–NCI, and NCI–SNOMED (40%) are the pair of ontologies used for the evaluation. In this experiment, precision, recall, and f-measure are evaluated as shown in (5.10),(5.11),(5.12). The definitions of different performance parameters are given below:

Precision = âPäLãGNQ0QåL / çF0äYKéLNäKON (5.10)

Recall = âPäLãGNQ0QåL / äPLtQF0LtéLNäKON (5.11)

$$\text{F-Measure} = \frac{\text{I}*\text{ãPLFQNQGM}*\text{éLFYKK}}{(\text{ãPLFQNQGMUéLFYKK})} \tag{5.12}$$

where *True Positive* represents the intersection between the alignments found by MPP-MLO and the reference alignments given along with the dataset. *Actual Results* represent the overall alignments found by MPP-MLO and the *Predicted Results* represent the reference alignment.

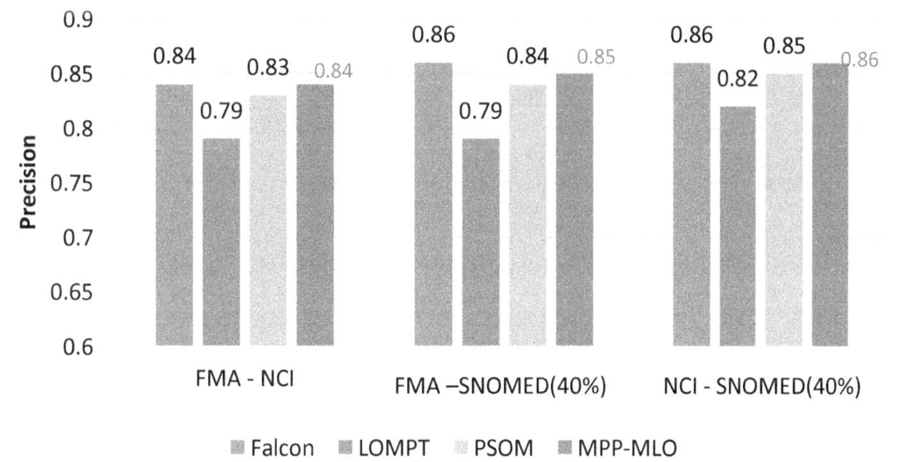

Figure 5.13 (a): Precision Comparison of Falcon, LOMPT, PSOM, and MPP-MLO

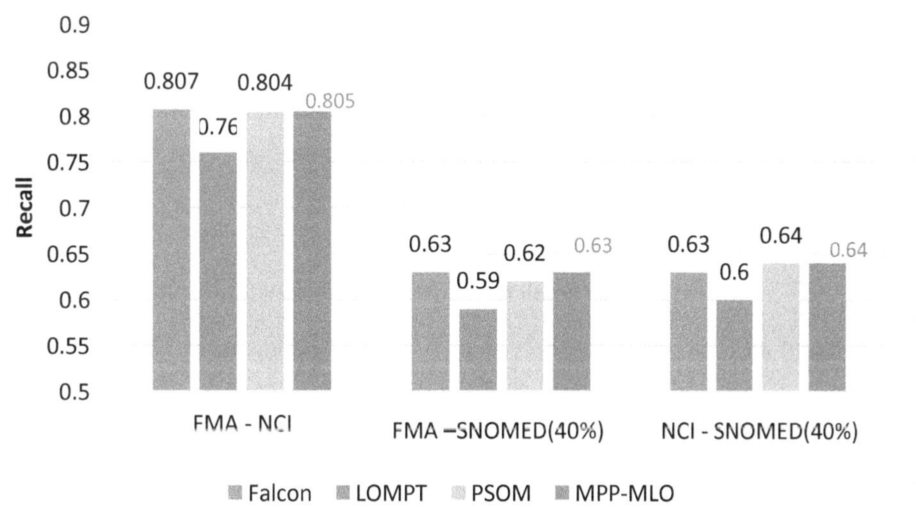

Figure 5.13 (b): Recall Comparison of Falcon, LOMPT, PSOM, and MPP-MLO

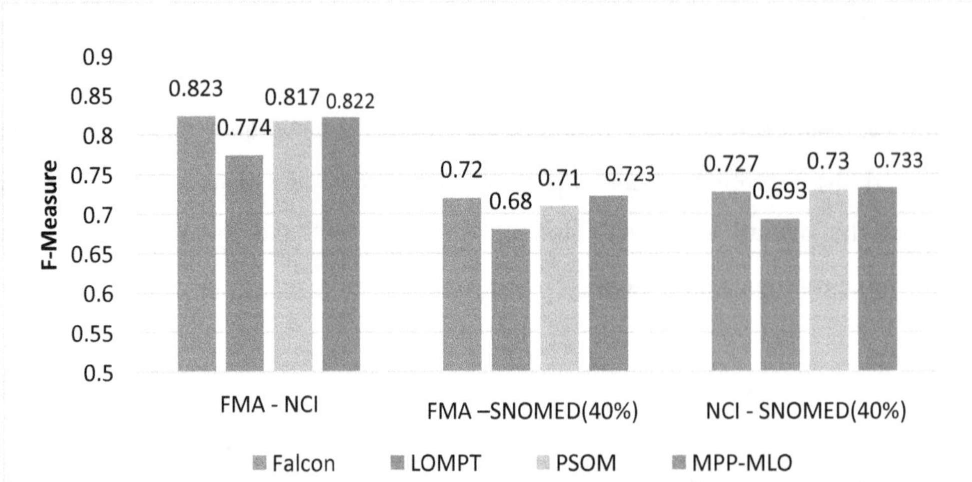

Figure 5.13 (c): F-Measure Comparison of Falcon, LOMPT, PSOM, and MPP-MLO

Based on the experiment and the results shown in Fig. 5.12 (a,b,c), it can be inferred that the MPP-MLO has depicted better accuracy as compared to *PSOM* and the *LOMPT*, due to multilevel partitioning and the IEI-Sub. Although MPP-MLO precision is less than *Falcon* with a small margin, this is because *Falcon* uses robust and high computational linguistic matcher to identify anchor which in turn contributes to overall findings of alignments. The F-measure also shows that the MPP-MLO is effective than the other ontology matching systems.

5.8.5 Comparision of Total Execution Time

Finally, the total execution time used by the complete ontology matching system for finding out the final alignments is compared in Table 5.3. The observations are as follows:

- There is almost 58.9% reduction in the execution time when compared with Falcon and specifically for NCI–SNOMED (40%), the reduction in execution time is around 61.7%,
- In the case of LOMPT, the reduction in execution time is almost 50.3%, and specifically for NCI–SNOMED, the reduction in execution time is 55.5%,
- In the case of PSOM, the execution time is almost the same, but the accuracy of the proposed system is more. As is can be proved seeing the results that MPP-MLO has better efficiency as compared to others.

Table 5.3: Comparison of the total execution time of Falcon, LOMPT, PSOM, and MPP-MLO

	FMA–NCI	FMA–SNOMED (40%)	NCI–SNOMED (40%)
Falcon	47,745	165,480	135,694
LOMPT	38,896	133,376	116,701
PSOM2	24,200	67,400	52,000
MPP-MLO	23,987	67,174	51,875

5.9 SUMMARY

In this work, a novel multilevel parallel partitioning based ontology matching technique is proposed, which targets efficiency and effectiveness over the existing ontology matching techniques. There is 58.7% reduction in execution time of the proposed system as compared to other existing approaches. In large scale ontology, the size of partitioned ontologies should be less and the similarity between selected sub-ontology pair should be high for better computation time and space. This is well achieved using partitioning at two levels without incurring extra overheads. The overall efficiency is increased by 78.9% using the concept of partitioning. The proposed system used MapReduce framework to handle the most time-consuming process of finding anchors and achieved better scalability using a parallel and distributed approach. On average, execution time reduced by 54.6% using the MapReduce framework. To discover the anchors set, a lightweight and efficient linguistic matcher called IEI-Sub is proposed. The execution time of IEI-Sub is reduced by 13.5% as compared to I-Sub. Also, for second level partitioning, non-overlapping clusters are formed using Entity score function and membership function, which further increase the quality of the clusters formed at the second level.

The next chapter presents the hybrid recommendation system for the end-user using the power of the semantic web and generated structured data. This system is developed to motivate common users to contribute collaboratively in developing the ontologies and structured information.

CHAPTER 6

HYBRID RECOMMENDATION SYSTEM BASED ON LINKED OPEN DATA AND SOCIAL NETWORK FEATURES

6.1 INTRODUCTION

Fetching desired information from websites or applications containing enormous data such as items, videos, pictures, and text etc. is a very challenging and time-consuming task. Current information retrieval and information filtering systems are highly inspired by the advancement done in Artificial Intelligence's approaches. Recommender System (RS) is a competent tool that assists users by providing a ranked list of items as per their requirements or preferences without being explicitly searching in the system. This system has proved to be an important tool to recommend items, thereby personalizing the applications for various domains such as tourism, marketing, movies, songs, hotels & restaurants, news, forecasting theories, and many more.

Various issues need to be taken care of while designing an appropriate recommendation system such as scalability, high computation and diversity. Other important challenges are mentioned below:

- One important issue that has majorly gained the attention of researchers is the *Cold Start Problem*, which arises at the time of registration of a new user or adding up a new resource or item in the system.
- While registration into a system, there would be no information about the user's interest or his rating for any particular item in the system, recommending an appropriate item at that time to the new user is very challenging. The quality of the recommender system degrades when there is insufficient information or no ratings are available [94].
- With the increasing e-commerce platforms, huge numbers of new users signing every day or there are less-active users in almost every application creates a serious issue for the recommendation systems [84].
- But there is still a lack of features, based on which the similarity between the users is calculated. Similarity measures should not be only confined to the rating

given by the users for particular items or just by comparing their basic demographic information such as age, location.

- There is a severe requirement to analyze more and different features that could describe users well enough depending upon various domains. For example, let's consider the *clothing domain*, two users with similar height and weight are most probable to like similar dresses. Therefore, it is highly required to build up a user's profile based on the different number of features as per the domain for which that recommender system needs to be developed.
- The similarity between the users should be calculated to improve the performance [96]f the recommendation system. The main problem lies in the standardization of the features which could successfully describe a user's attributes and provide related data. This data can further be used in representing user's profiles in various domains.

Utilizing the power of connected and structured linked data in the recommendation system holds a lot of research potential. The Linked Open Data (LOD) cloud is an enormous set of RDF statements interconnected together forming a cross-domain ontology graph and wrapping many domains, such as companies, people, geographical locations, movies, music, books, etc. DBpedia [96] is one of the largest LOD.

The proposed work focuses on solving *pure New user cold-start problem* by building user's profile based on LOD, collaborative features, and social network based features. A new approach is devised to compute item similarity based on ontology, and utilized it for predicting the rating of non-rated items. A method to calculate user's similarity based on collaborative features is proposed to deal with low accuracy and high computation time. The empirical results and comparative analysis of the proposed hybrid recommendation system dictate its better performance specifically for providing the solution to pure new user cold start problem.

6.2 PROPOSED HYBRID RECOMMENDATION SYSTEM

The framework of the proposed hybrid recommendation system is shown in Fig. 6.1. The system is designed to provide the best possible and efficient solution for pure new user cold start problem. The proposed system is broadly divided into the following three modules:

Module 1- Item Based Clustering

- First of all, the system utilizes the explicit *User-Item matrix* in which the rating is given to each item by the users already registered on that domain. The similarity between the items present in the system is calculated using *User-Item matrix* termed as *explicit user rating based similarity.*
- Also, the similarity between the items is calculated based on the ontology of that domain and termed as *ontology based similarity.* A new algorithm is proposed to calculate the item similarity based on ontologies. Suppose, the recommendation system is developed for movie based application, then the ontology on which the system store the movie information is utilized.
- Thereafter, the overall similarity between the items is calculated based on the average value of *ontology based similarity* and *item based similarity.* The item clusters are formed using *fuzzy c-means clustering* algorithm that utilizes the overall item similarity values calculated.
- Once similar item clusters are generated, the rating prediction algorithm is proposed to remove the sparsity in the *user-item matrix.* The algorithm works by predicting the ratings of the items which are not rated by the active user in the system.

Module 2- User Profile Generation

- Concurrently, the system creates user profile of the users registered on the system based on various features like LOD (Linked Open Data) and Social Network Graph feature.
- The similarity between each user's profile with every other user's in the system is required to be calculated. Traditional similarity measures are less accurate due to several drawbacks. Therefore, a more accurate similarity measure to calculate the similarity between the users is proposed.
- When a new user enters into the system using their Facebook Id and DBpedia ID (if any), the system automatically generates his profile using the *User Profile Generation Module*.

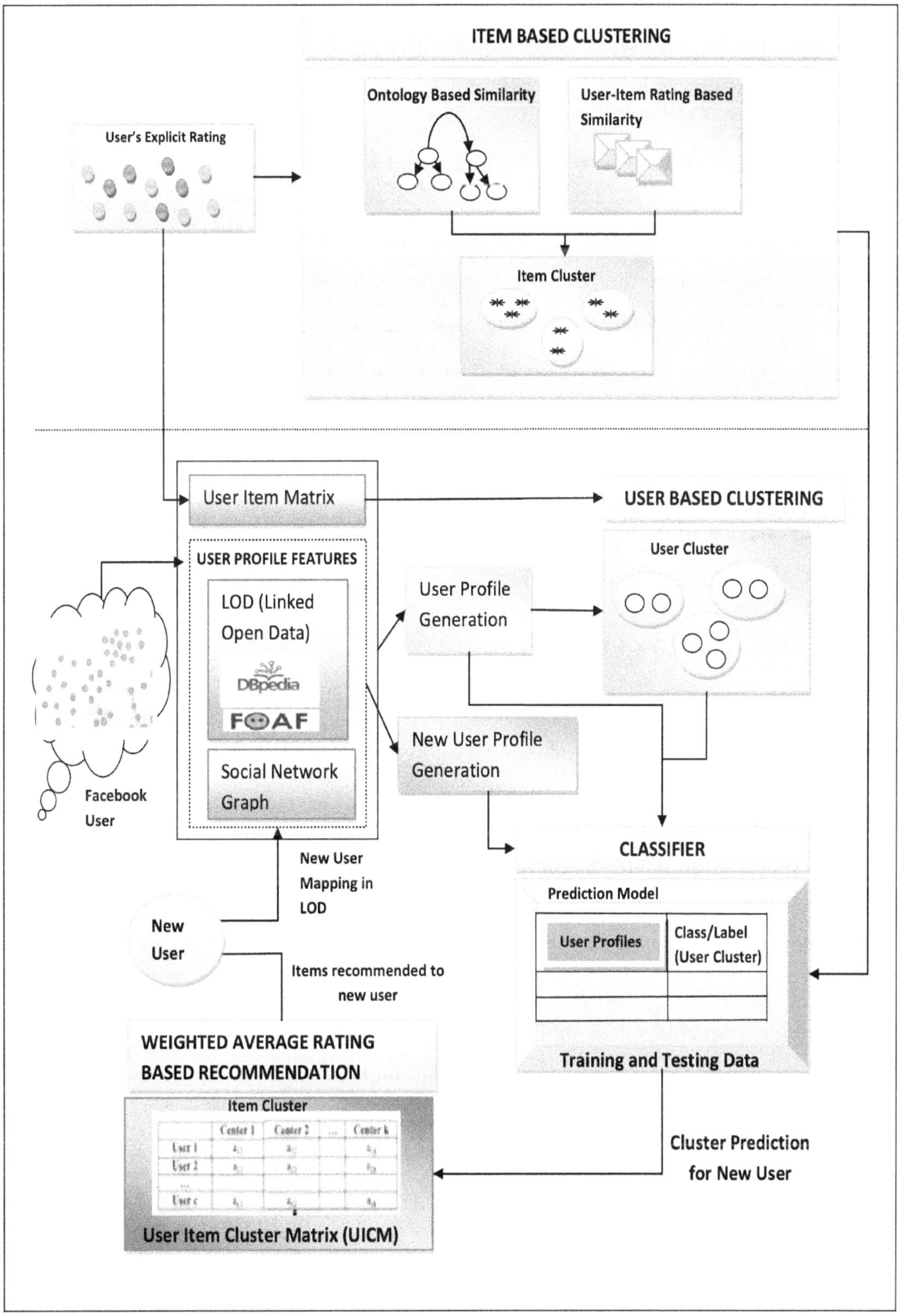

Figure 6.1: Framework of Proposed Hybrid Recommender System

- The classifier is used to classify the new users to a particular user cluster. The classifier is trained with the already registered user's profile. Once, new user's profile is generated, the classifier predicts the best suitable cluster to which the new user belongs.

Module 3- Weighted Average Rating based Recommendation

- Once, the new user is assigned to a user cluster, the recommender system then analyzes the rating provided to each item cluster by only those users, who are members of that same cluster. Each item cluster is assigned a weightage, based on the average rating given to each item cluster by these users.
- Finally, the items present in the item cluster with the highest weightage are recommended to the new user.

In the next section, *item based clustering* is discussed, which is computed using the item similarity based on explicit user rating and the ontologies.

6.3 ITEM BASED CLUSTERING

In this module, the overall similarity between the items is calculated based on their domain specific ontology and explicit rating provided by the user. The further sections described the process in more detail.

6.3.1 Item Similarity based on Ontology

Ontologies provide vast information in any domain which could be very beneficial in the recommendation system. Most of these researchers have considered only one attribute to calculate item similarity based on ontology, they somehow have neglected the multilevel and complex structure of ontologies.

Example Illustration:

Many researchers have only used *genre* of a movie to find a similar set of movies based on ontology. An abstract sample of the domain ontology illustrated in Fig. 6. 2, node *C* is defined as the as the target class. The class contains two attributes, *A1* and *A2*, and a subclass *SC*, which itself has its attributes, *A3, A4,* and *A5*. Assume, a movie recommendation system, if *C* is the movie class, then *A1* and *A2* could denote the *genre* and *directedBy* attributes, while *SC* could be the *Movie_origin* having its own attributes, *A3, A4,* and *A5* representing *Asia, Europe,* and *North America* respectively.

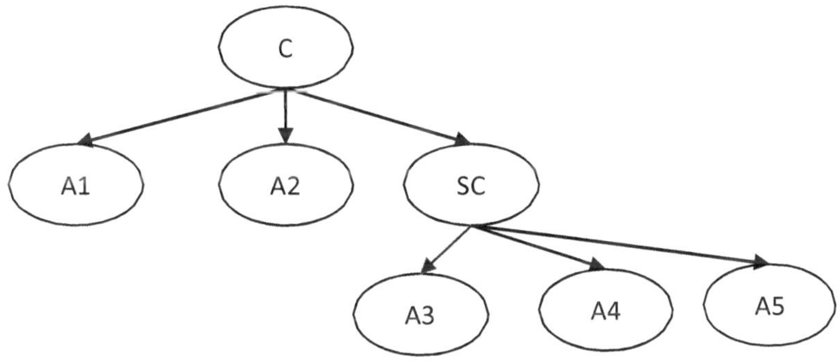

Figure 6.2: Sample Ontology

The other attributes such as *language* and *movie origin* are also important while analyzing the similarity between the movies. Therefore, considering only one attribute such as *genre* of a movie is not an appropriate solution and similarity among all the attributes should be calculated.

Ontologies represent the semantic description of any domain, so calculating the similarity between the two items based on their ontology is a very crucial task. The ontology is a complex and multilevel data structure. Therefore, calculation of the item similarity based on the ontology is divided into two sections:

- **Semantic Similarity between items**: This describes the technique to calculate the semantic similarity between the two items.
- **Similarity based on Ontology:** This similarity measures utilize the semantic similarity and further handles the computation required for multilevel data structure.

6.3.1.1 Semantic Similarity Calculation

In this section, item based semantic similarity is calculated using the *binary Jaccard similarity coefficient*. For two items to be similar, their own attributes, as well as their sub class's attributes, needs to be similar. The item class *C* has an attribute *At,* the value of this attribute could fall in m categories. Each item is considered as a binary vector V_c = ($v_{c,1}$, $v_{c,2}$, . . . , $v_{c,m}$) where a binary variable $v_{c,p}$ (p = 1, …, m) is defined as:

$V_{c,p}$ = 1, if Item belong to category p

$V_{c,,p}$= 0, If Item does not belong to category p

Then, the semantic similarity of items x and y for attribute At is presented below [165],[166]:

$$SSim(C_i.At, C_j.At) = \frac{!''''}{!''''\#!\$''\#!''\$} \qquad (6.1)$$

In Eq. (6.1), T_{01} , T_{10} and T_{11} respectively indicate the total number of categories for ($v_{ci,At}$ = 0; $v_{cj,At}$= 1), ($v_{ci,At}$ = 1; $v_{cj,At}$= 0) and ($v_{ci,At}$ = 1; $v_{cj,At}$ = 1).

Example Illustration of Semantic Similarity Calculation:

Consider the *movie class* of an ontology having *genres* as its attribute. The value of attribute could be *Comedy, Romantic, Fiction, Drama, Horror* and *Science* as represented in Table 6.1. Therefore, the number of categories to which this attribute belongs is *6*, therefore the value assigned to '*p*' is 6.

So, for each item their respective vectors can be represented as:

M1=(0,1,1,1,0,0),

M2=(1,0,0,1,0,0),

M3=(0,0,1,0,1,0),

M4=(1,1,0,1,0,0),

M5=(0,0,1,0,1,0)

where M1, M2, M3, M4, M5 are the binary vectors for movie 1, movie 2, movie 3, movie 4, movie 5 respectively.

Table 6.1: Movie-Genre Matrix

Movie	Genre					
	Comedy	Romantic	Fiction	Drama	Horror	Science
M1	0	1	1	1	0	0
M2	1	0	0	1	0	0
M3	0	0	1	0	1	0
M4	1	1	0	1	0	0
M5	0	0	1	0	1	0

The similarity between pairs of movies can be calculated using Eq. (6.1) and is given below:

SSim(M1,M2)= 1/(1+1+2) = ¼ = 0.25,

SSim(M1,M3)= 1/(1+1+1)=1/3=0.33,

SSim(M1,M4)= 2/(2+1+1)=2/4=0.5,

SSim(M1,M5)= 1/(1+1+2)=1/4=0.25,

SSim(M3,M5)= 2/(2+0+0)=2/2=1

SSim(M2,M4)= 2/(2+1+0)=2/3=0.66

where, SSim(M1,M2) is the similarity between *movie 1* and *movie 2* for an attribute *genre*. Correspondingly, the similarity between the same two items for all other attributes in the ontology can be calculated using Eq. (6.1).

6.3.1.2 Similarity based on Ontology

Unlike the traditional method, handling complex and multilevel data structures like ontologies as shown in Fig. 2 is very challenging. Ontologies contain the attribute of a class and also attributes of those attributes which itself is a class (i.e. subclass). In the sample set Fig. 2, *Class C* has three attributes, with the third attribute *SC* which itself is a class having three more attributes. The formula for calculating the overall semantic similarity between items I_i and I_j having the same ontology containing classes, subclasses, and attributes is explained below in detail.

In this method, *Similarity based on ontology* is calculated using the combination of the semantic similarity of the following:

- Semantic similarity of all the attributes corresponding to subclasses SC_i and SC_j of Item I_i and I_j respectively
- Semantic similarity between the attributes of class C_i and C_j of Item I_i and I_j respectively.

Using recursive computation, the average of the values is calculated, to obtain the similarity between items I_i and I_j until reaching the maximum depth. The suitable value of depth is set in the beginning. So, the *Similarity based on ontology* is calculated using Eq. (6.2) as explained below:

$S_{ontology}(I_i,I_j)$ = 2 ∑34" %%&▪ ()*.,- (-)⁾)0.,-(-)) / 5 (6.2)

where $S_{ontology}(I_i,I_j)$ is the similarity based on ontology between item I_i *and* I_j, if there is no attribute in the ontology which itself is a subclass, 6678(9&. :; ( ), 9-. :;(<) is the semantic similarity between classes C_i and C_j of two items I_i *and* I_j for a particular attribute '*At*' respectively, and *n* is the total number of attributes in the ontology of item domain.

If there are attributes in the ontology, which is also a subclass having its own attributes can be calculated using Eq. (6.3) as explained below.

$S_{ontology}(I_i,I_j)$ = 2 ∑34" %%&▪ ()*.,- (-)⁾)0.,-(-))# n ∑C4" >>*?(>@*.AB C ,>@0.AB(C)) / ? / 5 (6.3)

where,

- $S_{ontology}(I_i,I_j)$ is the *similarity based on ontology* between item I_i *and* I_j, if there is an attribute in the ontology which itself is a subclass,
- 6678(69&. :; (E) , 69-. :;( ) is the semantic similarity between subclasses SC_i *and* SC_j of two items I_i *and* I_j for a particular attribute '*At*' of subclass respectively,
- m is the total number of attributes of subclass in the ontology of item domain $1 \leq p \leq m$.
- 6678(9&. :; (<), 9-. :;(<) is the semantic similarity between classes C_i *and* C_j of two items I_i *and* I_j for a particular attribute '*At*' respectively, and
- *n* is the total number of attributes in the ontology of the item domain, $1 \leq k \leq n$.

Algorithm 6.1 shows the similarity computation based on the ontology of a particular domain. The output of the algorithm is the *Semantic Similarity Matrix*, SSM showing the semantic similarity between two items I_i *and* I_j based on ontology.

Examples Illustration:

Suppose *Movie_Origin* is Class of *Movie Ontology*, as shown in Fig. 6.3 and different continents are its attributes, continents can be further considered as subclass having its own attribute.

Algorithm: Similarity Computation Based on Ontology

```
Input: Item Ontology O(C,At,R), Set of Items I
Output: Semantic Similarity Matrix, SSM(I,I)
for each Ii ϵ I
        for each Ij ϵ I
                if(!isEqual(Ii.SC,Ij.SC))
                        Sontology(Ii,Ij) = ΣN L40 FFGH(IG.JK(L),I‖.JK(L)) / N
                else
                        Sontology(Ii,Ij) = [ΣN L40 FFGH(IG.JK(L),I‖.JK(L))#ΣH P40 FFGH(FIG.JK(P),FI‖.JK(P)) / H] / N
                end if
        end for
end for
```

Algorithm 6.1: Similarity Computation based on Ontology

If both the *movies* belong to the same *Continent*, then it is required to match this subclass's attributes like *country* i.e., country which is the origin of that movie. If both movies belong to the same country like *India*, then it is required to further match their attributes i.e. which *Cinema* it belongs to like *Bollywood, Tollywood, Punjabi,* etc, else it is not required to match their attributes.

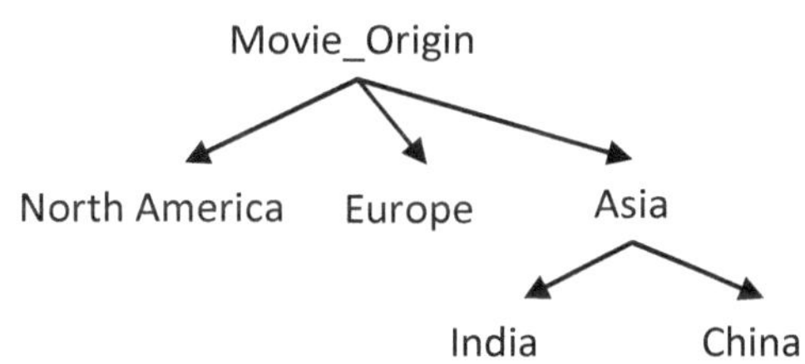

Figure 6.3: Snippet of Movie Ontology

6.3.2 Item Similarity based on Explicit User Rating

In this module, the similarity between items is calculated based on the explicit rating provided by the users in *User Item Rating Matrix*, *UIM*, where U is the set of users and I is the set of items, $r_{u,I}$ is the rating provided by the user u to item I as shown in Table 6.2.

In any system, the ratings are given to individual items by the users. The similarity between two items is determined by how similar are their rating patterns provided by the users. The similarity measure used here is, as given in Eq. (6.4),

$$Sim(I_i,I_j)=\sqrt{\sum_{UVW}^{5}\frac{(Q_{*R}SQ_{OR})^T}{(Q_{*R})^T S(Q_{OR})^T}} \tag{6.4}$$

where I_{iu} *and* I_{ju} are the value of the rating provided to Item I_i and Item I_j by user u respectively, n is the total number of users who rated both the items, $1\leq u\leq n$. Only the users who rated both the items are used for similarity calculation.

Table 6.2: User Item Rating Matrix, UIM

Items	I1	I2	I3	I4	I5
U1	r_{11}	r_{12}	-	r_{14}	r_{15}
U2	r_{21}	-	r_{23}	r_{24}	r_{25}
U3	r_{31}	r_{32}	-	r_{34}	r_{35}
U4	-	r_{42}	r_{43}	r_{44}	r_{45}
U5	r_{51}	r_{52}	r_{53}	-	-

6.3.3 Overall Item Similarity Score

The overall similarity score between the items is calculated based on the combination of similarity scores provided by ontology using Eqs. (6.2) and (6.3), and explicit user rating using Eq. (6.5) and it shown in Fig. 6.4.

$$Similarity\ (I_i,I_2)=\alpha * S_{ontology}(I_i,I_j)+\beta * Sim(I_i,I_j) \tag{6.5}$$

where $\alpha+\beta=1$, α, *and* β are the control values which could be adjusted by the experts of the domain. In this case, equal weightage is given to both the similarities measures i.e $\alpha=0.5$ *and* $\beta=0.5$. $Similarity(I_i,I_j)$ is the overall similarity score between two items, $S_{ontology}(I_i,I_j)$ is the similarity calculated based on ontology, and $Sim(I_i,I_j)$ is the similarity calculated based on explicit user's ratings as presented in Eq.(6.5).

Once the overall similarity is calculated for each item with every other item in the item set using Eq. (6.5), then *Overall Item Similarity Matrix (OISM)* as shown in Fig. 6.4, is formed which describes the overall similarity score among the items, in the item set.

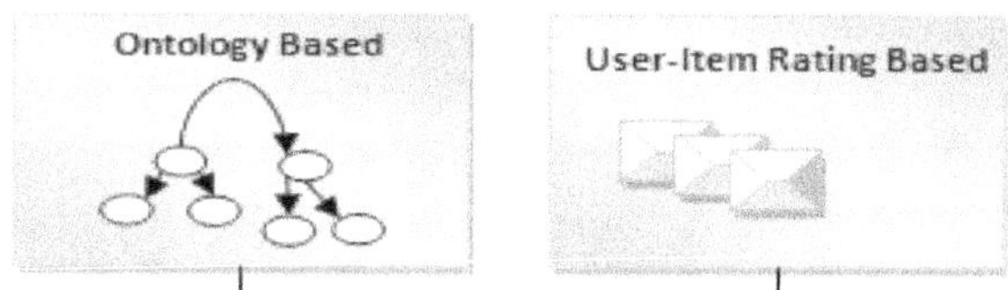

Items	I1	I2	I3	I4	I5
I1	-	A_{12}	A_{13}	A_{14}	A_{15}
I2	A_{21}	-	A_{23}	A_{24}	A_{25}
I3	A_{31}	A_{32}	-	A_{34}	A_{35}
I4	A_{41}	A_{42}	A_{43}	-	A_{45}
I5	A_{51}	A_{52}	A_{53}	A_{54}	-

Figure 6.4: Overall Item Similarity Matrix, OSM

In *OISM*, all rows and columns represent the total number of items in the item set and each cell A_{ij} represents the overall similarity score between item *i* and item *j*.

6.3.4 Item Clustering

In this proposed work, *Fuzzy C-means clustering* [167],[168] is used to cluster items, as it performs well with the sparse dataset. In most of the recommendation systems, only a few users provide ratings for the items resulting in the sparse explicit user-item matrix. In this research work, both content-based features are extracted from ontology and user rating data are considered, since considering only one of them will lead to low accuracy, overgeneralization, and overlapping of the cluster.

Once the cluster is formed, *User Item Cluster Matrix (UICM)* is created, where *U* is the set of user and *C* is the centers of all item's cluster, and the cell represents the value of average rating provided by user *u* to the item's cluster center *j* as shown in Fig. 6.5. Therefore the items which need to be analyzed are far less than the total number of items in the system, hence it improves the performance of the system [106].

The new matrix formed contains the center of each item cluster and the user's rating to each center. In Fig. 6.5, *m* denotes the number of all users, a_{uj} is the average rating of user *u* to *item cluster center j*, *n* implies the number of all items, R_{ij} indicates the rating of user *u* to *item j*, and *k* is the number of item centers.

The next section describes the Rating Prediction technique that only utilizes the ratings given by the similar users of a specific cluster.

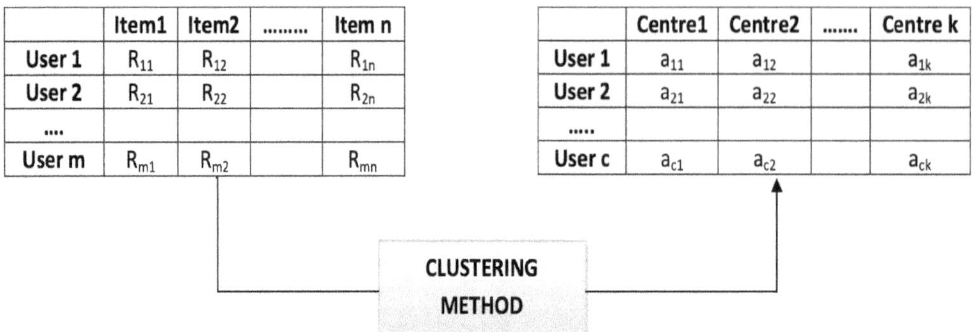

Figure 6.5: User Item Matrix, UIM converted to User Item Cluster Matrix

6.3.5 Rating Prediction

The *User Item Rating Matrix* contains number of empty cells in which the rating is not provided by the users. The proposed rating prediction technique predicts the rating based on the item cluster created in Section 6.3.3. For each unrated (target) item, the rating is predicted based on the ratings provided by the active user to the items which are similar to that unrated (target) item. Rating prediction is calculated in following two ways based on the available information:

1) The predicted rating is the collective sum of the ratings received by each similar item weighted by the similarity score between that particular similar item and the target item, divided by the sum of similarity scores of the similar items involved. The prediction of the rating of a target user u for an unrated item i is given in Eq. (6.6).

$$S_{u,i} = \frac{\sum_{t \in T} Similarity(i,t) * r_{u,t}}{\sum_{t \in T} Similarity(i,t)} \quad (6.6)$$

where $S_{u,i}$ is the Predicted Rating, for an item i by user u, $r_{u,t}$ is the rating for similar item t by user u; *Similarity(i,t)* is the similarity score between target item i and item t; and T is the total number of similar items under consideration.

2) In some scenarios, it could be possible that there would be no rating given to the top T similar items for a target item by the active user. In such scenario, even

after applying prediction using Eq. (6.7), some empty cells would still be present in the *User-Item Matrix*.

So, to overcome this problem, the remaining sparse cells could be predicted using an extended approach. In this approach, for an active user, his rating pattern to rate other items is considered along with the rating provided to the unrated (target) item by other users. The estimated rating of a target user *u* for an unrated item *i* using the proposed approach can be calculated as:

$$S_{u,i} = \alpha \frac{\overset{-}{\sum}_{34"} Z_{R,3}}{\grave{}} + b\frac{\overset{2}{\sum}_{c4",cdR} Z_{c,*}}{5} \qquad (6.7)$$

where

- α,β are the control parameters, where $\alpha+\beta=1$
- $S_{u,i}$ is the Predicted Rating
- K is the number of other items rated by u (target user), $1\leq k\leq K$
- $r_{u,k}$ is the rating given by u to other items K,
- n is the number of other users, where$1\leq q\leq n$, $q\neq u$, who provided a rating for target unrated item i.
- $r_{q,i}$ is the rating given to target item i by other users q, other than target user u.

α *and* β are the control values which could be adjusted by the experts of the domain. In this case, equal weightage is given to both the measures i.e. $\alpha=0.5$ *and* $\beta=0.5$.

The algorithm is presented in Algorithm 6.2 to predict the unrated value in explicit *User Item Rating Matrix, UIM(U,I)*, where *U* is the set of users and *I* is the set of Items. This algorithm will help in removing the sparsity in the *UIM(U,I)* and thus the output of this algorithm is *Dense User Item Rating Matrix*, *DUIM(U,I)* containing no sparsity, as described in Algorithm 6.2.

Let's take an example to describe in detail the working of the *Rating Prediction* module. In this example, a sample data set of *User Item Matrix* is considered with unrated values, creating a sparsity problem.

Algorithm: Rating Prediction

Input: Overall Item Similarity Matrix OISM(I,I), *User Item Rating Matrix*, UIM(U,I), User Set U, Item Set I
Output: *Dense User Item Rating Matrix*, DUIM(U,I)

```
for each user u ε U
        for each (item not rated by u) ε I
                if(rating given for similar item set)
                        S_u,i = Σkεn efgfhijfkl(f,k)*j_m,k / Σkεn efgfhijfkl(f,k)
                else
                        S_u,i = Σ_o40^p j_m,o / p + Σ_q40,qdm^r q,f / r
                end if
        end for
end for
```

Algorithm 6.2: Rating Prediction

Example Illustration of Rating Prediction:

Consider an example of explicit rating provided to each item by each user, which can be represented in a matrix as shown in Table 6.3. Suppose the matrix as shown in Table 6.3, contains rating given to movies by different users. Here '-' represents the sparsity, which means the user who has not rated that particular movie.

Table 6.3: Example of User Item Rating Matrix, UIM

	Item 1	Item 2	Item 3	Item 4
User 1	5	5	-	5
User 2	5	-	3	4
User 3	3	4	-	3
User 4	-	-	5	3
User 5	5	4	4	5
User 6	5	4	5	5

The similarity calculation based on user's explicit rating for two items I3 and I1 can be calculated as using Eq. (6.2) and Eq (6.4)

$$\text{Sim(I3,I1)} = \text{Sqrt}[((5-3)^2/(5^2+3^2)+(5-4)^2/(5^2+4^2)+(5-5)^2/(5^2+5^2)] = 0.59$$

$$S_{ontology}(I3,I1) = 0.33,$$

The overall similarity calculation based on ontology similarity and explicit user's rating can be calculated using (6.6)

$Similarity\ (I3,I1) = S_{ontology}(I3,I1) + Sim(I3,I1)\ )/2=0.46$

Similarly, we can calculate the overall similarity between two Items I3 and I2, as shown below

$Sim(I3,I2)= Sqrt[((4-4)^2 /(4^2 +4^2)+ (5-4)^2/(5^2 +4^2)] =0.15$

$S_{ontology}(I3,I2) = 0.25$

$Similarity\ (I3,I2) = S_{ontology}(I3,I2) + Sim(I3,I2)\ )/2=0.2$

Similarly, we can calculate the overall similarity between two Items I3 and I4, as shown below

$Sim(I3,I4)= Sqrt[((3-4)^2 /(3^2 +4^2)+ (5-3)^2/(5^2 +3^2)+ (4-5)^2/(4^2 +5^2)+ (5-5)^2/(5^2 +5^2)]=0.41$

$S_{ontology}(I1,I3)= 0.5$

$Similarity\ (I3,I4) = S_{ontology}(I1,I3) + Sim(I1,I3)\ )/2=0.45$

Therefore, the item most similar to item 3 is Item 1 and Item 4, so sparsity calculation to predict the rating value for Item 3 by user 1 would be calculated using Eq. (6.6)

$S_{13}= (0.46*5+0.45*5)/(0.46+0.45) = 5$

where S_{13} is the predicted rating for Item 3 by user 1 to remove sparsity. Similarly we could predict the rating value provided to Item 3 given by User 3, as shown. $S_{33}=(0.5*4+0.7*3)/(0.5+0.7) = 3.41 => 3$ where S_{33} is the predicted rating for Item 3 by user 3 to remove sparsity. Therefore UIM[3,3]=3, similarly other values can be predicted.

The next session describes in the detail the procedure for creating *User Profiles* based on Social network features, collaborative feature and LOD features.

6.4 USER PROFILE CREATION

User's profile is created and analyzed based on the following features:

- Social network features
- Collaborative features
- Linked Open Data Features

The use of features extracted from the LOD cloud to create user's profile is one of the distinguishing aspects of this framework. The number of features encoded in each group can vary depending upon the items in the recommender system and the domain of the recommender system. It can be more clearly described in Table 6.4.

Table 6.4: Comparison among the number of features encoded by each group

S.No.	Features Category	Number of Features
1.	Social Network Feature	4
2.	Collaborative Feature	No. of Items in Item Set
3.	LOD based features	Values vary with domain

Each user is represented by binary vector, containing 0s and 1s, depending upon whether that user falls into that feature or not.

Example Illustration:

Consider three users, *User 1, User 2,* and *User 3* in this example. Each user's *User Profile* is created based on the collaborative, LOD and social network based features. The user's profile is represented as vectors of 0's and 1's as shown in Table 6.5.

Table 6.5: Vector representing User Profile created based on features value

User	Feature Group												
	Collaborative Features					LOD based Features				Social Network based features			
User 1	0	1	1	0	1…	0	1	0	0…	0	1	0	0…
User 2	1	0	1	0	0…	0	1	1	1…	0	1	1	1…
User 3	1	0	0	0	1…	1	0	1	1…	1	0	1	1…

The next section describes in detail the social network analysis features used to create user profile.

6.4.1 User Registration

In our approach, it is very crucial to consider the number of facets to represent user depending upon domain rather than just analyzing user's demographic information such as age, gender, occupation only. In order to gather LOD-based features and social network features related to each user, an explicit requirement from the user side would be needed while registering in the system. Users have to specify their DBpedia ID (if any) and also they need to login into the application using their Facebook id ("Log In as Facebook User"). Due to privacy issues, permission is needed from the users to access basic information from their profile. The workflow to gather information about the user is shown in Fig. 6.6.

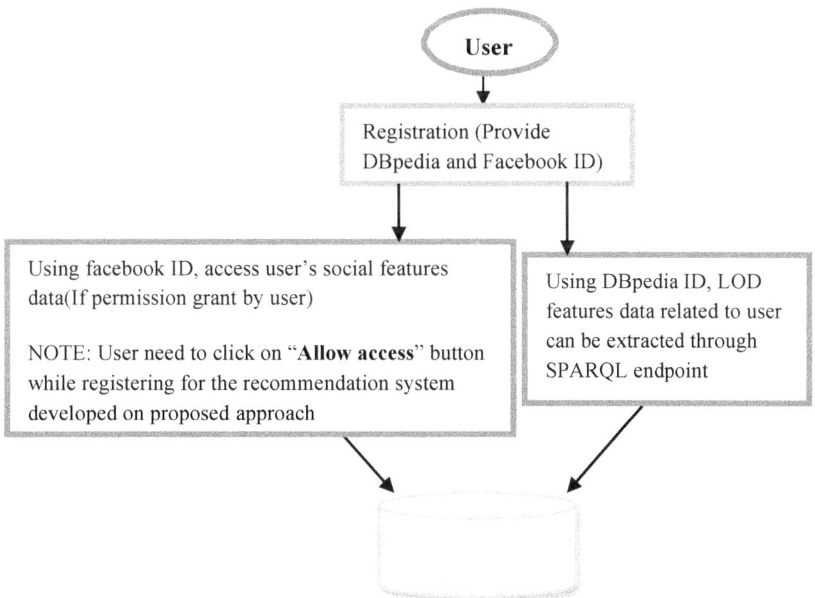

Figure 6.6: Workflow Diagram to gather information about user

Accessing User Information from Social Network

Facebook is one of the most famous social networking sites, almost all the web user has created their profile on Facebook. To access the information from Facebook, Facebook 4j API [169] is used to extract the required data. Fig. 6.7 shows how to create *app* and create a user authentication token using Graph API Explorer. Also, Fig. 6.8 shows the attributes and its data can be extracted using this API, if the user has granted permissions to do so.

6.4.2 Social Network Based Features

Social network analysis (SNA) is the field in which complete social configuration is anlyzed or processed using traditional network and graph theories. A network structure is composed of nodes (directional or unidirectional) and edges or links. Node could describe any person or thing depending upon requirement and links or ties describe the links between them.

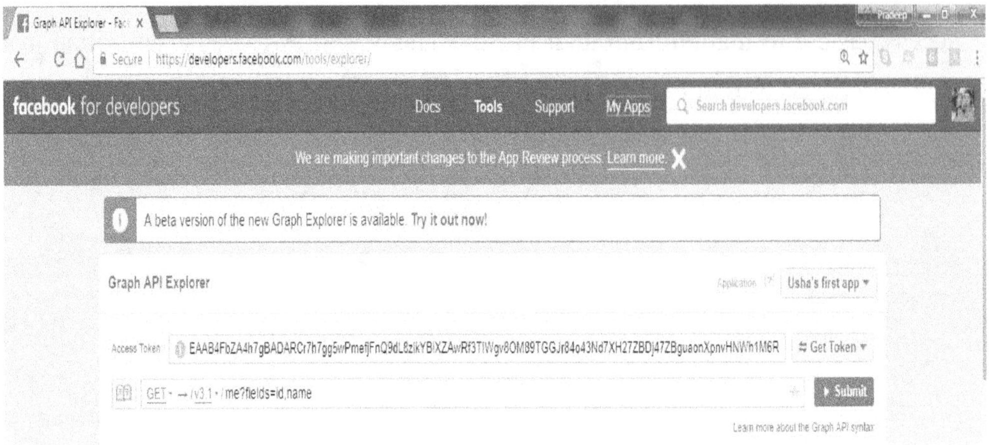

Figure 6.7: Graph API Explorer

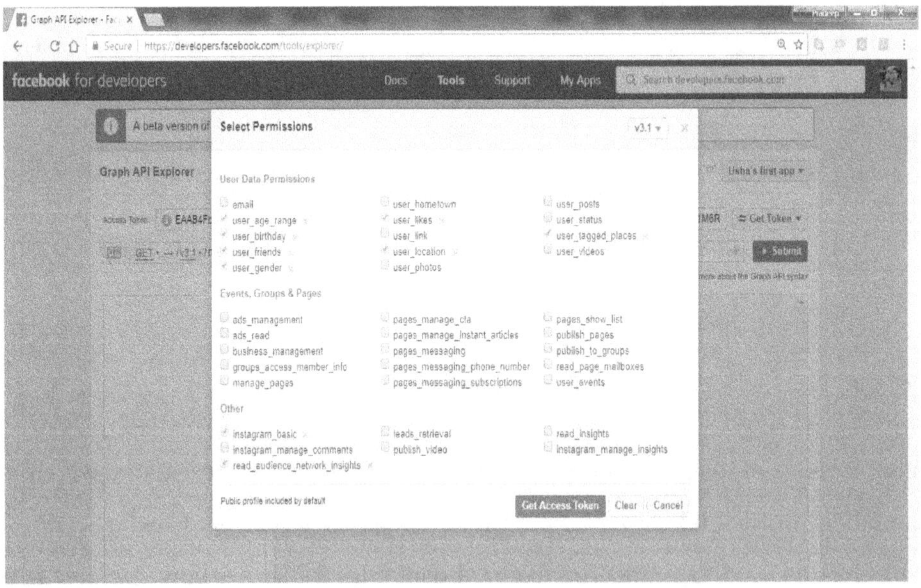

Figure 6.8: Facebook's user account permissions

A sample social network is shown in Fig. 6.6. In this proposed work, following social network features are used and included in the user profile creation

- **Centrality**

  In network, theory centrality is defined as a factor that recognizes the most significant nodes in the given network. Community structure describes the property of low cohesion and high coupling for the grouping of nodes in a given network. Node is termed as more central if it has a higher degree

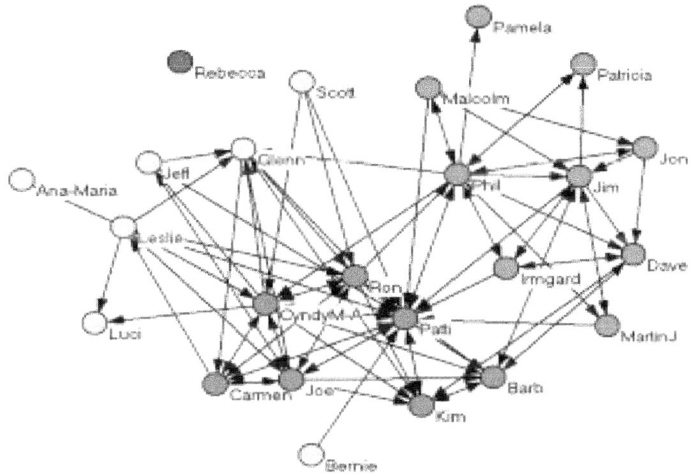

Figure 6.9: Sample of Social Network.

- **Clustering Coefficient** is defined as a measurement of the degree by which nodes can cluster together in the given graph. A graph $G= (V,E)$ formally contains set of vertices and edges. An edge represents the connection between two vertices. For example, an edge e_{ij} connects vertex v_i with vertex v_j."

  The neighborhood N_i for a vertex v_i is defined as those neighbors which are directly connected to it.

  $$N_i = \{v_j : e_{ij} \varepsilon E \vee e_{ji} \varepsilon E\}$$

  where K_i is defined as the number of vertices, $|N_i|$, in the neighborhood, N_i, of a vertex.

- **Degree for a vertex v can be defined as:**
  - **In-degree**, is "the number of edges started at v. A higher degree node would be more esteemed (choices received)."
  - **out-degree**, is the number of edges concludes at v. Node degree distribution is one of the most important properties of a graph. The higher degree node would be more central (choices made)."

6.4.3 Collaborative Features

This class of features models the information encoded in the *User-Item Matrix* which contain ratings provided by the users for particular items [170]. Table 6.6 shows an example representing the collaborative features modeling user's likes and dislikes. Each user is modeled by extracting the corresponding column vector.

Table 6.6: Example of a matrix modeling users' like and dislike

	User 1	User 2	User 3	User 4	User 5	………	User N
Inception	1	0	1	0	0	………	1
Spider-Man	1	0	0	0	1	………	0
Blade Runner	0	1	1	0	0	………	1

Columns of the matrix represent the inclinations articulated by users and the rows represent the rating that each item got from all the users in the system.

Drawbacks of existing User Similarity measures based on Explicit Ratings

In most of existing research work, various similarity measures such as Pearson Correlation, Cosine similarity, Jaccard coefficient, etc. had been widely used but has certain limitations as described below:

- These methods are inefficient in dealing with datasets which is sparser and very less rating provided by users.
- Calculating similarity using traditional methods is more convincing, if users have given ratings to more common items. It is very likely that different people have different tendencies of giving ratings as some users always used to give a rating on the higher side even though they don't like the item so much and vice versa.
- The traditional similarity measures don't take these thing into account. Many researchers had encoded the user's rating's absolute value into *1*, if user "likes" item and *0* is user "dislikes" item but this strategy will eventually become complex while finding similar users.

The proposed work focuses both on local and global contexts while analyzing user's preferences. The similarity measure is an extension to the similarity measure proposed by the authors in [93].The final similarity value is divided by the summation of the average rating of each factor. The improved method is called as AWPSS (Average weighted Proximity-Significance-Singularity).

In Eqs. (6.8, 6.9 & 6.10), the first factor is *Proximity factor*, it only considers the difference between the two ratings. The next factor is *Significance* that gives more importance to the ratings if the distance between the two ratings from the median rating is more. The third factor is *Singularity* it specifies how other ratings are different from these two ratings.

Proximity ($r_{u,p}$, $r_{v,p}$) = 1 − W / W#uvw (S|yz,{SZ|,c|) (6.8)

Significance ($r_{u,p}$, $r_{v,p}$) = W / W#uvw (S|yz,{SZ?}~|. |y,{SZ?}~|) (6.9)

Singularity ($r_{u,p}$, $r_{v,p}$) = 1 − W / W#uvw (S|(Äz,{ÅÄ,{ / T) SÇc) (6.10)

where μ_p is the average rating of item p. $r_{u,p}$ is the rating of item p by user u. Each factor belongs to (0,1) in our model. The extended similarity method called as AWPSS (Average weighted Proximity-Significance-Singularity) is defined in Eq. (6.11)

$$\text{AWPSS}\ (r_{u,p}, r_{v,p}) = \alpha^{*}\ \text{Proximity}\ (r_{u,p}, r_{v,p}) + \beta^{*}\text{Proximity}\ (r_{u,p}, r_{v,p}) + \gamma^{*}\text{Singularity}\ (r_{u,p}, r_{v,p}) \quad (6.11)$$

where $\alpha+\beta+\gamma=1$, α, β *and* γ are the control values which could be adjusted by the experts of the domain. In this case, equal weightage is given to all the similarities measures i.e $\alpha=0.33$ *and* $\beta=0.33$ *and* $\gamma=0.33$.

6.4.4 Linked Open Data Based Features

All the features considered to create user profile describe numerous facets of the users and represented using vector. However, extending this vector by using LOD attributes is one of the novel approaches of this work to generate a user's profile. The LOD cloud is standard and an important source to acquire descriptive features to model the users.

- Consider the recommendation system is for the clothing domain, then to find the similarity between users, it depends more on their height, weight, bust size rather than their location, occupation, etc.
- Only DBpedia has standardized these attributes of defining any user's profile. Although DBpedia contains information to well-known people only, but it has been linked with other many databases as well which could further provides information about users.

- In the future, as the Linked Data grows, more and more information would be available covering users from all over the world, where each user will be uniquely identified by URI.
- Most of the domain existed currently are closed domain, as they do not share information among each other. With the growing benefits provided by Linked Open Data, many domains in the future might collaborate and share information with each other and contribute to further growth of LOD.
- User's privacy and authentication issues would play a major role in linking the data from around the world.

Also, in DBpedia, information about the users or any other items is freely available in the LOD cloud in RDF format. Using SPARQL query end-point, this information can be easily be extracted. To obtain information from the LOD, the URI of the resource is required.

As shown in Table 6.7, attributes representing various facets of the user are gathered from DBpedia LOD cloud. Each feature is represented using two things: $[property, value]$, different users could have the same or different value for each entity. To represent the feature corresponding to each user, a *vocabulary* of LOD-based features is built. The value of each feature in the vocabulary was set to *1* if the user is described through that RDF property, *0* otherwise. It means the value *0* represents the information that is not related to the user and *1* represents information is related to that user.

6.4.5 User Similarity

In this module, the similarity between the users is calculated based on the following:

- Social network features
- Collaborative features
- Features extracted from LOD cloud

Table 6.7: Partial representation of the vector modeling the LOD-based features extracted from DBpedia for the User 1, User 2, User 3

Basic LOD based Features	User 1	User 2	User 3
(dbo:birthPlace, dbr:Germany)	1	0	0
(dbo:birthPlace, dbr:India)	0	1	1
(dbo:birthSign, dbr:Scorpion)	0	0	1
(dbo:College, dbr:IIT Delhi)	0	1	0
(dbo:Employer, dbr:Amazon)	1	0	0
(dbo:age, dbr:36)	1	0	1
(dbo:age, dbr:22)	0	1	1
(dbo:Discipline, dbr:Arts)	1	0	0
(dbo:sex, dbr:Female)	0	0	1
(dbo:Profession, dbr:Racer)	1	0	1
(dbo:Profession, dbr:Dancer)	0	1	0
(dbo:tattoo, dbr:Shiva)	1	0	0
(dbo:skinColor, dbr:brown)	0	1	1

Each user is represented by binary vector, containing 0s and 1s, depending upon whether that user falls into that feature or not. Each user in User Set is considered as a binary vector $U= (u_{f1}, u_{f2}, \ldots, u_{fm})$ where a binary variable u_f ($f= 1, \ldots, m$) is defined as:

$u_f = 1$, if user belongs to that p

$u_f = 0$, If user does not belong to that p

where m is the total number of features contained in collaborative and LOD based feature group. The similarity between each user to other corresponding users in the user set is presented in Eq. (6.12):

$$U_{sim}(U_i,U_j) = \frac{\text{!""}}{\text{!""\#!\$"\#!"\$}} \tag{6.12}$$

Here, T_{01}, T_{10} and T_{11} respectively indicate the total number of categories for ($u_{if}= 0$; $u_{jf}= 1$), ($u_{if}= 1$; $u_{jf}= 0$) and ($u_{if}= 1$; $u_{jf}= 1$).

Example Illustration:

Consider *User Profile* of three users, *User 1, User 2,* and *User 3* based on the set of features selected as shown in Table 6.8.

Table 6.8: Vector representing User Profile created based on features value

User	User Profile												
User 1	0	1	1	0	1	0	1	0	0	0	1	0	0
User 2	1	0	1	0	0	0	1	1	1	0	1	1	1
User 3	1	0	0	0	1	1	0	1	1	1	0	1	1

The similarity between the users can be calculated by applying the Eq. (6.12) on the given date and following the same computation process as explained in detailed in Section 6.3.1.1.

6.4.6 User Clustering

In this proposed system, *Fuzzy C-means clustering (FCM)* [167] is used to cluster similar items as well as users. FCM provides soft clustering in which each data point is provided with the membership value which describes how much that point belongs to that particular cluster. Also, it works best for a large dataset with many features or dimensions. In this work, three groups of features are considered for generating user clusters, since considering only one of them will lead to low accuracy, overgeneralization, and overlapping of the cluster.

The next section describes the weighted average recommendation technique to classify new user and provide recommendation.

6.5 WEIGHTED AVERAGE RECOMMENDATION

In this proposed work, the *pure new user cold start problem* is formulated and computes *top-N* recommendations for a *new user*, who just registered in the system. It is considered that new user has not rated any item in the system and not even has searched for any of the items. Following steps described the technique in more detail:

- When a user enters in a system, new user profile is generated using *User profile generation* module.
- Some good performing classification algorithms, namely *Logistic Regression, Random Forest and Naïve Bayes* (NB) are implemented to analyze the results from each of them.

- The prediction model is developed for a classifier using various attributes and class labels. Numbers of *User Profile* Features are used, as attributes for the classifier and *user clusters* as class labels.
- The classifier is trained with 70% of the data and the rest 30% of data is used as test data.
- After creating the *user clusters*, *new user* is classified in one of the *user cluster* by the classifier and the recommendation is given to *new user* based on the rating provided by the other users present in the same cluster. Thus, it results in improving performance since the cluster that should be analyzed includes much fewer users compared to the number of all items [171]

An algorithm for weighted average recommendation system is shown in Algorithm 6.3.

Algorithm 3: Weighted Average Recommendation

Input: User Profile, Item Clusters I, User Cluster U, User Item Matrix
Output: N Items recommended to new user

1. When a new user logs in to the system, his profile will be generated by system using "User Profile Generation" module.
2. Then classifier will analyze the user and can predict the "User Cluster" to which this new user belongs to.
3. Once the "User Cluster" is found to which new user belongs to, the system will analyze the rating provided to each "Item cluster" by only those users who are present in this predicted "User Cluster".
4. The average weight of the rating given to each Item cluster by the user present in the predicted cluster is calculated.
5. Item cluster with the highest rating value is recommended to the new user.

Algorithm 6.3: Weighted Average Recommendation

The next section describes the experiment done by analyzing the real-world data sets for the comparative analysis of the proposed approach with the other existing approaches.

6.6 EXPERIMENTAL SETUP

In this section, two real-world data sets are used to evaluate the proposed recommender system which deals with *pure user cold start problem*. Also, the results are compared with the existing state-of-the-art recommendation systems.

6.6.1 Dataset Description

This work is evaluated using the following two datasets:

MovieLens Dataset [172]**:** This is one of the most famous datasets used for the evaluation of recommender systems. There are 6040 and 3952 numbers of users and movies respectively in the dataset. The rating has been given on a 5-star scale in this dataset. Only those users are selected for evaluations who have given at least 20 ratings to the items in the system. Therefore this dataset includes 10,00209 anonymous ratings based on the number of movies and users.

Yahoo! Webscope R4 dataset [173]**:** Yahoo! Research Alliance Webscope program provided this dataset, in which rating is given on 5-star scale and the dataset is divided into two sets: training and testing datasets. The training set includes 7642 users, 11,915 movies and 211,231 ratings. The testing set includes 2309 users, 2380 movies and 10,136 ratings.

In this study, LOD features are extracted from DBpedia SPARQL endpoint[96] and Facebook 4j API [169] has been used to gather information about the user. Also, Web crawler WebSPHINX [174] has been used to crawl content related to items from IMDb [175]. For these evaluations, randomly 80% of the data are used for the training set and the remaining 20% of data are used for the testing set.

6.6.2 Result Analysis and Discussions

The proposed recommender system is developed using PHP (7.1) language, under a 4 GHz processor, 8GB RAM, and 64- bit Microsoft Windows 2010. The proposed approach is compared and evaluated with related researches such as recommendation engine using Pearson nearest neighbor algorithm[176], user and item-based prediction method with EM clustering, Singular Value Decomposition (SVD) and ontology [177],item based prediction methods with EM clustering and SVD with ontology [177], and user and item based with SVD , EM clustering and no contribution of ontology.

The proposed approach is represented with user and item based along with ontology and Linked Open Data.

6.6.2.1 Scalability Analysis

In the first experiment, the effectiveness of the proposed approach which is based on ontology based similarity, clustering, and LOD is evaluated. Throughput is defined as the number of recommendations per second, is and used for evaluation. MovieLens and Yahoo! Webscope R4 datasets are used to show the effectiveness of the proposed method in improving the scalability of the overall system.

- In Figure 6.10(a-b), it can be observed that the performance of the proposed method as compared to the state-of-the-art techniques.
- Throughput is presented as a function of the cluster size. It could be clearly inferred from the graph that, the throughput of proposed approach based on ontology similarity, clustering, and LOD is slightly higher than other approaches.
- Due to clustering, only portion of the items/ users is analyzed by the recommendation system, hence it is efficient as opposed to systems using the nearest neighbour approach. Therefore, in case of nearest neighbour, increase in the size of the cluster is not impacting throughput as it needs to scan all nearest neighbours.

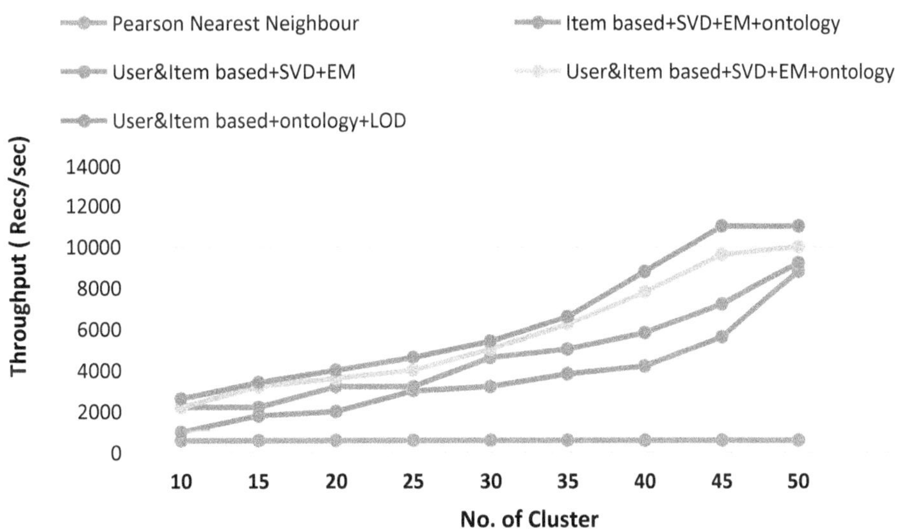

Figure 6.10-(a): Scalability using MovieLens Dataset

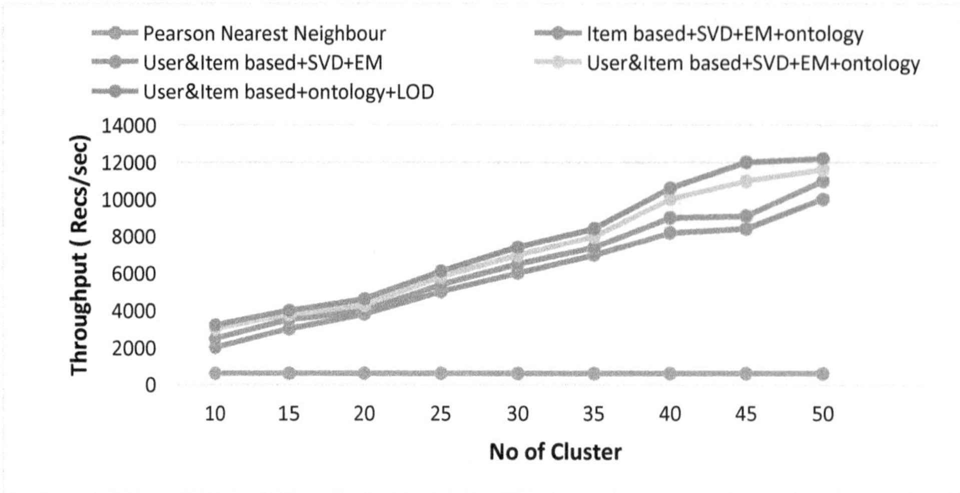

Figure 6.10-(b): Scalability using Yahoo Webscope Dataset

6.2.2.2 Predictive Accuracy

Mean Absolute Error (MAE) is the statistical metrics to analyze the predictive accuracy. In this experiment, the MAE between the predicted and the actual ratings is measured. MAE is presented in Eq. (6.13)

$$MAE(pred, act) = \sum_{i=1}^{N} \frac{|pred_{i} - act_{i}|}{n} \quad (6.13)$$

where N is the number of items on which a user u has expressed an opinion. The proposed method analyzed using MAE for predictive accuracy and compared with Pearson nearest neighbor algorithm, item-based prediction method with clustering, SVD and ontology, and user- and item-based prediction methods with clustering and SVD. For this evaluation, different numbers of neighbors (k) are considered (k = 10, 20, 30, 40, 50, 60, 70, 80, 90 and 100).

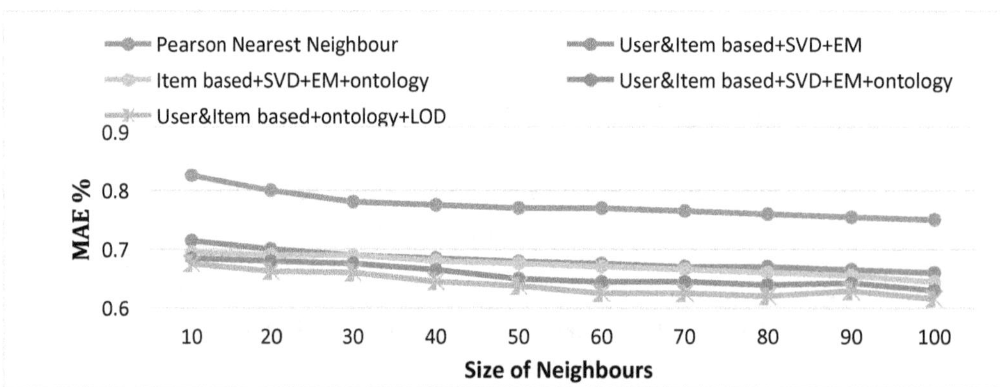

Figure 6.11-(a): MAE using MovieLens Dataset

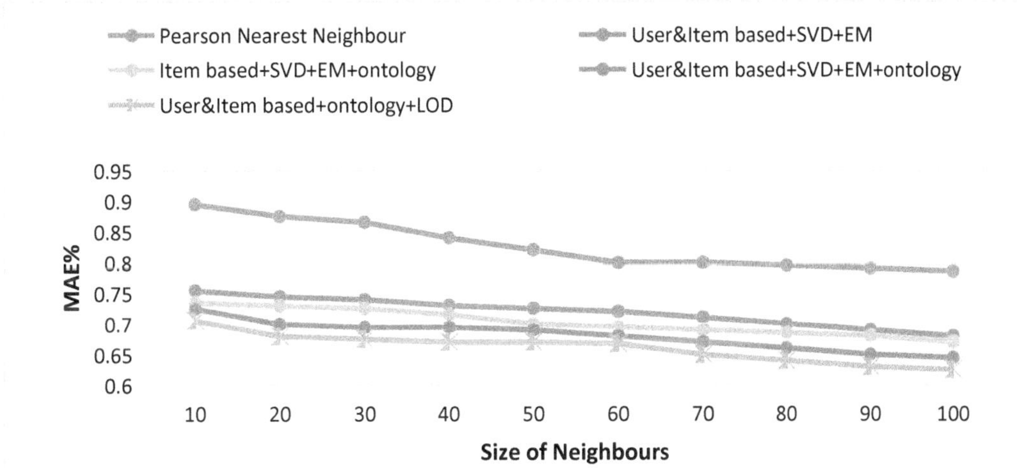

Figure 6.11-(b): MAE using Yahoo Webscope Dataset

Fig. 6.11(a-b) shows the MAE for various approaches plotted against different neighborhood size on two datasets MovieLens and Yahoo Webscope respectively. It is found that the proposed approach based on item-user ontology, clustering and LOD performed very well in accuracy as compared to other approaches. Also, it can be clearly observed that with the use of ontology, the accuracy of the system is improved, as MAE of Item-based+SVD+EM+ontology is lower than the User and item based+SVD+EM.

6.6.2.3 Decision-support accuracy

In a hybrid based recommender system, the decision support accuracy metric play a very crucial role in analyzing the overall performance of the recommender system. These types of metrics compare the recommended items with the relevant items. The metrics which come under this category are Precision, Recall, and F-measure.

The precision in Eq. (6.14) calculates the fraction of items that are relevant from the list of results retrieved, while the recall in Eq. (6.15) calculates the fraction of relevant items that have been retrieved.

$$\text{Precision}=\frac{\text{!á}}{\text{!á\#àá}} \quad (6.14)$$

$$\text{Recall}=\frac{\text{!á}}{\text{!á\#àâ}} \quad (6.15)$$

where, *FN* is the number of false non-relevant predictions, *TR* is the number of true relevant predictions and *FR* is the number of false relevant predictions. A metric that considers both values is the F1-measure as shown in Eq. (6.16),

$$\mathrm{F1} = \frac{\text{(W\#ä}^{\text{T}}\text{).ÉZÑÜ\&ä\&å5.ZÑÜYXX}}{\text{ä}^{\text{T}}\text{.ÉZÑÜ\&ä\&å5\#ZÑÜYXX}} \qquad (6.16)$$

It calculates the mean of the recall and the precision, β is be used to weight the influence of one of both, where $\beta > 1$ raises the significance of the precision and on the other hand, using $\beta < 1$, the influence of recall is increased. So, $\beta = 1$ is considered for a balanced F-measure. The proposed method is evaluated based on the different number of top recommendations, such that N = 10, 20, 30, 40, and 50. Tables 6.9 and 6.10 shows that the F1 measures and the precision values for different *Top-N* recommendations. It can be inferred from the Table 6.9 that in comparison to nearest neighbour algorithm, precision obtained by the proposed method is significantly high. It is also observed in that F1-measures of the proposed system which deals with ontology and LOD has outperformed other methods, majorly nearest neighbour approach. These results prove that our recommendation system is efficient and scalable as compared to nearest neighbor algorithm. Here:

Method A = User- and Item-based + SVD + EM + Ontology,

Method B = Item-based + SVD + EM + Ontology,

Method C = User- and Item- based + SVD + EM,

Method D = Nearest Neighbor

Table 6.9: F1-measure and the precision values for different Top-N recommendations (MovieLens dataset)

Top N	Proposed System		Method A		Method B		Method C		Method D	
	Precision	F1-Metric	Precision	F1-Metric	Precision	F1-Metric	Precision	F1-Metric	Precision	F1-Metric
Top-5	0.803	0.813	0.787	0.797	0.771	0.773	0.719	0.721	0.564	0.583
Top-10	0.806	0.817	0.796	0.807	0.782	0.784	0.736	0.739	0.582	0.601
Top-15	0.822	0.832	0.816	0.827	0.802	0.804	0.747	0.749	0.592	0.615
Top-20	0.833	0.844	0.821	0.833	0.809	0.811	0.757	0.76	0.601	0.622
Top-25	0.846	0.857	0.833	0.844	0.823	0.825	0.769	0.77	0.628	0.65
Top-30	0.839	0.849	0.831	0.84	0.819	0.821	0.757	0.762	0.603	0.605
Top-35	0.832	0.843	0.823	0.832	0.806	0.808	0.75	0.751	0.581	0.59
Top-40	0.829	0.84	0.819	0.83	0.801	0.803	0.739	0.741	0.573	0.579
Top-45	0.821	0.835	0.818	0.827	0.793	0.795	0.733	0.732	0.556	0.558
Top-50	0.819	0.832	0.813	0.822	0.783	0.785	0.723	0.722	0.541	0.546

Table 6.10: F1 measures and the precision values for different Top-N recommendations (Yahoo Webscope dataset)

Top N	Proposed System		Method A		Method B		Method C		Method D	
	Precision	F1-Metric	Precision	F1-Metric	Precision	F1-Metric	Precision	F1-Metric	Precision	F1-Metric
Top-5	0.768	0.786	0.757	0.767	0.714	0.727	0.669	0.694	0.494	0.516
Top-10	0.786	0.798	0.766	0.777	0.737	0.757	0.683	0.707	0.517	0.534
Top-15	0.803	0.814	0.783	0.792	0.74	0.764	0.688	0.709	0.528	0.549
Top-20	0.808	0.817	0.786	0.797	0.747	0.771	0.692	0.711	0.536	0.557
Top-25	0.802	0.817	0.788	0.797	0.749	0.776	0.697	0.714	0.542	0.565
Top-30	0.824	0.832	0.789	0.801	0.757	0.779	0.704	0.724	0.551	0.571
Top-35	0.826	0.835	0.791	0.803	0.761	0.785	0.715	0.727	0.564	0.582
Top-40	0.825	0.838	0.799	0.805	0.764	0.791	0.721	0.734	0.571	0.594
Top-45	0.827	0.839	0.809	0.814	0.772	0.793	0.727	0.744	0.585	0.608
Top-50	0.839	0.843	0.815	0.821	0.784	0.798	0.739	0.762	0.617	0.631

6.6.2.4 Features Performance

Evaluation and analysis of features is done to gain insights on how different set of features used to create *user profile* is improving the accuracy and performance of the proposed recommendation system. The performance of features is measured individually and in combination. In Table 6.11, it is observed that LOD feature itself has increased the F-measure of the proposed system as compared to other individual features such as demographic-based or social network features. Also, it can be seen that combining LOD+SN+demographic features do not provide any major increase in the performance of the recommender system. With the increase in the top N recommendation system, the performance of the system increased significantly.

Table 6.11: F1 measures and the precision values of feature performance

Top N	Precision LOD	F1-Metric LOD	Precision LOD + D	F1-Metric LOD + D	Precision LOD + SN + D	F1-Metric LOD + SN + D	Precision SN	F1-Metric SN
Top-5	0.68	0.76	0.4	0.571	0.4	0.4	0.4	0.4
Top-10	0.68	0.8	0.5	0.5	0.4	0.16	0.4	0.45
Top-15	0.77	0.82	0.33	0.47	0.6	0.48	0.47	0.47
Top-20	0.73	0.84	0.4	0.56	0.55	0.43	0.6	0.6
Top-25	0.85	0.86	0.32	0.6	0.48	0.48	0.6	0.6
Top-30	0.8	0.88	0.67	0.76	0.57	0.33	0.66	0.66
Top-35	0.97	0.97	0.56	0.7	0.63	0.58	0.6	0.75

6.7 SUMMARY

6.7 SUMMARY

The proposed system is contributed to overcome various issues of recommendation systems such as accuracy, throughput, sparsity, and *new user cold start* problem.

- To enhance the efficiency of recommender systems, new methods are devised to calculate semantic similarity between two items based on ontology and explicit user rating.
- Users' similarity is determined using various features like LOD, Social Network, and collaborative, that increases the accuracy in finding similar users and clustering them.
- The experimental evaluation of the proposed system is done on two real world datasets using MAE, precision, recall and F1 measures performance metrics.

It is evaluated that the system is favorable in improving the throughput, accuracy, decreasing the sparsity, and dealing with *new user cold start* problem.

The next chapter describes the semantic search engine based on the natural language processing and the RDF. It allows users common users to retrieve precise results and motivate them for structured data creation.

CHAPTER 7

SEMANTIC SEARCH ENGINE BASED ON NLP AND RDF

7.1 INTRODUCTION

The traditional search retrieval algorithms of Web 2.0 have become outdated in retrieving the precise and accurate information from the growing Web 3.0, known as Semantic Web. The more advanced and strategic techniques compliant with the semantic web would be highly needed to find the desired information from evolving semantically linked data. The semantically enriched information is the need of the hour, it is vital to make this information accessible to the general user. It is logical to assume that the general user lacks in understanding the ontology structure of the system or structured language to retrieve data such as SPARQL. Interpreting the requirement directly into SPARQL is indeed very challenging for the common user [178][179]. Also, the knowledge base in some domain specific application gradually extended and updated. Therefore, there might be cases in which there is no relevant information present in the knowledge base in accordance with user query, in such scenarios, alternatives methodology needs to be adapted to retrieve the relevant information from other sources.

In this work, a semantic search engine is proposed which includes the following:

- Natural Language Processing technique is used for automated formulation of SPARQL queries from the given user query.
- To reduce ambiguity and improving the top search results, weightage score is assigned to each mapping between the user query word and the resource in the ontology.
- To overcome the limitation of keyword-based search, this approach does not rely only on the frequency of keywords that occurred in the web document. However, the underlying semantic structure of the web documents retrieved from Google and the triplets retrieved from the Semantic Wiki is analyzed and the co-occurrence matrix based on the user query triplets is formulated.

- Formulation of *Term Frequency matrix* and *Co-occurrence matrix* from the RDF triplets to improve the context relevance issue and further decomposing it to generate priority vector.
- Many domain specific applications which deal with handling natural language user queries often result into *no result found issue*, therefore in this approach, an alternate technique to redirect user query over the semantic structured web is devised to overcome this issue.
- To increase the relevancy in retrieving the documents from the web, the frequency of co-occurrence which is far less than the term frequency is used which further eliminates the less relevant web documents from the corpus.

7.2 PROPOSED SEMANTIC SEARCH ENGINE FRAMEWORK

In this section proposed architecture of semantic search engine is explained as shown in Fig. 7.1. The architecture is divided into two phases, *Result Retrieval from domain KB* and *Result Retrieval from Web*, each of the phases is explained in brief below:

Phase 1: (Result Retrieval from created Domain Knowledge Base)

1. In this phase, pre-processing is applied to the query submitted by the user in *natural language*. The pre-processing involves sentence segmentation, tokenization, and stop words removal, determining each token's part of Speech (POS), and conducting lemmatization. As a result, a set of query terms $QT = \{t1, t2, . . . , tn\}$, which retains the input order, is retrieved.
2. The tokens generated are analyzed for interrogatives such as *when, which, who* and for functions such as *how many, max* etc.
3. The interrogatives and the function terms are kept aside to be used in creating SPARQL structure. Finally, a set of user query terms are generated.
4. Each term in the query is mapped with the most similar resource in the ontology using proposed *Term Ontology Mapping technique*.
5. A weightage function is proposed to assign weight to each of the mapping done in previous step
6. SPARQL is constructed based on the finding of the above steps.
7. Finally, the SPARQL query is applied on domain KB using Jena ARQ2 engine, and results are displayed to users.

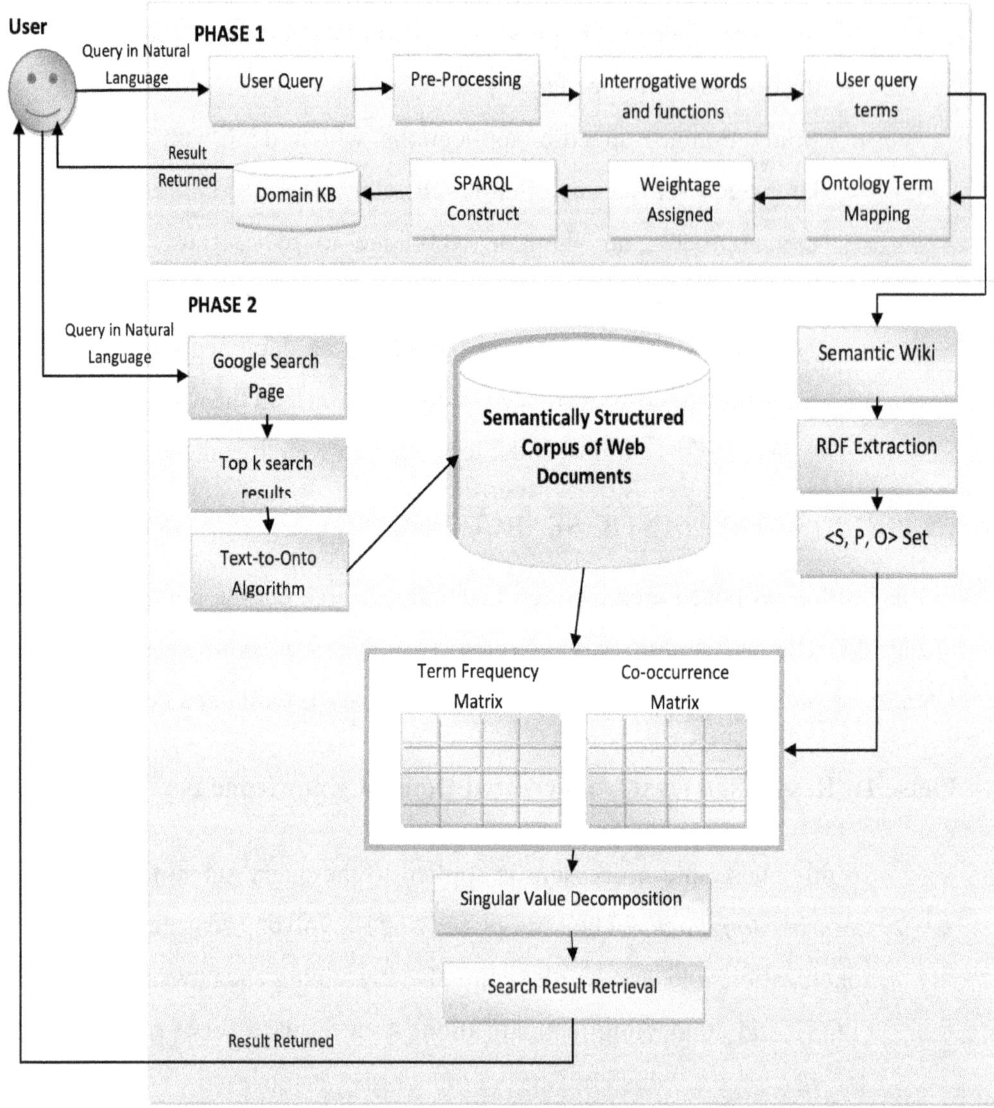

Figure 7.1: Proposed Semantic Search Engine Framework

Phase 2: (Result Retrieval from Web 2.0)

If the query does not return any result due to lack of related information from the domain KB, the query is further directed to Web 2.0.

1. Query in natural language is redirected to the Google search page.
2. Top *k* search results retrieved are taken into consideration and converted into a semantically structured document.
3. *Text2Onto* algorithm is applied for converting unstructured web documents into semantically annotated web documents.

4. The semantically annotated documents are added into the Web document corpus.
5. Semantic crawl agent uses the query term generated in the first phase and utilizes the real-world semantic wiki to generate the <S,P,O> sets related to the user query.
6. Considering each term, of the user query, the *Term Frequency Matrix* is generated and <S,P,O> set is used to generate the *Co-occurrence Matrix.*
7. *Singular value decomposition* is used to find out the best possible query vector and the corresponding web documents are retrieved.
8. Finally, results are returned to the user.

The flowchart of the proposed system as shown in Fig. 7.2 depicts the abstract flow of the proposed system.

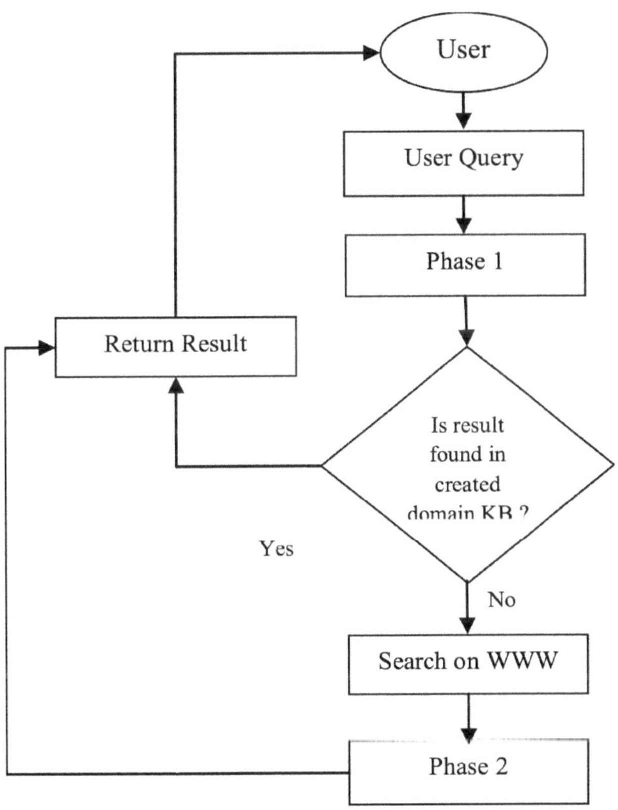

Figure 7.2: Flow Chart of Proposed Semantic Search Engine

7.3 PHASE 1 OF SEMANTIC SEARCH ENGINE

In this section, the conversion from user query in natural language to SPARQL is explained in detail. The phase mainly explains the pre-processing, term ontology mapping, weightage assignment, and finally SPARQL conversion process.

7.3.1 User Query

The user is not well versed in writing structured query such as SPARQL to retrieve the desired result, so to allow mass participation, there need to find some way to overcome this problem. So, in the proposed system, users can comfortably enter their queries in natural language.

Example Illustration: Suppose the user entered query is *What is the genre of movie directed by Kangana Ranaut?* This query is taken as an example to show the processing of different sections.

7.3.2 Pre-Processing

In this phase, pre-processing is applied on the query submitted by the user. The pre-processing involves sentence segmentation, tokenization, and stop words removal, determining each token's part of Speech (POS), and conducting lemmatization. As a result, a set of query terms $QT = \{t1, t2, . . . ,tn\}$, which retains the input order, is retrieved. All these pre-processing tasks is implemented by *NLTK in Python*, which is a famous library for NLP [180].

Interrogative words or function

After retrieving set of query terms, the function or interrogative terms present in the query set are identified for the further conversion process. These identified terms are kept separately to be used in the final SPARQL conversion process.

a) **Interrogatives:** The query terms such as *where, who, which, when* etc. are identified as interrogatives. The search target defines the search requirement of the user. The interrogatives are considered as search targets and the modification in these terms could affect the final SPARQL query conversions.

b) **Functions:** The query terms such as *maximum, how many* are required to be included in the final SPARQL such as *ORDER BY, COUNT*, etc. This allows aggregating the resources as per the requirement.

Example Illustration: Continuing with the same example, after pre-processing module, following are the set of query terms generated:

Set of Query Terms= What Genre movie directed Kangana Ranauat

Interrogative term= What.

7.3.3 Term Ontology Mapping

On completion of pre-processing, the terms generated from the user is further mapped to the domain resources present in the ontology based on similarity computation. The triplet paths mapped with the user's query terms are identified and weightage is assigned to each triplet path. Finally, the process is followed by the SPARQL conversion process,

7.3.3.1 Index Creation

In this section, all the resources present in the domain ontology are indexed. The snippet of the indexed domain ontology for the movie domain is shown in Table 7.1.

- The index created comprises of the URI of the resources, their type and the annotated values taken from comments, labels, and titles.
- The URI of the resources indexed may belong to the Classes, Data or Object Properties, Instances, and the Literals.
- The literal values represent the value of type integer, string, numeric, etc.
- The annotation values are mainly intended to assist humans to understand more about the resources and therefore considered as an important parameter to be included in the Index creation.

The abstract model of mapping query terms with the ontology resources in index is shown in Fig. 7.4.

Table 7.1: Index of Movie Ontology Resource

URI	Type	Annotation (Comments)
mv:MovieArtist	Class	Movie Artist, Actor, Hero,Heroine,Actress
mv:Manikarnika	Instance	Manikarnika, Jhansi ki Rani
mv: KanganaRanaut	Instance	KanganaRanaut, name of actress, heroine
mv:hasRuntime	DataProperty	Runtime, Length of movie
mv:hasGenre	DataProperty	Genre, type, field
mv:directedBy	ObjectProperty	Director, directed by, direction given by
45	Integer	45, Forty Five
Hindi	Literal	Hindi Language, Regional Language

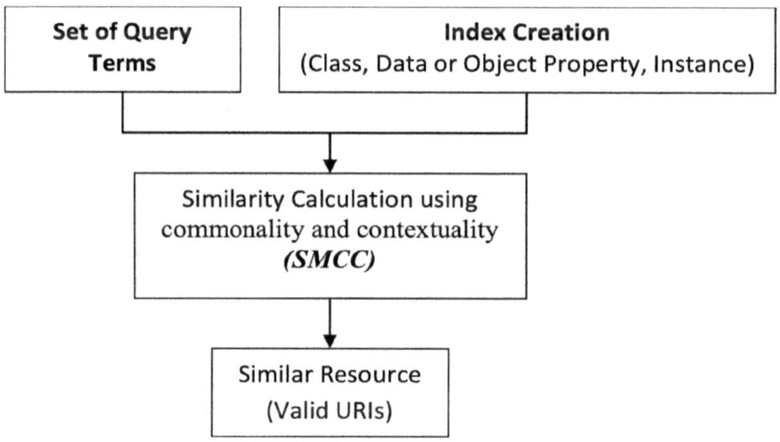

Figure 7.3: Mapping between Query Terms and Index Created

As shown in Fig. 7.3, each term in the user query is compared with the values of these annotations for finding the best possible match of the query term with the resources using proposed *similarity measure based on commonality and contextuality (SMCC)* as described in next section.

7.3.3.2 Similarity Measure (SMCC)

It has been proven that "difference should play a less important role on the computation of the overall similarity''[155]. Therefore, each query term is matched with the annotation values using a proposed *similarity measure based on commonality and contextuality (SMCC).*

- The *commonality technique* is the normalization of the common substring to the length of the input strings. In this process, if the maximum common string is found while comparing the two matching strings, then it is removed. This is a repeated process that executes till minimum string length is not achieved. Length of *2* characters is chosen as the minimum string length. The length of the generated substrings is scaled to the string length.
- The *contextual similarity* between the terms is calculated using *Word2vec* [181] which creates the vector of the possible contextual terms related to the given terms and similarity between them is calculated.

Consider p and q as two strings, the similarity among them is described below in Eq. (7.1).

$$SMCC(p,q) = \alpha * \frac{\text{\#* }\sum \text{\$\%\& ( )) (\&*+,-\&-)}}{\text{\$\%\&(1)3\$\%\&(4)}} + \beta * word2vec(p,q) \tag{7.1}$$

where $\alpha+\beta=1$, α, and β are the control values. If any one of the commonalities or the contextuality similarity measure has zero value, then $\alpha=\beta=1$.

The query term is mapped to the URI resource of the domain ontology if the similarity value computed is above the threshold value. In this work, the threshold value is taken (>= 0.7). The resources that has similarity value greater than 0.7 are termed as *Valid URIs* and further taken into consideration for exploring all the possible triplets paths.

Example Illustration:

1. Suppose the two strings are:
   - *String 1 = director*
   - *String 2 = directed*

   Here, the lengthy common string is *direct* and it is removed. The leftover string is *or* and *ed*, and in the next iteration there is no common string. The length of the total common substring is 6 as *direct* is *6 characters* long.

   The computed similarity value between these strings is 2*6/(8+8) = 0.75. And the similarity using word2vec is 0.72. Therefore, the total similarity as per Eq. (7.1) is:

   SMCC(director,directed)= (0.5*0.75+0.5*0.72) =0.73

2. In another scenario, suppose the two strings are *movie* and *film*, there is no similarity based on commonality but the *word2vector* will give 0.71 as similarity value.

The next section describes the technique to assign weightage to the triplets to identify possible triplet paths.

7.3.3.3 Weightage Assignment to Triplets

Each triplet consists of <S,P,O> subject, predicate, and object. Therefore, a data structure is proposed to define the triplet path, with each row representing different *data or object relation* value present in the domain ontology.

The data structure consists of the Relation, its type, corresponding domain and range, and the triplet path. The triplet path is composed of *domain* as its *subject*, *property/relation* as its *predicate*, and the *range* as its *object*. Table 7.2 shows the snippet of the proposed data structure.

Table 7.2: Snippet of Triplet Path data structure

Relation	Type	Domain	Range	Triplet Path
mv:directedBy	Object Property	mv: Movie	mv: Person	mv: Movie-- mv:directedBy-- mv: Person
mv:hasGenre	Data Property	mv: Movie	Rdfs:Literal	mv: Movie-- mv:hasGenre-- Rdfs:Literal
mv:HasRuntime	Data Property	mv: Movie	Rdfs:Literal	mv: Movie-- mv:HasRuntime -- Rdfs:Literal

After mapping user query terms to the corresponding resource URI, *Valid URIs are identified.* These *Valid URIs* are assigned *weightage* in the *Triplet Path Data Structure* to find out the possible Triplet paths relevant to the user query as shown in Fig.7.4.

On the basis of generality [182], each triplet path is assigned a weight Wr. Higher is the generality of a triplet path if there are more number of connections between the edge and node (domain and range) of the path as compared to those that have less connection.

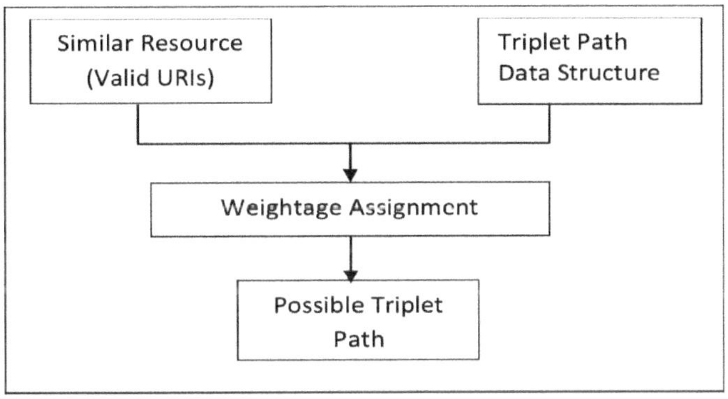

Figure 7.4 Weightage Assignment

The weight represents the ratio between the number of instance level triplets connected with the property of the path and the total number of triplets having the same domain and range irrespective of the property connecting them using Eq. (7.2).

$$W_r = \frac{5(6(),,,,8\&-\%)}{5(6(),*,,8\&-\%)} \tag{7.2}$$

where ‘x’ is the number of triplet paths, ‘r’ is the property containing the domain and range and ‘*’ is any property connecting the same domain and range. The interpretation of the generality is the probability of the triplet path present in the user query.

In the construction of the user query graph, the arc is identified using the triplet path whose weight is greater than the threshold value. To find the shortest path connecting the nodes, *A* algorithm* [183] has been used. Finally, it is converted into the SPARQL query. The next section described in detail the process of conversion to SPARQL query.

7.3.4 Conversion to SPARQL Query

In this process of conversion, it’s very crucial to deal with the interrogative query terms and the functions terms identified in the pre-processing Section 7.3.2.

7.3.4.1 Dealing with Interrogatives

The interrogative terms in the query clearly reflect the user’s intentions or aim. In the English language, the interrogatives are placed at the beginning of the question. On the basis of the interrogatives' dependency, they are divided into two categories namely *Dependent Interrogatives* and the *Independent Interrogatives*.

- The terms such as *which or what* are the types of *dependent interrogatives* preceding the *Class* of resources. In such scenarios, the query is rearranged, the *class* resources are placed at the end of the query and the dependent interrogative term is removed from it.
- For example, the user query terms are *what genre movie directed KanganaRanaut*, in this *what* is removed and thus the query rearranged as *movie directed KanganaRanaut genre*.
- The terms such as *where, who, when* or *which* are not preceded by class resources. All such interrogative terms are removed from query and *owl:Thing* is added at the end as the mapped resources. For example, the user query is, *Who is the manager of Royal club?* In this query, *who* is removed and the *owl:Things* is added at the end as mapped resources.
- Although particular class could be referred, such as *who*, class is *foaf:Person*, but *owl:Thing* is the suitable option if the class representing people is not known in any ontology.

The interrogatives describe the target of the given user query and this is required which creating the basic structure of SPARQL query. The next section describes the process of creating SPARQL basic structure.

7.3.4.2 Basic Structure

The basic structure of SPARQL query contains two clauses namely 'select' and 'where'. This is further explained in detailed below:

- The target which needs to be searched is specified by the clause 'select' and corresponding to it, a variable was assigned. The triplet set which could restrict the target variable is specified in 'where' clause.
- The shortest path derived using the A* algorithm in the previous section is directly translated into the conditional triplets.

- After the basic structure of the query has been formed, the function terms identified in pre-processing phase such as FILTER, LIMIT, OFFSET, ORDER BY etc. is added in the structure of the SPARQL query, if required.
- All the time related constraints of the query could be processed using the SPARQL time related functions such as days(), months() and year().
- If there is a requirement for number of result information, the COUNT function could be used in the 'select' clause. Other function terms such as LIMIT or ORDER BY could be added in the SPARQL structure.

Example Illustration:

Fig. 7.5 represents the conversion into a SPARQL query. The examples show that the select clause uses the target variable belonging to the class *Genre* as discussed while handling interrogatives terms. Also, the *where* clause represents the shortest path that has been translated directly. The relationship among the nodes has already been defined as per the unit path triplets. For example, the property *p1* is binding the node *x1 with ?m1* and has direction from *m1 to x1*. This relationship could be described using triplet *(?m1, p1, x1)*.

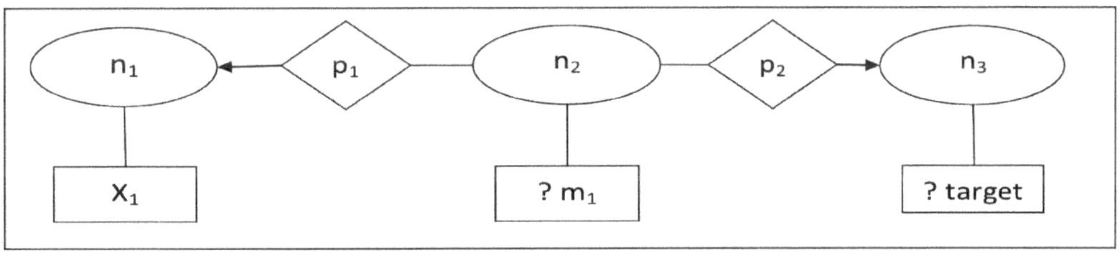

Figure 7.5: Creation of Query Graph

Finally, conversion of the query graph into its SPARQL query is represented below:

```
SELECT ?genre
WHERE {
?m1        p1      X1
?m1        p2      ?target
?m1rdf:type    n2
?targetrdf:type    n3
}
```

Example Illustration:

```
SELECT ?genre
WHERE {
?movie directedby ?KanganaRanaut
?movie hasGenre ?genre
?movie rdf:tye Movie
?target rdf:type Genre
}
```

The above example is SPARQL query for the user query, *what is the genre of the movie directed by Kangana Ranaut?*. The detailed algorithm for Phase 1 is shown in Algorithm 7.1.

Finally, the query generated in SPARQL is processed by the Jena ARQ2 Engine [184]. There is a Jena model uploaded corresponding to the domain ontology, therefore the Jena ARQ2 Engine could access this model and execute the query. The search results generated due to processing the SPARQL query on the knowledge base are returned to the user.

If the result is not retrieved from the domain knowledge base, after executing the SPARQL query, then the user query is redirected to the *Phase 2* of the proposed system. The next section discusses about the Phase 2 of the proposed Semantic Search Engine.

7.4 PHASE 2 OF SEMANTIC SEARCH ENGINE

If no results are retrieved from the domain Knowledge base related to the user's natural language query in phase 1, then that query is directed to Phase 2 for further processing from Web 2.0.

7.4.1 Result Retrieval from Web 2.0

The user query in natural language is redirected further to the Google search engine page if no result is returned from the developed domain KB. The top *k* results can be considered the relevant results for an optimal value of k. In this proposed system, the value of k is taken as 10, as suggested in literature that the search results after 10th position get less than 5% of traffic [185]. The top *k* search results are crawled and parsed by the proposed system.

Algorithm: Phase 1 of Search Engine

Input: User Query in natural language (U_{NL})
Output: Result generated from SPARQL query.
begin
ValidURL = null;
P_{query}= null;
STEP 1: Load user query U_{NL}
STEP 2: For pre-processing, apply NLTK on U_{NL} from python library and generate
Query Terms $Q_T = \{t_1, t_2, \ldots\ldots, t_x\}$
Interrogative Terms $I_T = \{i_1, i_2, \ldots\ldots, i_y\}$
Function Terms $F_T = \{f_1, f_2, \ldots\ldots, f_z\}$
STEP 3: Generate indexes for URI from the domain ontology in the form
<URI , Type , Annotations>
STEP 4: Load $Q_T = \{t_1, t_2, \ldots\ldots, t_x\}$ and URI indexes for Term Ontology Mapping
STEP 5: // Calculating Term Ontology Mapping
For each URI (URI_q), from URI set
For each query term *p* from Q_T
For each word *q* from annotations A(q)
$$SMCC(p,q)\ \alpha * \frac{2\sum i\ len(commonstring)}{len(p)3len(q)} + \beta * word2vec(p,q)$$
Similarity (p,A(q)) = max ($\sum_{iL\delta} SMCC(p,q)_{(n)}$)
if (Similarity (p,A(q)) > Threshold (0.7))
ValidURL = ValidURL U URI_q
endif
endfor
endfor
endfor
STEP 6: Load triple path store, S_T from domain ontology represented using data structure
<Relation , Type , Domain, Range, Triple Path>
STEP 7: // Finding Possible Triple Path
For each URI_i in valid URI set, ValidURI
For each Triplet path $T_j$from Triple Store, S_T
If (URI_ipresent in T_j)
Possible Triple Path,
$TP_p= TP_p U\ T_j$
Endif
Endfor
Endfor
STEP 8: // Assign Weightage
For each path *r* in Possible Triple Path, TP_p
Calculate the weightage,
$$W_r = \frac{x(dom,r,range)}{x(dom,*,range)}$$
If (W_r> Threshold value)
User Query Path,
$P_{query}= P_{query}U\ W_r$
Endif
Endfor
STEP 9: Apply A* algorithm to find the shortest path between the identified path's nodes to form Query Graph
STEP 10: Conversion of Query Graph into SPARQL query syntax
STEP 11: SPARQL query processed by Jena ARQ2 Engine and result returned to the user.
end

Algorithm 7.1: Phase 1 of Proposed Semantic Search Engine

The next section described about the Text2Onto tool that is used to convert the top *k* documents retrieved from the web into the structured document.

7.4.2 Text2Onto Process

Text2Onto [21], is an improvised version of Text2Onto and is developed at the AIFB Institute of University, Karlsruhe, Germany. The Text2Onto tool is chosen for the following reasons:

- A combination of various machine learning techniques along with linguistic processing approaches has been used by Text2Onto. GATE framework was used for linguistic processing by Text2Onto.
- In Text2Onto, Linguistic processing starts with tokenization followed by sentence splitting. The annotation set created, is given as input to POS tagger which allocates to all tokens its suitable syntactic categories.
- Lastly, lemmatizing is done using a morphological analyzer and stemming using stemmer. The learning process is then begun to recognize the concepts and the relations based on linguistic and machine learning heuristics.
- Several measures have been adopted by Text2Onto to analyze the relevance of a particular term with the corpus. Various algorithms have been used by Text2Onto to calculate the measures such as entropy, Term Frequency Inverse Document Frequency (TFIDF), and Relative Term Frequency (RTF).
- Further, there are several algorithms for utilizing the hyponym of Word Net structure, employing linguistic heuristics and matching Hearst patterns for learning about relations.
- Text2Onto uses sources such as databases, dictionaries, free texts, legacy ontologies, and semi-structured texts as its input. This learning process outcome is the domain related ontology containing its specific and not related concepts.
- The non-related concepts are removed to fine tune the domain ontology. Therefore, only the domain related concepts are present in the resultant ontology generated after the learning process. The complete process is iterative and administered by the ontology engineers to better refine and complete the ontology.

The next section described the technique of RDF generation.

7.4.3 RDF Generation

The semantic web is all about storing the semantically structured data, and the RDF triples are the strong metadata that represents the data on the web. RDF snippets are suggested as strong indicators for retrieving useful and required information from the web. The RDF structure indicates the context of the content and helps in filtering the ambiguous web page based on its context. The triple structure of RDF is <Subject-Predicate-Object>, i.e. <S,P,O>.

- In this process, Semantic crawl Agent has been used which takes each unique user query term as an input to obtain its relevant RDF structure <S,P,O> from the real world Semantic Wikis.
- The semantic crawl agent is considered as intelligent software which is able to retrieve RDF entities from the Semantic Wikis. Semantic wiki consists of the RDF triple structure which represents the content on the pages.
- It is also the reflection of the real-world Semantic Web. RDF triples <S,P,O> are extracted from the Semantic Wiki with the aim of fetching all the contexts of the user query.
- The individual entities forming triples, may have a high correlation with many closely linked domain, but taking the triples together, means the co-occurrence of the <S,P,O> pattern when searched, they reflect the clear domain indication.
- Therefore, instead of querying individual entities, their triplets co-occurrences are considered for querying which will represent the clear domain to which the user query belongs to.

This eventually will remove the ambiguous results and the most related results will be retrieved by the user. The output generated from this process is the set of <S,P,O> set according to the user query.

The next section describes the process of Term Frequency Matrix created using the corpus of semantically structured documents.

7.4.4 Term Frequency Matrix

The general structure of the *Term Frequency Matrix (TF_{QW})* has been shown in Table 7.3. In the Term Frequency matrix, each query term generated after pre-processing has been evaluated for its frequency in every web document page of the corpus. Many traditional approaches formulate the Term Frequency Matrix using query terms for the purpose of Information Retrieval from the web pages.

However, in this work, Term Frequency matrix along with the Co-occurrence matrix created using RDF triple <S,P,O> has been used which restricts its co-occurrence in the number of web pages. The matrix in Table 7.3 represents the 'x' number of unique user query terms on the one rows and 'y' number of web pages along with the columns from the corpus. The cell value 'N_{xy}' represents the frequency of query term 'x' in web document 'y'.

Table 7.3: Term Frequency Matrix *(TF_{QW})*

Documents/ query	**Web Doc 1**	**Web Doc 2**	**Web Doc 3**	**Web Doc 4**	**……**	**Web Doc y**
Query T1	N_{11}	N_{12}	N_{13}	N_{14}	……	N_{1y}
Query T2	N_{21}	N_{22}	N_{23}	N_{24}	……	N_{2y}
Query T3	N_{31}	N_{32}	N_{33}	N_{34}	……	N_{3y}
…	……	……	……	……	……	……
Query Tx	N_{x1}	N_{x2}	N_{x3}	N_{x4}	……	N_{xy}

The next section described the co-occurrence matrix, which is utilized to finally retrieve the precise search results.

7.4.5 Co-occurrence Matrix

The general structure of *Co-occurrence Matrix (CO_{RW})* using RDF triple <S,P,O> is depicted in Table 7.4. The matrix represents the frequency of co-occurrence of the triple i.e. the occurrence of the <S-P-O> together in each web page from the corpus.

- This process removes the terms that are irrelevant to the domain represented by the user query due to the restricted co-occurrence of the RDF triples. This strategy of co-occurrence of the Subject-Predicate-Object is formulated due to the triple structure of the RDF schema.
- The co-occurrence of the RDF triple acts as a strong indicator and thus contributes indirectly in handling context irrelevance and reduces search results the ambiguity.

The co-occurrence matrix in Table 7.4 shows the 'x' number of RDF triplet set generated by the semantic crawl agent represented on the one rows and 'y' number of web pages represented along with the columns from the web corpus. The cell value 'N_{xy}' represents the frequency of RDF triplet <Sx,Px,Qx> co-occurrence in web document 'y'.

Table 7.4: Co-occurrence Matrix *(CO_{RW})*

Documents/ Triplets	**Web Doc 1**	**Web Doc 2**	**Web Doc 3**	**Web Doc 4**	**……**	**Web Doc y**
<S1-P1-O1>	CN_{11}	CN_{12}	CN_{13}	CN_{14}	……	CN_{1y}
<S2-P2-O2>	CN_{21}	CN_{22}	CN_{23}	CN_{24}	……	CN_{2y}
<S2-P2-O2>	CN_{31}	CN_{32}	CN_{33}	CN_{34}	……	CN_{3y}
…	……	……	……	……	……	……
<Sx-Px-Ox>	CN_{x1}	CN_{x2}	CN_{x3}	CN_{x4}	……	CN_{xy}

Like in traditional schemes, relying on term frequency or Inverse Document Frequency, the combination of the co-occurrence matrix using RDF triplet and term frequency matrix has been included in this proposed system.

Therefore, it resulted in reducing the irrelevancy in such a semantic environment and further helps in decreasing the computational complexity. Thereafter, both the matrices i.e., Term Frequency and the co-occurrence are subjected to Singular Value Decomposition, which could further condense the matrices into Query Term Priority Vector (PV_{QT}). Next section gives the details about it.

7.4.6 Singular Value Decomposition

Singular Value Decomposition has been applied to the Term Frequency Matrix along with the Co-occurrence Matrix of RDF triple. This technique will further reduce both the matrix into Query Term Priority Vector. The generated Query Term Priority Vector has been linked to the most relevant query terms. The algorithm depicted in Algorithm 7.2 takes RDF triple generated using semantic crawl agent and the web pages corpus as an input and will generate the Query Term Priority Vector as an output.

The next section describes the process of results retrieval and the retrieved results are presented to the user.

7.4.7 Search Result Retrieval

The reason behind enriching the top search results to the users through this approach is that it does not take into account blindly the frequency of occurrences of the user query terms in the web documents. However, the knowledge hidden in the schema level has been used for the solution and it is retrieved from the metadata structure linked to it.

- The derivation of the co-occurrence matrix using RDF structure <S,P,O> acts as a strong indicator for the query term as it has been obtained from the real world Semantic Wiki knowledge base.
- Moreover, the focus is on formulating the Query Term Prioritization Vector based on the convergence of co-occurrence RDF triple matrix and the Term Frequency Matrix using Singular Value Decomposition.
- The query term frequencies $\{X_{11},X_{12},X_{13,\ldots,}X_{xy}\}$ of the Term Frequency Matrix are shown in Table 7.3. However the frequencies of Subject-Predicate-Object co-occurrence $\{CX_{11},CX_{12},CX_{13,\ldots,}CX_{xy}\}$ are depicted in Table7.4.
- It is obvious that the frequency of co-occurrence 'CX' is very less as compared to the query term frequency 'X', i.e. $CX_{xy}<X_{xy.}$ Therefore, it removes the less related web pages and thus improves the relevancy while obtaining Query Term Prioritization Vector which considers the incidence between the co-occurrence RDF matrix and the Term Frequency Matrix.
- Moreover, as the co-occurrence matrix provides strong indication while retrieving the document from the semantic web, it overtakes other traditional approaches such as Page Rank, TF-IDF etc.

The Query Term Priority Vector generated provides the highly relevant query terms. The web document containing <S,P,O> RDF triple belonging to the highly relevant terms are retrieved and shown to the user in the order of highest frequency. Therefore, the entire web document which contains the relevant query term triple and has a frequency greater than the threshold will be presented to the user. The detailed algorithm for Phase 2 is described in Algorithm 7.2.

The next section describes in detail about the evaluation of the proposed system and its comparison analysis with the existing systems.

Algorithm: Phase 2 of Search Engine

Input: Preprocessed User Query Terms (U_{QT})
Output: Relevant Web Pages URL.
begin
STEP 1: User query redirected on Web 2.0
STEP 2: Process Top k search results and place in document corpus D_k
STEP 3: Semantically structured web document corpus, D_{ss}= null
 for each document $d_i D_k$
  Apply Text2Onto algorithm
  $D_{ss} = D_{ss} U\ d_i$
 end for
STEP 4: Extract RDF triplets from Semantic Wiki using U_{QT}
STEP 5: Load each RDF triplet from Triplet Store T_R
STEP 6: for each triplet in T_R
 LookUp web document in $D_{ss}$and generate
  a) Term Frequency Matrix (TF_{QW}) depicting the occurrence of query terms in $D_{ss.}$
  b) Co-occurrence Matrix (CO_{RW}) depicting the occurrence of RDF triplet T_R in $D_{ss.}$
STEP 7: Apply Singular Value decomposition on above matrix.
STEP 8: Formulate the Query Term Prioritization Vector (PV_{QT}) depicting highly related terms.
STEP 9: Web document URLs containing highly relevant terms <S,P,O> triplet are returned to the user.
End

Algorithm 7.2: Phase 2 of Proposed Semantic Search Engine

7.5 EXPERIMENTAL SETUP

A detailed experimental evaluation has been done to compare the proposed approach of the semantic search engine with the existing approaches. The proposed system prototype has been implemented using *Java* 8, under 4 GHz processor, 8GB RAM and 64-bit Microsoft Windows 2010. Various libraries and plug-ins have been used additionally.

The plug-ins are used such as *Jena* for accessing ontology, *Text2Onto* for converting web documents in a structured format, *AgentSpeak* extension Jason for semantic crawl agent and *Lucene* library for indexing the resources of the domain ontology. Ontology was created for the *Movie* domain using the proposed system EasyOnto, a platform for developing domain ontology. Movie domain ontology consists of 35 classes, 44 data properties, 53 object properties, and 633 individuals, comprising a total of 3,933 axioms. The performance metrics parameters are represented in Eq. (7.3-7.7).

$$Precision = \frac{\text{QR)S\%,(T6('R)\%\&+*,\%+,-\%U\%68\&6,\%\$\%U8\&+}}{\text{QR)S\%,(T6('R)\%\&+*,\%+,-\%U\%6}} \tag{7.3}$$

$$Recall = \frac{\text{QR)S\%,(T6('R)\%\&+*,\%+,-\%U\%68\&6,\%\$\%U8\&+}}{\text{QR)S\%,(T6('R)\%\&+*,\%\$\%U8\&+}} \tag{7.4}$$

F-measure = #∗V,%'-∗-(&∗W%'8$$ / V,%'-∗-(&3W%'8$$ (7.5)

Accuracy = V,%'-∗-(&3 W%'8$$ / # (7.6)

FDR (False Discovery Rate) = 1 – Positive Predicted Value (7.7)

7.5.1 Dataset Preparation

The interaction with 178 people has been done and they were requested to provide the natural language query for the *Movie* domain. All these people were unfamiliar with the terms ontology, semantic web, and SPARQL. 135 queries has been collected and few people were reluctant in responding properly. Three domain experts were given the task of manually evaluating the system. The experts analyzed the feasible answers that should be generated from the user queries, also, they analyzed the correctness of the SPARQL query generated by the proposed system. To measure the performance metrics such as precision, recall, f-measure, etc, the manual evaluation was necessary.

7.5.2 Result Analysis and Discussion

The experiment was done based on various criteria and generated results are analyzed in comparisons with other existing semantic web or Knowledge base search approaches such as OTNLS [186], SQG_NLS [118], SWQ_RDF [128], UPSIR [125], IWSF [130].

7.5.2.1 Performance Metrics

The existing approaches such as OTNLS, SQG_RDF, SWQ_RDF, UPSIR, and IWSF were taken into consideration and evaluated for the same dataset as the proposed approach for the same 135 queries. It is clearly depicted in Fig. 7.6 that the proposed approach outstands in comparison with other semantic based search techniques. There are several reasons for such high value performance of the proposed approach. The incorporation of the efficient semantic similarity measure and the assigning weightage to the possible query path helps in the creation of precise SPARQL query. In scenarios where desired information is not available in Knowledge Base, an alternative solution to handle use query is presented. Also, the idea of using the co-occurrence matrix

<Subject, Predicate, Object> depicts the relevancy of user query with the web pages.

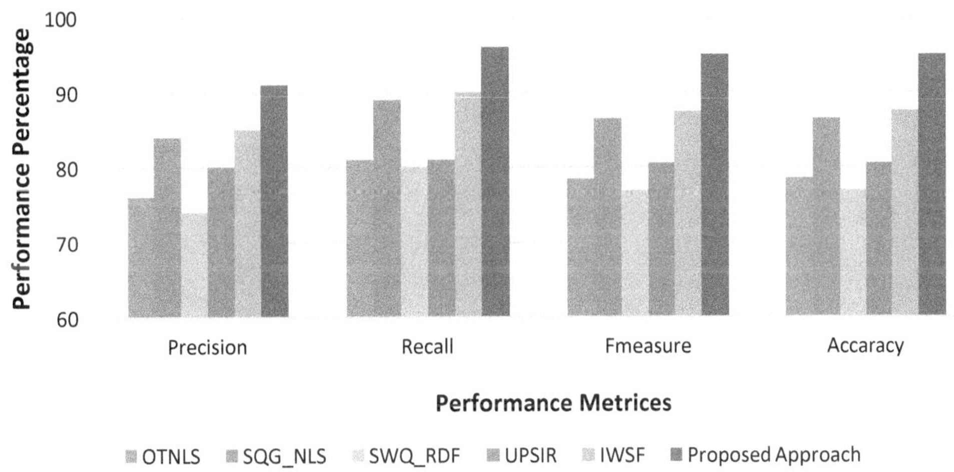

Figure 7.6: Comparison based on Performance Metrics

SWQ_RDF shows the lowest performance measure with 74% precision, 80% recall, 76.9% F-measure, and 77% accuracy. The proposed approach shows improvement in precision with 16.48%, 7.69%, 18.68%, 12.09, and 6.59% in comparison to OTNLS, SQG_NLS, SWQ_RDF, UPSIR, and IWSF respectively. On average, the performance improvement shown by the proposed method for precision, recall, f-measure, and accuracy is 12.31%, 12.29%, 13.76, 13.68% respectively.

7.5.2.2 False Discovery Rate

False Discovery Rate indicates the number of false or incorrect search results retrieved by the web search engine for a particular user query. The importance of calculating the FDR is to analyze the percentage of the search results which are excluded by the user for a particular search query. Although, various statistical tools for FDR computation are available, but mentioned technique in Eq. (7.7) is the easiest method for calculating FDR value with respect to search engines. The quality of search engines is considered as high if the value of FDR is low. This implies that the search engine able to retrieve the most appropriate search results for a specific query.

It can be observed from Fig. 7.7, that the proposed system has the lowest value of FDR as compared with other systems. SWQ_RDF shows the highest value of FDR as 0.33. The proposed approach is better than OTNLS, SQG_NLS, SWQ_RDF, UPSIR and

IWSF showing 31.58%, 21.05%, 73.68%, 47.37%, 15.79% reduction in FDR value.

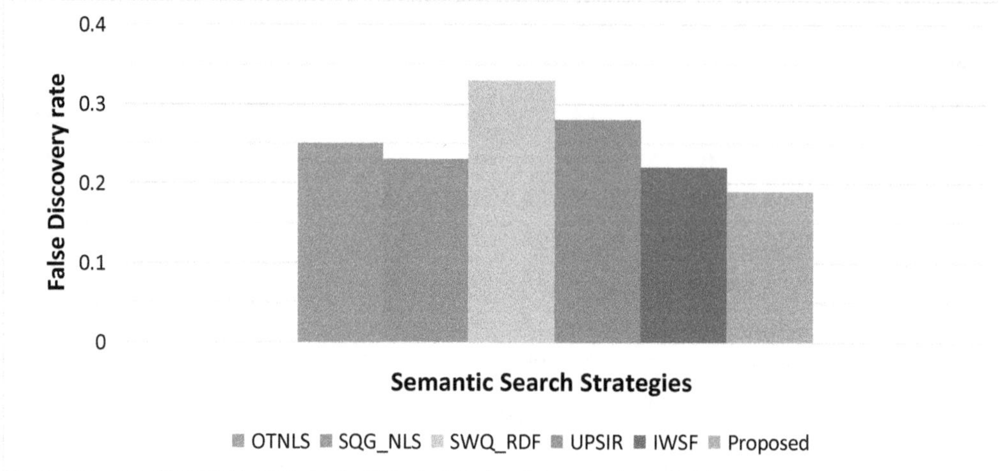

Figure 7.7: False Discovery Rate comparison

The lowest value of FDR reflects that the proposed system provides very less inappropriate and rejected recommendations, thereby it is proven to be an appropriate semantic search engine. RDF triple co-occurrence matrix and the efficient semantic similarity, ISI are the reasons for such low value of FDR.

7.5.2.3 SMCC Performance Metrics

The evaluation of the effectiveness and the appropriateness of the approaches incorporated in proposed framework had been done and its relative performance in the context of the semantic similarity measure chosen is depicted in Fig. 7.8. The traditional measures of similarity such as Cosine similarity, Jaccard similarity had been replaced with the proposed similarity measure SMCC. It is evident from the experiment that the high performance was depicted by the proposed SMCC measure as compared to the other similarity measures.

It is observed that the adaptation of Cosine Similarity yields 85% precision, 86% recall, 85.5% F-measure, and 85.5% accuracy. However, using the Jaccard Similarity measures shows improvements in the performance matrix as compare with the Cosine Similarity. The values for precision, recall, F-measure and accuracy are 86%, 88%, 87%, 87% respectively.

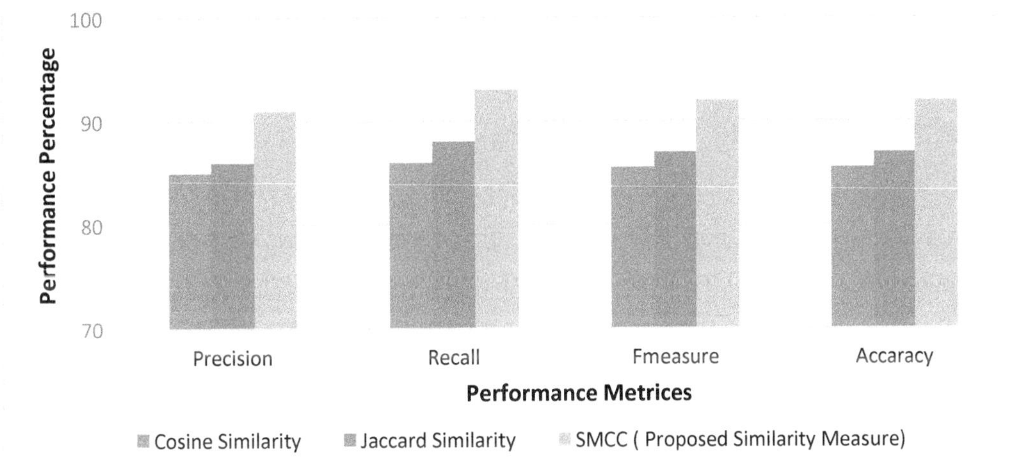

Figure 7.8: SMCC Performance Metrics

The proposed SMCC similarity measure outstands in performance as it is hybrid and efficient for a semantic space. There is an average 6% increase in precision 6.5% in the recall, 6.2% in F-measure, and 6.3% in the accuracy as compared to *Cosine and Jaccard similarity.*

7.5.2.4 Co-occurrence Matrix Performance Metrics

In Fig. 7.9, it is observed that including RDF triple Co-occurrence matrix in the proposed system has greatly contributed in increasing the efficiency as compared to classical TF-IDF. In this experiment, the co-occurrence matrix has been replaced by the TF-IDF matrix to compare the statistics, it has been observed using the co-occurrence matrix, the Precision is increased by 10.9%, and recall increased by 8.3%. If TF-IDF has been used, it would reduce the F-measure from 94% to 84.9% and decrease the accuracy by 9.6%.

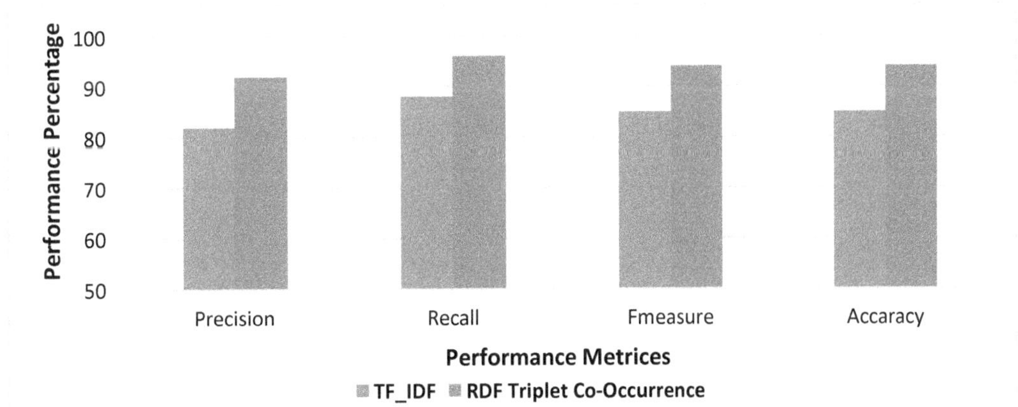

Figure 7.9: Performance metrics using Co-occurrence Matrix

The reason behind these numbers is quite clear as this approach for semantic search depends on the knowledge inferred from the RDF triple. TF-IDF could be appropriate while querying the traditional web, as it depends on the number of occurrences of the query term in the web pages, unlike Semantic Web. The co-occurrence matrix depends upon the co-occurrence of RDF triple which represents the knowledge, instead of depending merely on the occurrence of query terms in web documents; therefore, it increases the overall performance in comparison to the TF-IDF.

7.6 SUMMARY

To overcome the limitations of Web 2.0 and the challenge faced by common user in retrieving the information from the domain specific ontology, an efficient semantic search engine has been proposed and following are the key findings:

- The SPARQL query has been automatically generated according to the user query submitted in natural language.
- Also, assigning the weightage score to each triple path and finding the possible triple path as per query also reduces the ambiguity.
- The proposed semantic similarity measure (SMCC), increases the effectiveness and the appropriateness of the approach.
- Further, redirecting the user query to Web 2.0, greatly increases the performance measures. The proposed approach increases the overall precision, recall, and f-measure by 9.74%, 9.02%, 9.88%, 9.83% respectively.
- The formulation of the *Term Frequency matrix* and the *Co-occurrence matrix* improves the context relevance and reduces the false discovery by 37.89%.

The next chapter concludes the thesis work and discusses the scope for future enhancements.

CHAPTER 8

CONCLUSION & FUTURE SCOPE

8.1 CONCLUSION

In this research, a collaborative system for community based semantic information sharing has been developed which allows the common users to contribute and share knowledge in creating ontologies; and developing structured data. The system is designed for users with different levels of expertise. The developed system provides the capability for ontology matching to allow interoperability with the other applications. Domain knowledge base is generated using the developed ontologies and structured data. The users can take advantage of created structured data for getting better recommendations and precise search results.

Following are the major contributions of the research carried out in this thesis

1. **Collaborative Ontology and structured data creation**
   EasyOnto system has been developed for collaboratively creating lightweight ontologies and structured data for further information sharing. It allows users with different levels of expertise to share their perspectives in developing domain specifications.
1. **Ontology Matching System to allow Interoperability**
   Multilevel Parallel Partitioning for Efficiently Matching Large Ontologies (MPP-MLO) mechanism has been developed to align the created ontologies and establish interoperability between Semantic Web applications that use different but related ontologies.
2. **Hybrid Recommendation System**
   A hybrid recommendation system has been designed and developed which deals with accuracy, scalability, and new User Cold Start Problems based on Linked Open Data and Social Network features. This system is developed to motivate common users to contribute collaboratively in developing structured data.
3. **Semantic Search Engine**
   A Semantic Search Engine has been developed based on natural language processing and RDF. It also incorporates Google search results as input and

processes them with the help of Semantic Web technologies in order to increase the degree of relevance and higher precision to recall ratio. At the first level, a user search query will be carried out from the created Knowledge base, which is further redirected to the Google search engine, in case no results are received from knowledge base

The various milestone achieved by the developed Community Based Semantic Information System are:

- **Domain-Independent System**

  The proposed system is operational on a variety of domains. The domain-independent behavior of the system is achieved by not restricting the module of the system to any specific domain.
- **Collaborative Ontology Development**

  This system allows accelerating the ontology acquisition phase which involves mass participation and removes the need for involvement of domain experts in the initial phases of ontology development.
- **Scalability**

  In the large scale ontology matching system, the size of the partitioned input ontologies should be less for reduced computational complexity. In MPP-MLO, on an average, 54.6% reduction in execution time using MapReduce framework. The execution time of IEI-Sub is reduced by 13.5% as compared to I-Sub. Overall Execution s almost 58.9% reduction in the execution time as compared to existing approaches.
- **Improved Accuracy**

  The proposed hybrid recommendation system shows 33.75% improvement in overall system precision and 29.4% improvement in accuracy using LOD features. The proposed semantic search engine also shows 37.88% less inappropriate and overall 12.30% improvement in precision as compared to existing approaches.
- **Improved Evaluation**

  It has been observed that the performance of the proposed systems is fairly high as compared to existing systems due to the convergence of social and semantic web technologies.

- **Contribution towards Linked Open Data**

  Using the *EasyOnto* platform, the community can able to contribute towards Linked Open Data initiatives.

Some of the future extensions of the research are depicted in next section.

8.2 FUTURE SCOPE

In this thesis, a community based semantic application has been designed and implemented that includes lightweight ontology development, ontology matching, recommendation engine, and semantic search engine. Some of the possible extensions and issues that could be further explored or extended by researchers in the near future are as follows:

1. **Heavyweight Collaborative Ontology Creation Tool**

   An effort could be made in developing a collaborative tool for developing heavyweight (more expressiveness) ontologies for users with different expertise levels.
2. **Structuring existing web resources**

   The thesis work focused on creating new structured data. The research work can be extended to extract structured information from existing web resources and semantically annotate it with the help of Mining techniques, summarization and NLP (Natural Language Processing) techniques.
3. **Automatic domain-specific feature selection**

   In the proposed hybrid recommendation system, the user profile feature selection could be automated depending upon the domain.
4. **Cross-Domain Integration**

   As the proposed system is domain independent, in the future cross-domain integration can be carried out.

REFERENCES

1. Leah, V.: Technical Report on the Introduction of Semantic Web. (2020)

2. Chhaya, K., Khanzode Librarian, A., Raisoni, G.H., Sarode, R.D.: Evolution of World Wide Web: From WEB 1.0 TO 6.0. Online

3. Spivak, N.: How the WebOS Evolves?, https://novaspivack.typepad.com/nova_spivacks_weblog/2007/02/steps_towards_a.html

4. Tim Berners-Lee, Hendler, J., Lassila, O.: The Semantic Web. Sci. Am. (2001)

5. Semantic Web - W3C, https://www.w3.org/standards/semanticweb/

6. Tim Berners-Lee, Dan Connolly, Ralph R. Swick: Web Architecture: Describing and Exchanging Data. W3C Note. (1999)

7. Mikroyannidis, A.J.: Toward a social semantic web. Computer (Long. Beach. Calif). 40, 113–115 (2007). https://doi.org/10.1109/MC.2007.405

8. BBC NEWS | Technology | Web users "getting more ruthless," http://news.bbc.co.uk/2/hi/technology/7417496.stm

9. Bojars, U., Breslin, J.G., Peristeras, V., Tummarello, G., Decker, S.: Interlinking the social web with semantics. IEEE Intell. Syst. 23, 29–40 (2008). https://doi.org/10.1109/MIS.2008.50

10. Lee Feigenbaum: Semantic Web Landscape 2009, https://www.slideshare.net/LeeFeigenbaum/semantic-web-landscape-2009

11. Kumar Sloni, D., Sharma, V.K.: Safe Semantic Web and Security Aspect Implication for Social Networking. Int. J. Comput. Appl. Eng. Sci. II, (2011)

12. Specia, L., Motta, E.: Integrating folksonomies with the semantic web. In: Lecture Notes in Computer Science (including subseries Lecture Notes in Artificial Intelligence and Lecture Notes in Bioinformatics). pp. 624–639. Springer Verlag (2007)

13. Xu, L., Zhichen, F., Ting, Y., Mao, Jianchang, S., Difu: Towards the Semantic Web: Collaborative Tag Suggestions, https://www.researchgate.net/publication/200110821_Towards_the_Semantic_Web_Collaborative_Tag_Suggestions

14. John G. Breslin, Uldis Bojārs, Alexandre Passant, Sergio Fernández, Stefan Decker: SIOC: Content Exchange and Semantic Interoperability Between Social Networks. In: W3C Workshop on the Future of Social Networking (2009)

15. Howard, R.: The Virtual Community, Revised Edition | The MIT Press. MIT Press (2000)

16. Graves, M., Constabaris, A., Brickley, D.: FOAF: Connecting people on the Semantic Web. In: Knitting the Semantic Web. pp. 191–202. Taylor and Francis (2009)

17. Guarino, Nicola: Ontologies and knowledge bases: towards a terminological clarification. Towards Very Large Knowledge Bases, IOS Press (1995)

18. Mizoguchi, R.: Tutorial on Ontological Engineering: Part 1: Introduction to Ontological Engineering. New Gener. Comput. 21, 365–884 (2003). https://doi.org/10.1007/bf03037311

19. Ferndndez, M., G6mez-P~rez, A., Juristo, N.: METHONTOLOGY: From Ontological Art Towards Ontological Engineering. (1997)

20. Studer, R., Grimm, S., Abecker, A.: Semantic web services: Concepts, technologies, and applications. Springer Berlin Heidelberg (2007)

21. Cimiano, P., Völker, J.: Text2Onto A framework for ontology learning and data-driven change discovery. In: Lecture Notes in Computer Science. pp. 227–238. Springer Verlag (2005)

22. Sahoo, L., Das, D., Datta, S.: A Survey on Recommendation System. Artic. Int. J. Comput. Appl. 160, 975–8887 (2017). https://doi.org/10.5120/ijca2017913081

23. Basiri, J., Shakery, A., Moshiri, B., Hayat, M.Z.: Alleviating the Cold-Start Problem of Recommender Systems Using a New Hybrid Approach.

24. Guha, R., McCool, R., Miller, E.: Semantic search. In: Proceedings of the 12th International Conference on World Wide Web, WWW 2003. pp. 700–709. ACM Press, New York, New York, USA (2003)

25. Vargas, H., Buil-Aranda, C., Hogan, A., López, C.: RDF Explorer: A Visual SPARQL Query Builder. In: Lecture Notes in Computer Science (including subseries Lecture Notes in Artificial Intelligence and Lecture Notes in Bioinformatics). pp. 647–663. Springer (2019)

26. Bernstein, A., Kaufmann, E., Kaiser, C., Kiefer, C.: Ginseng : A Guided Input Natural Language Search Engine for Querying Ontologies. (2006)

27. Kaufmann, E., Bernstein, A., Fischer, L.: NLP-Reduce: A "na¨ıvena¨ıve" but Domain-independent Natural Language Interface for Querying Ontologies.

28. Siorpaes, K., Hepp, M.: myOntology: The Marriage of Ontology Engineering and Collective Intelligence. Bridg. Gep between Semant. Web Web 20 SemNet 2007. 2, 1–12 (2007)

29. Schaffert, S., Bry, F., Baumeister, J., Kiesel, M.: Semantic Wiki. Informatik-Spektrum. 30, 434–439 (2007). https://doi.org/10.1007/s00287-007-0195-z

30. Dall'Agnol, J.M.H., Tacla, C.A., Freddo, A.R., Molinari, A.H., Paraiso, E.C.: The use of well-founded argumentation on the conceptual modeling of collaborative ontology development. In: Proceedings of the 2011 15th International Conference on Computer Supported Cooperative Work in Design, CSCWD 2011. pp. 200–207 (2011)

31. Buffa, M., Gandon, F., Ereteo, G., Sander, P., Faron, C.: SweetWiki: A semantic wiki. Web Semant. 6, 84–97 (2008).

https://doi.org/10.1016/j.websem.2007.11.003

32. Krötzsch, M., Vrandečić, D., Völkel, M.: Semantic MediaWiki. In: Lecture Notes in Computer Science (including subseries Lecture Notes in Artificial Intelligence and Lecture Notes in Bioinformatics). pp. 935–942. Springer Verlag (2006)

33. Zaini, N., Omar, H.: An online system to support collaborative knowledge acquisition for ontology development. In: ICCAIE 2011 - 2011 IEEE Conference on Computer Applications and Industrial Electronics. pp. 543–548 (2011)

34. Wang, S., Wang, W., Zhuang, Y., Fei, X.: An ontology evolution method based on folksonomy. J. Appl. Res. Technol. 13, 177–187 (2015). https://doi.org/10.1016/j.jart.2015.06.015

35. Jiménez Ruiz, E., Grau, B.C., Horrocks, I., Berlanga, R.: Supporting concurrent ontology development: Framework, algorithms and tool. Data Knowl. Eng. 70, 146–164 (2011). https://doi.org/10.1016/j.datak.2010.10.001

36. Geng, Q., Deng, S., Jia, D., Jin, J.: Cross-domain ontology construction and alignment from online customer product reviews. Inf. Sci. (Ny). 531, 47–67 (2020). https://doi.org/10.1016/j.ins.2020.03.058

37. Kurilovas, E., Juskeviciene, A.: Creation of Web 2.0 tools ontology to improve learning. Comput. Human Behav. 51, 1380–1386 (2015). https://doi.org/10.1016/j.chb.2014.10.026

38. Mkhinini, M.M., Labbani-Narsis, O., Nicolle, C.: Combining UML and ontology: An exploratory survey. Comput. Sci. Rev. 35, 100223 (2020). https://doi.org/10.1016/j.cosrev.2019.100223

39. Borodin, A. V., Zavyalova, Y. V.: An ontology-based semantic design of the survey questionnaires. Conf. Open Innov. Assoc. Fruct. 10–15 (2017). https://doi.org/10.23919/FRUCT.2016.7892177

40. MacGregor, R.M.: Inside the LOOM description classifier. ACM SIGART Bull. 2, 88–92 (1991). https://doi.org/10.1145/122296.122309

41. Heflin, Jeff, H., James, L., Sean: SHOE: A Knowledge Representation Language for Internet Applications. (2000)

42. Kent, R.E.: Conceptual Knowledge Markup Language: An Introduction. (2018)

43. Karp, Peter, C., Vinay, T., Jerome: XOL: An XML-Based Ontology Exchange. Presented at the March (2000)

44. Connolly, Dan, H., Frank, H., Ian, M., Deborah, P., Schneider, Peter, S., Lynn: DAML+OIL: Reference Description. (2001)

45. Corcho, O., Fernández-López, M., Gómez-Pérez, A.: Methodologies, tools and languages for building ontologies. Where is their meeting point?, (2003)

46. Algergawy, A., Massmann, S., Rahm, E.: A clustering-based approach for large-

scale ontology matching. In: Lecture Notes in Computer Science (including subseries Lecture Notes in Artificial Intelligence and Lecture Notes in Bioinformatics). pp. 415–428. Springer, Berlin, Heidelberg (2011)

47. Hu, W., Qu, Y., Cheng, G.: Matching large ontologies: A divide-and-conquer approach. Data Knowl. Eng. 67, 140–160 (2008). https://doi.org/10.1016/j.datak.2008.06.003

48. Sure, Y., Angele, J., Staab, S.: OntoEdit: Guiding Ontology Development by Methodology and Inferencing.

49. Graffoo - Graphical Framework for OWL Ontologies, https://essepuntato.it/graffoo/

50. Paul Kogu: DARPA Agent Markup Language (DAML) Unified Modeling Language (UML)-Based Ontology Toolset (UBOT), https://www.researchgate.net/publication/235110733_DARPA_Agent_Markup_Language_DAML_Unified_Modeling_Language_UML-Based_Ontology_Toolset_UBOT

51. Bārzdiņš, J., Bārzdiņš, G., Čerāns, K., Liepiņš, R., Sproģis, A., RenarsLiepins, lumiilv: OWLGrEd: a UML Style Graphical Notation and Editor for OWL 2.

52. Anzo - Semantic Web Standards, https://www.w3.org/2001/sw/wiki/Anzo

53. Domingue, J.: Tadzebao and WebOnto: discussing, browsing, and editing ontologies on the Web. undefined. (1998)

54. TopBraid Composer - Maestro Edition — TopQuadrant, Inc, https://www.topquadrant.com/products/topbraid-composer/

55. Kalyanpur, A., Parsia, B., Hendler, J.: A tool for working with web ontologies, (2005)

56. Spyns, P., Tang, Y., Meersman, R.: An ontology engineering methodology for DOGMA. Appl. Ontol. 3, 13–39 (2008). https://doi.org/10.3233/AO-2008-0047

57. Corcho, Ó., Fernández-López, M., Gómez-Pérez, A., Vicente, Ó.: WebODE: An Integrated Workbench for Ontology Representation, Reasoning, and Exchange. In: Lecture Notes in Computer Science (including subseries Lecture Notes in Artificial Intelligence and Lecture Notes in Bioinformatics). pp. 138–153. Springer Verlag (2002)

58. Tudorache, Tania Noy, N.: Collaborative Prot eg. World Wide Web Internet Web Inf. Syst. 1–3 (2007)

59. Islam, N., Siddiqui, M.S., Shaikh, Z.A.: TODE: A dot net based tool for ontology development and editing. In: ICCET 2010 - 2010 International Conference on Computer Engineering and Technology, Proceedings (2010)

60. Hu, W., Chen, J., Cheng, G., Qu, Y.: ObjectCoref & Falcon-AO: Results for OAEI 2010. In: CEUR Workshop Proceedings. pp. 158–165 (2010)

61. Aumueller, D., Do, H.H., Massmann, S., Rahm, E.: Schema and ontology

matching with COMA++. In: Proceedings of the ACM SIGMOD International Conference on Management of Data. pp. 906–908 (2005)

62. Saraladha, K., Aghila, G., Sathiya, B.: LOMPT: An efficient and scalable ontology matching algorithm. Procedia Eng. 38, 2272–2287 (2012). https://doi.org/10.1016/j.proeng.2012.06.274

63. Hu, W., Qu, Y.: Falcon-AO: A Practical Ontology Matching System. SSRN Electron. J. (2018). https://doi.org/10.2139/ssrn.3199401

64. Wang, P.: Lily Results on SEALS Platform for OAEI 2011.

65. Hamdi, F., Safar, B., Niraula, N.B., Reynaud, C.: TaxoMap alignment and refinement modules: Results for OAEI 2010. (2010)

66. Noy, N.F., Noy, N.F., Musen, M.A.: Anchor-PROMPT: Using Non-Local Context for Semantic Matching. Proc. Work. Ontol. Inf. Shar. Int. Jt. Conf. Artif. Intell. (IJCAI. 63--70 (2001)

67. Seddiqui, M.H., Aono, M.: Anchor-flood: Results for OAEI 2009. CEUR Workshop Proc. 551, 127–134 (2009)

68. Li, Y., Jianhui, Z., Liu, J., Hou, Y.: Matching Large Scale Ontologies Based on Filter and Verification. Math. Probl. Eng. 2020, (2020). https://doi.org/10.1155/2020/8107968

69. Mountasser, I., Ouhbi, B., Frikh, B.: Hybrid large-scale ontology matching strategy on big data environment. ACM Int. Conf. Proceeding Ser. 282–287 (2016). https://doi.org/10.1145/3011141.3011185

70. Xue, X., Chen, J.: Using Compact Evolutionary Tabu Search algorithm for matching sensor ontologies. Swarm Evol. Comput. 48, 25–30 (2019). https://doi.org/10.1016/j.swevo.2019.03.007

71. Laadhar, A., Ravat, F., Ghozzi, F., Teste, O., Megdiche, I., Gargouri, F.: Partitioning and local matching learning of large biomedical ontologies. Proc. ACM Symp. Appl. Comput. Part F1477, 2285–2292 (2019). https://doi.org/10.1145/3297280.3297507

72. Vigo, M., Matentzoglu, N., Jay, C., Stevens, R.: Comparing ontology authoring workflows with Protégé: In the laboratory, in the tutorial and in the 'wild.' J. Web Semant. 57, 100473 (2019).https://doi.org/10.1016/j.websem.2018.09.004

73. Matentzoglu, N., Vigo, M., Jay, C., Stevens, R.: Inference Inspector: Improving the verification of ontology authoring actions. J. Web Semant. 49, 1–15 (2018). https://doi.org/10.1016/j.websem.2017.09.004

74. Stevens, R., Lord, P., Malone, J., Matentzoglu, N.: Measuring expert performance at manually classifying domain entities under upper ontology classes. J. Web Semant. 57, 100469 (2019). https://doi.org/10.1016/j.websem.2018.08.004

75. Zhuang, L., Schouten, K., Frasincar, F.: SOBA: Semi-automated Ontology Builder for Aspect-based sentiment analysis. J. Web Semant. 60, 100544 (2020).

https://doi.org/10.1016/j.websem.2019.100544

76. Kiourtis, A., Nifakos, S., Mavrogiorgou, A., Kyriazis, D.: Aggregating the syntactic and semantic similarity of healthcare data towards their transformation to HL7 FHIR through ontology matching. Int. J. Med. Inform. 132, 104002 (2019). https://doi.org/10.1016/j.ijmedinf.2019.104002

77. Rentina API Documentaion | Free API Documentation Tool | Cortical.io | Cortical.io, https://www.cortical.io/retina-api-documentation/

78. Levenshtein Distance, https://people.cs.pitt.edu/~kirk/cs1501/Pruhs/Spring2006/assignments/editdistance/Levenshtein Distance.htm

79. Ouali, I., Ghozzi, F., Taktak, R., Hadj Sassi, M.S.: Ontology alignment using stable matching. Procedia Comput. Sci. 159, 746–755 (2019). https://doi.org/10.1016/j.procs.2019.09.230

80. Vennesland, A.: Matcher composition for identification of subsumption relations in ontology matching. Proc. - 2017 IEEE/WIC/ACM Int. Conf. Web Intell. WI 2017. 154–161 (2017). https://doi.org/10.1145/3106426.3106503

81. Ngo, D.H., Bellahsene, Z.: Overview of YAM++—(not) Yet Another Matcher for ontology alignment task. J. Web Semant. 41, 30–49 (2016). https://doi.org/10.1016/j.websem.2016.09.002

82. Saruladha, K., Ranjini, S.: COGOM: Cognitive Theory Based Ontology Matching System. Procedia Comput. Sci. 85, 301–308 (2016). https://doi.org/10.1016/j.procs.2016.05.237

83. Sathiya, B., Geetha, T. V, Saruladha, K.: PSOM 2-partitioning-based scalable ontology matching using MapReduce. Sadhana. 42, (2046). https://doi.org/10.1007/s12046-017-0742-5

84. Al-Shamri, M.Y.H., Bharadwaj, K.K.: Fuzzy-genetic approach to recommender systems based on a novel hybrid user model. Expert Syst. Appl. 35, 1386–1399 (2008). https://doi.org/10.1016/j.eswa.2007.08.016

85. Burke, R.: Hybrid recommender systems: Survey and experiments. User Model. User-adapt. Interact. 12, 331–370 (2002). https://doi.org/10.1023/A:1021240730564

86. Leung, C.W., Chan, S.C., Chung, F.: An empirical study of a cross-level association rule mining approach to cold-start recommendations. Knowledge-Based Syst. 21, 515–529 (2008). https://doi.org/10.1016/j.knosys.2008.03.012

87. Fernández-Tobías, I., Cantador, I., Tomeo, P., Anelli, V.W., Di Noia, T.: Addressing the user cold start with cross-domain collaborative filtering: exploiting item metadata in matrix factorization. User Model. User-adapt. Interact. 29, 443–486 (2019). https://doi.org/10.1007/s11257-018-9217-6

88. Roy, S., Guntuku, S.C.: Latent factor representations for cold-start video recommendation. In: RecSys 2016 - Proceedings of the 10th ACM Conference on Recommender Systems. pp. 99–106. Association for Computing Machinery,

Inc (2016)

89. Rohani, V.A., Kasirun, Z.M., Kumar, S., Shamshirband, S.: An Effective Recommender Algorithm for Cold-Start Problem in Academic Social Networks. Math. Probl. Eng. 2014, 1–11 (2014). https://doi.org/10.1155/2014/123726

90. Meng, C., Cheng, Y., Jiechao, C., Peng, Y.: A Method to Solve Cold-Start Problem in Recommendation System based on Social Network Sub-community and Ontology Decision Model. Presented at the November 1 (2013)

91. Li, C., Wang, F., Yang, Y., Li, Z., Zhang, X.: Exploring social network information for solving cold start in product recommendation. In: Lecture Notes in Computer Science (including subseries Lecture Notes in Artificial Intelligence and Lecture Notes in Bioinformatics). pp. 276–283. Springer Verlag (2015)

92. Poirier, D., Fessant, F., Tellier, I.: Reducing the cold-start problem in content recommendation through opinion classification. In: Proceedings - 2010 IEEE/WIC/ACM International Conference on Web Intelligence, WI 2010. pp. 204–207 (2010)

93. Liu, H., Hu, Z., Mian, A., Tian, H., Zhu, X.: A new user similarity model to improve the accuracy of collaborative filtering. Knowledge-Based Syst. 56, 156–166 (2014). https://doi.org/10.1016/j.knosys.2013.11.006

94. Ahn, H.J.: A new similarity measure for collaborative filtering to alleviate the new user cold-starting problem. Inf. Sci. (Ny). 178, 37–51 (2008). https://doi.org/10.1016/j.ins.2007.07.024

95. Adomavicius, G., Tuzhilin, A.: Toward the next generation of recommender systems: a survey of the state-of-the-art and possible extensions. IEEE Trans. Knowl. Data Eng. 17, 734–749 (2005). https://doi.org/10.1109/TKDE.2005.99

96. Auer, S., Bizer, C., Kobilarov, G., Lehmann, J., Cyganiak, R., Ives, Z.: DBpedia: A nucleus for a Web of open data. In: Lecture Notes in Computer Science (including subseries Lecture Notes in Artificial Intelligence and Lecture Notes in Bioinformatics). pp. 722–735. Springer, Berlin, Heidelberg (2007)

97. Heitmann, B., Hayes, C.: Using Linked Data to Build Open, Collaborative Recommender Systems. undefined. (2010)

98. Passant, A.: dbrec - Music recommendations using DBpedia. In: Lecture Notes in Computer Science (including subseries Lecture Notes in Artificial Intelligence and Lecture Notes in Bioinformatics). pp. 209–224. Springer, Berlin, Heidelberg (2010)

99. Piao, G., Breslin, J.G.: Measuring semantic distance for linked open data-enabled recommender systems. In: Proceedings of the ACM Symposium on Applied Computing. pp. 315–320. Association for Computing Machinery (2016)

100. Musto, C., Semeraro, G., Lops, P., De Gemmis, M., Narducci, F.: Leveraging social media sources to generate personalized music playlists. In: Lecture Notes in Business Information Processing. pp. 112–123. Springer Verlag (2012)

101. Bostandjiev, S., O'Donovan, J., Höllerer, T.: Tasteweights: A visual interactive

hybrid recommender system. In: RecSys'12 - Proceedings of the 6th ACM Conference on Recommender Systems. pp. 35–42 (2012)

102. Son, L.H., Cuong, K.M., Minh, N.T.H., Van Canh, N.: An application of fuzzy geographically clustering for solving the cold-start problem in recommender systems. In: 2013 International Conference on Soft Computing and Pattern Recognition, SoCPaR 2013. pp. 44–49. Institute of Electrical and Electronics Engineers Inc. (2013)

103. Musto, C., Lops, P., de Gemmis, M., Semeraro, G.: Semantics-aware Recommender Systems exploiting Linked Open Data and graph-based features. Knowledge-Based Syst. 136, 1–14 (2017). https://doi.org/10.1016/j.knosys.2017.08.015

104. Nilashi, M., Ibrahim, O., Bagherifard, K.: A recommender system based on collaborative filtering using ontology and dimensionality reduction techniques. Expert Syst. Appl. 92, 507–520 (2018). https://doi.org/10.1016/j.eswa.2017.09.058

105. Almazro, D., Shahatah, G., Albdulkarim, L., Kherees, M., Martinez, R., Nzoukou, W.: A Survey Paper on Recommender Systems. (2010)

106. Bassiliades, N., Symeonidis, M., Meditskos, G., Kontopoulos, E., Gouvas, P., Vlahavas, I.: A semantic recommendation algorithm for the PaaSport platform-as-a-service marketplace. Expert Syst. Appl. 67, 203–227 (2017). https://doi.org/10.1016/j.eswa.2016.09.032

107. Celdrán, A.H., Pérez, M.G., García Clemente, F.J., Pérez, G.M.: Design of a recommender system based on users' behavior and collaborative location and tracking. J. Comput. Sci. 12, 83–94 (2016). https://doi.org/10.1016/j.jocs.2015.11.010

108. Tarus, J.K., Niu, Z., Yousif, A.: A hybrid knowledge-based recommender system for e-learning based on ontology and sequential pattern mining. Futur. Gener. Comput. Syst. 72, 37–48 (2017). https://doi.org/10.1016/j.future.2017.02.049

109. Martín-Vicente, M.I., Gil-Solla, A., Ramos-Cabrer, M., Pazos-Arias, J.J., Blanco-Fernández, Y., López-Nores, M.: A semantic approach to improve neighborhood formation in collaborative recommender systems. Expert Syst. Appl. 41, 7776–7788 (2014). https://doi.org/10.1016/j.eswa.2014.06.038

110. Gonzalez Camacho, L.A., Alves-Souza, S.N.: Social network data to alleviate cold-start in recommender system: A systematic review. Inf. Process. Manag. 54, 529–544 (2018). https://doi.org/10.1016/j.ipm.2018.03.004

111. Nouali, O., Belloui, A.: Using semantic web to reduce the cold-start problems in recommendation systems. In: 2nd International Conference on the Applications of Digital Information and Web Technologies, ICADIWT 2009. pp. 525–530 (2009)

112. Ilyas, Q.M., Kai, Y.Z., Talib, M.A.: A conceptual architecture for semantic search engine. In: Proceedings of INMIC 2004 - 8th International Multitopic

Conference. pp. 605–610. Institute of Electrical and Electronics Engineers Inc. (2004)

113. Mukhopadhyay, D., Banik, A., Mukherjee, S., Bhattacharya, J., Kim, Y.-C.: A Domain Specific Ontology Based Semantic Web Search Engine. (2011)

114. Dong, H., Hussain, F.K., Chang, E.: Transport service ontology and its application in the field of semantic search. In: Proceedings of 2008 IEEE International Conference on Service Operations and Logistics, and Informatics, IEEE/SOLI 2008. pp. 820–824 (2008)

115. Sinha, S., Dattagupta, R., Mukhopadhyay, D.: Designing an ontology based domain specific Web search engine for commonly used products using RDF. In: ACM International Conference Proceeding Series. pp. 612–617. ACM Press, New York, New York, USA (2012)

116. Fatima, A., Luca, C., Wilson, G.: New framework for semantic search engine. In: Proceedings - UKSim-AMSS 16th International Conference on Computer Modelling and Simulation, UKSim 2014. pp. 446–451. Institute of Electrical and Electronics Engineers Inc. (2014)

117. Styperek, A., Ciesielczyk, M., Szwabe, A.: SPARQL - Compliant semantic search engine with an intuitive user interface. In: Lecture Notes in Computer Science (including subseries Lecture Notes in Artificial Intelligence and Lecture Notes in Bioinformatics). pp. 201–210. Springer Verlag (2014)

118. Song, S., Huang, W., Sun, Y.: Semantic query graph based SPARQL generation from natural language questions. Cluster Comput. (2017). https://doi.org/10.1007/s10586-017-1332-3

119. Heibi, I., Peroni, S., Shotton, D.: Enabling text search on SPARQL endpoints through OSCAR. Data Sci. 2, 205–227 (2019). https://doi.org/10.3233/ds-190016

120. Arenas, M., Grau, B.C., Kharlamov, E., Marciuska, S., Zheleznyakov, D.: Faceted search over ontology-enhanced RDF data. CIKM 2014 - Proc. 2014 ACM Int. Conf. Inf. Knowl. Manag. 939–948 (2014). https://doi.org/10.1145/2661829.2662027

121. Wang, X., Yang, L., Zhu, Y., Zhan, H., Jin, Y.: Querying Knowledge Graphs with Natural Languages. In: Lecture Notes in Computer Science (including subseries Lecture Notes in Artificial Intelligence and Lecture Notes in Bioinformatics). pp. 30–46. Springer (2019)

122. Wang, C., Xiong, M., Zhou, Q., Yu, Y.: PANTO: A portable natural language interface to ontologies. In: Lecture Notes in Computer Science (including subseries Lecture Notes in Artificial Intelligence and Lecture Notes in Bioinformatics). pp. 473–487. Springer Verlag (2007)

123. Yahya, M., Berberich, K., Elbassuoni, S., Ramanath, M., Tresp, V., Weikum, G.: Natural Language Questions for the Web of Data. Association for Computational Linguistics (2012)

124. Ferré, S.: SQUALL: A controlled natural language as expressive as SPARQL 124.1. In: Lecture Notes in Computer Science (including subseries Lecture Notes in Artificial Intelligence and Lecture Notes in Bioinformatics). pp. 114–125 (2013)

125. John, P.M., Arockiasamy, S., Thangiah, P.R.J.: A personalised user preference and feature based semantic information retrieval system in semantic web search. Int. J. Grid Util. Comput. 9, 256–267 (2018). https://doi.org/10.1504/IJGUC.2018.093987

126. Ramesh, C., Rao, K.V.C., Govardhan, A.: Ontology based web usage mining model. In: Proceedings of the International Conference on Inventive Communication and Computational Technologies, ICICCT 2017. pp. 356–362. Institute of Electrical and Electronics Engineers Inc. (2017)

127. Yasodha, S., Dhenakaran, S.S.: ONTOPARK: Ontology based page ranking framework using resource description framework. J. Comput. Sci. 10, 1776–1781 (2014). https://doi.org/10.3844/jcssp.2014.1776.1781

128. Chooralil, V.S., Gopinathan, E.: A Semantic Web query Optimization Using Resource Description Framework. In: Procedia Computer Science. pp. 723–732. Elsevier B.V. (2015)

129. Bansal, R., Jyoti, Bhatia, K.K.: Ontology-based ranking in search engine. In: Advances in Intelligent Systems and Computing. pp. 97–109. Springer Verlag (2018)

130. Ahamed, B.B., Ramkumar, T.: An intelligent web search framework for performing efficient retrieval of data. Comput. Electr. Eng. 56, 289–299 (2016). https://doi.org/10.1016/j.compeleceng.2016.09.033

131. Zhang, Y., Vasconcelos, W., Sleeman, D.: OntoSearch: An Ontology Search Engine. In: Research and Development in Intelligent Systems XXI. pp. 58–69. Springer London (2007)

132. Rajasurya, S.: Semantic Information Retrieval Using Ontology in University Domain. Int. J. Web Semant. Technol. 3, 55–68 (2012). https://doi.org/10.5121/ijwest.2012.3406

133. Kamath, S.S., Piraviperumal, D., Meena, G., Karkidholi, S., Kumar, K.: A semantic search engine for answering domain specific user queries. In: International Conference on Communication and Signal Processing, ICCSP 2013 - Proceedings. pp. 1097–1101 (2013)

134. Singhal Google, A.: Modern Information Retrieval: A Brief Overview. (2001)

135. Narula, G.S., Yadav, U., Duhan, N., Jain, V.: Evolution of foaf and sioc in semantic web: A survey. (2018)

136. Gruber, T.: Collective knowledge systems: Where the Social Web meets the Semantic Web. Web Semant. 6, 4–13 (2008). https://doi.org/10.1016/j.websem.2007.11.011

137. Ankolekar, A., Krötzsch, M., Tran, T., Vrandecic, D.: The two cultures: Mashing

up web 2.0 and the semantic web. In: 16th International World Wide Web Conference, WWW2007. pp. 825–834. ACM Press, New York, New York, USA (2007)

138. Mika, P.: Ontologies are us: A unified model of social networks and semantics. Web Semant. 5, 5–15 (2007). https://doi.org/10.1016/j.websem.2006.11.002

139. Liu, J., Gruen, D.M.: Between ontology and folksonomy: A study of collaborative and implicit ontology evolution. In: International Conference on Intelligent User Interfaces, Proceedings IUI. pp. 361–364. ACM Press, New York, New York, USA (2008)

140. Cattuto, C., Benz, D., Hotho, A., Stumme, G.: Semantic Analysis of Tag Similarity Measures in Collaborative Tagging Systems. (2008)

141. Broder, A.Z., Fontoura, M., Gabrilovich, E., Joshi, A., Josifovski, V., Zhang, T.: Robust classification of rare queries using web knowledge. Proc. 30th Annu. Int. ACM SIGIR Conf. Res. Dev. Inf. Retrieval, SIGIR'07. 231–238 (2007). https://doi.org/10.1145/1277741.1277783

142. Bedi, P., Banati, H., Thukral, A.: Social semantic retrieval and ranking of eResources. In: Proceedings - 2nd International Conference on Advances in Recent Technologies in Communication and Computing, ARTCom 2010. pp. 343–347 (2010)

143. Obitko, M.: Ontologies - Description and Applications. Lab. Intell. Decis. Mak. Control Ser. Res. Reports. 1–36 (2001)

144. PostgreSQL: Documentation: 9.3: Routine Database Maintenance Tasks, https://www.postgresql.org/docs/9.3/maintenance.html

145. Raad, J., Cruz, C., Cruz, C.A.: A Survey on Ontology Evaluation Methods. (2015). https://doi.org/10.5220/0005591001790186ï

146. Cullot, N., Cullot, N., Ghawi, R., Yétongnon, K.: DB2OWL: A Tool for Automatic Database-to-Ontology Mapping.

147. (PDF) Collaborative Protege., https://www.researchgate.net/publication/221022547_Collaborative_Protege

148. Laboratory, Y., Gruber, T.R.: KNOWLEDGE S A Translation Approach to Portable Ontology Specifications A Translation Approach to Portable Ontology Specifications. (1993)

149. Kirsten, T., Thor, A., Rahm, E.: Instance-based matching of large life science ontologies.

150. Resource Description Framework (RDF): Concepts and Abstract Syntax, https://www.w3.org/TR/2009/REC-rdf-concepts-20090303/

151. Babalou, S., Kargar, M.J., Davarpanah, S.H.: Centralized Clustering Method To Increase Accuracy In Ontology Matching Systems. 45, 1–10 (2013)

152. Sathiya, B., Geetha, T. V., Saruladha, K.: PSOM2—partitioning-based scalable

ontology matching using MapReduce. Sadhana - Acad. Proc. Eng. Sci. 42, 2009–2024 (2017). https://doi.org/10.1007/s12046-017-0742-5

153. Rahm, E.: Towards Large-Scale Schema and Ontology Matching. In: Schema Matching and Mapping. pp. 3–27. Springer Berlin Heidelberg (2011)

154. Winkler, W.E.: The State of Record Linkage and Current Research Problems. Stat. Res. Div. US Census Bur. 1–15 (1999). https://doi.org/10.1.1.39.4336

155. Stoilos, G., Stamou, G., Kollias, S.: A string metric for ontology alignment. Lect. Notes Comput. Sci. (including Subser. Lect. Notes Artif. Intell. Lect. Notes Bioinformatics). 3729 LNCS, 624–637 (2005). https://doi.org/10.1007/11574620_45

156. Euzenat, J., Ferrara, A., Meilicke, C., Pane, J., Scharffe, F., Shvaiko, P., Stuckenschmidt, H., Ondřejˇondřejšváb-Zamazal, O., Svátek, V., Trojahn, C.: First Results of the Ontology Alignment Evaluation Initiative 2010.

157. Apache Hadoop 2.7.3 – Hadoop: Setting up a Single Node Cluster., https://hadoop.apache.org/docs/r2.7.3/hadoop-project-dist/hadoop-common/SingleCluster.html

158. Nezhadi, A.H., Shadgar, B., Osareh, A.: ONTOLOGY ALIGNMENT USING MACHINE LEARNING TECHNIQUES. Int. J. Comput. Sci. Inf. Technol. 3, (2011). https://doi.org/10.5121/ijcsit.2011.3210

159. Levenshtein, V.: Binary codes capable of correcting deletions, insertions, and reversals. Sov. Phys. Dokl. 10, 707–710 (1966)

160. Lin, F., Sandkuhl, K.: A survey of exploiting WordNet in ontology matching. In: IFIP International Federation for Information Processing. pp. 341–350. Springer, Boston, MA (2008)

161. Zhang, H., Hu, W., Qu, Y.: Constructing virtual documents for ontology matching using mapreduce. In: Lecture Notes in Computer Science (including subseries Lecture Notes in Artificial Intelligence and Lecture Notes in Bioinformatics). pp. 48–63. Springer, Berlin, Heidelberg (2012)

162. Hu, W., Jian, N., Qu, Y., Wang, Y.: GMO: A graph matching for ontologies. In: CEUR Workshop Proceedings. pp. 41–48 (2005)

163. Falcon-AO: A practical ontology matching tool - Home, http://ws.nju.edu.cn/falcon-ao/

164. Ontology Alignment Evaluation Initiative::2013, http://oaei.ontologymatching.org/2013/

165. Ranjbar Kermany, N., Alizadeh, S.H.: A hybrid multi-criteria recommender system using ontology and neuro-fuzzy techniques. Electron. Commer. Res. Appl. 21, 50–64 (2017). https://doi.org/10.1016/j.elerap.2016.12.005

166. Shambour, Q., Lu, J.: A trust-semantic fusion-based recommendation approach for e-business applications. Decis. Support Syst. 54, 768–780 (2012). https://doi.org/10.1016/j.dss.2012.09.005

167. Baraldi, A., Blonda, P.: A survey of fuzzy clustering algorithms for pattern recognition. I. IEEE Trans. Syst. Man Cybern. Part B. 29, 778–785 (1999). https://doi.org/10.1109/3477.809032

168. Katarya, R., Verma, O.P.: An effective web page recommender system with fuzzy c-mean clustering. Multimed. Tools Appl. 76, 21481–21496 (2017). https://doi.org/10.1007/s11042-016-4078-7

169. Code Examples | Facebook4J - A most easily usable Facebook API wrapper in Java, https://facebook4j.github.io/en/code-examples.html

170. Herlocker, J.L., Konstan, J.A., Borchers, A., Riedl, J.: An algorithmic framework for performing collaborative filtering. In: Proceedings of the 22nd Annual International ACM SIGIR Conference on Research and Development in Information Retrieval, SIGIR 1999. pp. 230–237. Association for Computing Machinery, Inc, New York, New York, USA (1999)

171. Gong, S.: A Collaborative Filtering Recommendation Algorithm Based on User Clustering and Item Clustering. J. Softw. 5, 745–752 (2010). https://doi.org/10.4304/jsw.5.7.745-752

172. MovieLens, https://movielens.org/

173. Webscope | Yahoo Labs, https://webscope.sandbox.yahoo.com/catalog.php?datatype=i&did=67

174. WebSPHINX: A Personal, Customizable Web Crawler, https://www.cs.cmu.edu/~rcm/websphinx/

175. IMDb: Ratings, Reviews, and Where to Watch the Best Movies & TV Shows, https://www.imdb.com/

176. Ahuja, R., Solanki, A., Nayyar, A.: Movie recommender system using k-means clustering and k-nearest neighbor. In: Proceedings of the 9th International Conference On Cloud Computing, Data Science and Engineering, Confluence 2019. pp. 263–268. Institute of Electrical and Electronics Engineers Inc. (2019)

177. Porcel, C., Martinez-Cruz, C., Bernabé-Moreno, J., Tejeda-Lorente, Á., Herrera-Viedma, E.: Integrating Ontologies and Fuzzy Logic to Represent User-Trustworthiness in Recommender Systems. Procedia Comput. Sci. 55, 603–612 (2015). https://doi.org/10.1016/j.procs.2015.07.050

178. Han, L., Finin, T., Joshi, A.: GoRelations: An intuitive query system for DBpedia. In: Lecture Notes in Computer Science (including subseries Lecture Notes in Artificial Intelligence and Lecture Notes in Bioinformatics). pp. 334–341. Springer, Berlin, Heidelberg (2012)

179. Damljanovic, D., Agatonovic, M., Cunningham, H.: Natural language interfaces to ontologies: Combining syntactic analysis and ontology-based lookup through the user interaction. In: Lecture Notes in Computer Science (including subseries Lecture Notes in Artificial Intelligence and Lecture Notes in Bioinformatics). pp. 106–120. Springer, Berlin, Heidelberg (2010)

180. Natural Language Toolkit — NLTK 3.5 documentation, https://www.nltk.org/

181. Word embedding demo, http://bionlp-www.utu.fi/wv_demo/

182. Lee, M., Kim, W., Park, S.: Searching and ranking method of relevant resources by user intention on the Semantic Web. Expert Syst. Appl. 39, 4111–4121 (2012). https://doi.org/10.1016/j.eswa.2011.09.127

183. A-Star Algorithm Python Tutorial - An Introduction To A* Algorithm In Python, https://www.simplifiedpython.net/a-star-algorithm-python-tutorial/

184. jena-arq 2.9.4 javadoc (org.apache.jena), https://www.javadoc.io/doc/org.apache.jena/jena-arq/2.9.4/index.html

185. No. 1 Position in Google Gets 33% of Search Traffic [Study], https://www.searchenginewatch.com/2013/06/20/no-1-position-in-google-gets-33-of-search-traffic-study/

186. Sander, M., Waltinger, U., Roshchin, M., Runkler, T.: Ontology-Based Translation of Natural Language Queries to SPARQL. 42–48 (2014)

LIST OF PUBLICATIONS OUT OF THESIS

List of Published Papers

S.No.	Title of Paper along with volume, Issue no., year of publication	Journal	Publisher	Impact Factor	Whether Referred or Non-referred ?	Whether you paid any money or not for publication	Link
1	Efficient Retrieval of data using Semantic Search Engine based on NLP and RDF	Journal of Web Engineering (**SCIE Indexed**)	**River Publication**	**0.6**	Referred (**SCIE, SCOPUS**)	**No**	https://journals.riverpublishers.com/index.php/JWE/article/view/5909
2.	MPP-MLO: Multilevel Parallel Partitioning for Efficiently Matching Large Ontologies , Mar,2021	Journal of Scientific and Industrial Research (JSIR), ISSN: 0975-1084	NISCAIR	1.056	Referred (**SCIE, SCOPUS**)	No	http://nopr.niscair.res.in/handle/123456789/56476
3.	Dealing with Pure New User Cold-Start Problem in Recommendation System Based on Linked Open Data and Social Network Features,Vol. 2020, June,2020	Mobile Information Systems, ISSN: 1875-905X	Hindawi	1.8	Referred (**SCIE, SCOPUS**)	No	https://doi.org/10.1155/2020/8912065
4.	Evolution of FOAF and SIOC in Semantic Web: A Survey, Vol. 654, 2018	Big Data Analytics, Advances in Intelligent Systems and Computing, ISSN: 2194-5357	Springer	-	Referred (**SCOPUS**)	No	https://link.springer.com/chapter/10.1007/978-981-10-6620-7_25
	EasyOnto: A	Big Data Analytics,					https://www.springer

5.	Collaborative Semiformal Ontology Development Platform, Vol. 652, 2018	Advances in Intelligent Systems and Computing, ISSN: 2194-5357	Sprin ger	-	Referred (**SCOPUS**)	No	p rofession a l.de/en/ea syonto-a-collaborati ve-semiforma -ontology- d evelopme nt-platfor/151 03410
6.	Development and Visualization of Domain Specific Ontology using Protégé, Vol. 9, April 2016	Indian Journal of Science & Technology, ISSN 0974-5645	-	-	Referred (**SCOPUS**)	N o	https://indj st.org/articl es/develop ment-and-visualizatio n-of- domain-specific-ontology-using-protege
7.	Lexical, Ontological and Conceptual Framework of Semantic Search Engine (LOC-SSE), Vol. 8, Dec, 2016	BIJIT-BVICA M Internationa l Journal of Information Technology, ISSN 2511-2112	Spri nger	-	Referred (**UGC-Care**)	N o	http://bvica m.in/INDI ACom/BJI T/downloa ds/pdf/issu e16/05.pdf
8.	Ontology Engineering and Development Aspects: A Survey, Vol. 9, 2016	International Journal of Education and Management Engineering (IJEME), , ISSN 2305-8463	ME CS	-	Referred	N o	https://ww w.semantic scholar.org /paper/Ont ology-Engineerin g-and-Developme nt-Aspects%3 A-A-Yadav-Narula/6cd 8857fe376 36517e56e cd945e6bc 5de46b850 e
9.	A Novel Approach for Precise Search Results Retrieval based on Semantic Web Technologies, 2016	3rd Internationa l Conference on Computing for Sustainable	IEE E	-	Referred (**SCOPUS**)	N o	https://ieee xplore.ieee. org/docum ent/772448 7

		Global Developme nt, **SCOPUS, IEEE**					
10.	An Overview of Social Semantic Web Framework, Vol. 654, 2016	3rd Internationa l Conference on Computing for Sustainable Global Developme nt	IEE E	-	Referred (**SCOPUS**)	N o	https://ieee xplore.ieee. org/docum ent/772436 9
11.	Semantically related tag recommendation using folksonomized ontology, 2016	3rd Internationa l Conference on Computing for Sustainable Global Developme nt, **SCOPUS, IEEE**	IEE E	-	Referred (**SCOPUS**)	N o	https://ieee xplore.ieee. org/docum ent/772490 0
12.	Relevant Page Retrieval and Query Recommendation using Semantic Analysis of Queries, Vol. 4, 2013	International Journal of Scientific & Engineering Research, ISSN 2229-5518	-	-	Referred	N o	https://ww w.ijser.org/ paper/Rele vant-Page- Retrieval- and-Query- Recommen dation- using- Semantic- Analysis- of- Queries.ht ml

www.ingramcontent.com/pod-product-compliance
Lightning Source LLC
LaVergne TN
LVHW082334200926
848481LV00012B/3340
* 9 7 9 8 2 3 2 0 7 3 1 2 1 *